IMAGES
of America

SPINK COUNTY

ON THE COVER: Children at play—Lucille Issenhuth, on the right, plays dolls with Pauline Pool. Edward C. Issenhuth is seated on the front step of his home, and an unidentified woman stands in the doorway. The house is still a private home. (Courtesy of Spink County Museum.)

IMAGES
of America

SPINK COUNTY

Alan L. Evans, PhD, and Mary Lou Schwartz
for the Spink County Historical Society

ARCADIA
PUBLISHING

ISBN 978-0-7385-9352-4

Published by Arcadia Publishing
Charleston, South Carolina

Printed in the United States of America

Library of Congress Control Number: 2011936765

For all general information, please contact Arcadia Publishing:
Telephone 843-853-2070
Fax 843-853-0044
E-mail sales@arcadiapublishing.com
For customer service and orders:
Toll-Free 1-888-313-2665

Visit us on the Internet at www.arcadiapublishing.com

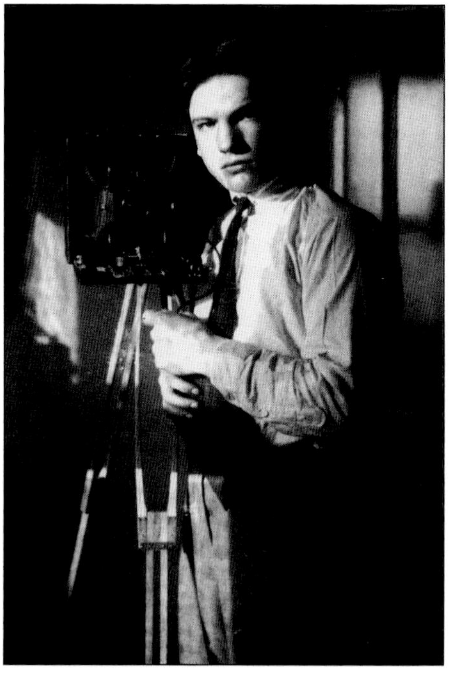

We dedicate this to the early photographers of Spink County. Particularly noteworthy are O. Lenz Conde, pictured above, and P.G. Anderson, Linrooth, and O'Brien, all of Redfield.

Contents

ACKNOWLEDGMENTS

As we neared the completion of this pictorial history of Spink County, it became clear that writing and compiling this book has been a team endeavor. We hope even the casual reader of this book takes note of these, the acknowledgments, in order to share in our gratitude to the team that has made this history possible.

Inspiration for starting on the book project came from Earl Grandpre of Conde. His dedication to preserving memories of the past by generous loan of his considerable collection of photographs and writings, plus his wealth of spoken recollections, whets the historical appetite. Mutual friends Marion Jensen and son Doug—also history enthusiasts—contributed a sizable number of historical photographs and photographic postcards. Published author Rod Evans made available his extensive collection of photographs of the town of Mellette plus a trove of treasured photographs of our mutual ancestors. Glenn and Ruth Overby, who also share my ancestry, similarly made available their remarkable photographic assemblage. Russell McNeely provided access to his collection of postcards. John Solheim and Kathy Maddox, as well as local histories written by Bethal Schmidt, provided much information about southern Spink County. We would have been lost without Dana Harlow's *Prairie Echoes* and Letha Nolan's *Spink County Area History*. Without the generous support of the Spink County Historical Society members and museum, in terms of extraordinary collection of photographs, historical information, plus office use, this book would not have been possible.

The technical process of scanning historical photographs and documents to make them suitable for the high standards of Arcadia Publishing has proven surprisingly difficult. For much of the time this book was in progress, John Pearson of Arcadia has been a patient teacher and mentor. His successor, Jeff Ruetsche, was similarly supportive as we approached completion. Walter Stevenson, extremely knowledgeable in digital preparation, was a most supportive, patient, and skilled technician; his generosity with his time and talent has been invaluable.

We, the authors, knew each other only casually through our mutual membership on the board of the Spink County Historical Society. When the letter came to the board from Arcadia Publishing stating their interest in publishing a pictorial history of Spink County, we teamed together without really knowing our compatibility. We have gotten along fine and have been mutually excited as we dove into the extraordinary history of Spink County. It is our hope that our effort brings as much satisfaction to you, the reader, as it has brought to us, the authors.

Unattributed photographs are courtesy of the Spink County Museum.

INTRODUCTION

Native Americans and French fur traders were the earliest inhabitants of what is now Spink County. Abbie Gardner, taken hostage after an Indian massacre at Spirit Lake, Iowa, was the first white female in the county area. A memorial commemorates the cooperation of a local band of Native Americans and Stephen Riggs, an early missionary teacher, in her successful rescue and return to Iowa.

In summer, the flat, rich ground of Spink County, long ago the floor of a primordial lake, is a patchwork of squares of growing wheat, corn, soybeans, and pasture. This fertile quilt, punctuated by many water-filled prairie potholes, drains into the meandering James River, which flows, in general, from north to south.

In early 1873, the legislature established those first county boundaries. The Homestead Act of 1862 laid the groundwork for new settlements. While some walked or pushed carts, most settlers took advantage of reasonably priced emigrant cars provided by the railroad to get within 60 or 70 miles of a land claim made earlier the previous fall by family members and associates. For the rest of the way, a wood-wheeled wagon, often pulled by a pair of oxen, and containing seed, a sod-busting plow, a tent, farming and building tools, perhaps a cook stove, pots, pans, food provisions, and maybe even a bureau, a bed, a table, and some chairs, carried the family to its land. A milk cow, tethered to the wagon or driven by one of the youngsters, often brought up the rear. This little procession was dwarfed by the endless expanse of prairie grass beneath the open sky. Land, practically free—what an extraordinary opportunity!

The development of railroads provided a gridiron of transportation. Surveyors attempted to plot out Spink County, but Drifting Goose, a Yanktonias Sioux, along with his band of warriors, thwarted the project twice. After an incident with their capturing a flag man, swiping his clothes and boots and sending him across the hot July prairie, they did come to an understanding with the surveyors. The crews were able to continue their task.

In 1878, Frank Fisher established the first settlement near Belcher's Ford on the James River. Early on the site became a popular recreation area hosting the first public Fourth of July event in 1880. As a WPA project during 1936–1937, Fisher's Grove provided employment to surrounding inhabitants.

For thousands of years, Native Americans tended small plots of corn and squash along the riverbank. The last farming tribe, the Mandan, was largely wiped out because their hospitality shown to the members of the Lewis and Clark expedition exposed the native population to smallpox and other diseases. Now, the James River and points on Timber Creek would serve as popular settlements. The rich fertile ground extended five miles north toward Old Ashton.

Drifting Goose led a band of Sioux Indians who originally lived on Armadale Island about eight-and-a-half miles northeast of Mellette. They skillfully managed to both resist and appease the arriving settlers as they staked their hopes and dreams to garner sections of homestead and tree claims. As more settlers arrived, Drifting Goose became more concerned about the Indian lands. He had not consented when the Yanktonians conceded the land in 1838, so he felt the land still belonged to him. He and his band mounted a campaign of terror against the settlers, stopping short of killing anyone.

Pres. Rutherford Hayes signed the proclamation June 27, 1879, declaring part of Tetonka Township for Drifting Goose and his band. Legend has it that land speculators were also supporting the Indian leader. They knew if the land were part of a reservation, they could profit by timing its release.

The area settlers protested. In the winter of 1879, William H. Hedges, homesteader and surveyor for the Chicago & North Western Railroad, braved the elements and rode horseback throughout the township securing settlers' signatures. Once submitted to the president, he revoked the proclamation, releasing the land back to the public domain on July 11, 1880. This forced the Indian leader and his band to eventually leave the area for Crow Creek Reservation.

Marvin Hughitt, early president of the Chicago & North Western, saw the potential in the prairies and expanded the railroad as a business enticement. He advertised the land as the most productive grain lands in the world. What followed was a steady influx of emigrant cars. Settlers depended on the trains for food, fuel, and building materials. At Redfield, passengers could make connections in four directions with daily exchanges of a hundred people. Twenty-four hours a day, freight trains moved in and out of Redfield in those four directions. Other communities in the county developed along the rail lines including Ashton, Athol, Conde, Crandon, Doland, Duxbury, Frankfort, Gallup, Hitchcock, Mansfield, Mellette, Northville, Spotswood, Tulare, and Turton.

The railroad was also influential in starting the first school in Spink County. As early as 1881, the crew's children learned their math and reading in a claim shanty. So many children attended that it necessitated the pupils taking turns sitting. By the end of the century, each of the surrounding towns supported a school often sharing space with a local church. Rural schools popped up around student populations and dotted the countryside.

Moving through the next 75 years, Spink County residents continued a variety of experiences. Redfield was in a bid for the state capital site but also experienced a prairie war to rightfully gain the county seat records from Old Ashton. And while Redfield well-driller Peter Norbeck was the first native-born South Dakotan to become governor, Ashton claimed Deacon Philippe, the winning pitcher for the first World Series. Doland had Hubert Humphrey as its native son.

Farming and ag-related business, including pheasant hunting, have driven the county's economy. Redfield holds the honor of being the Pheasant Capital of the World thanks to the efforts of early hunters releasing six Chinese pheasants.

One

THE BEGINNINGS

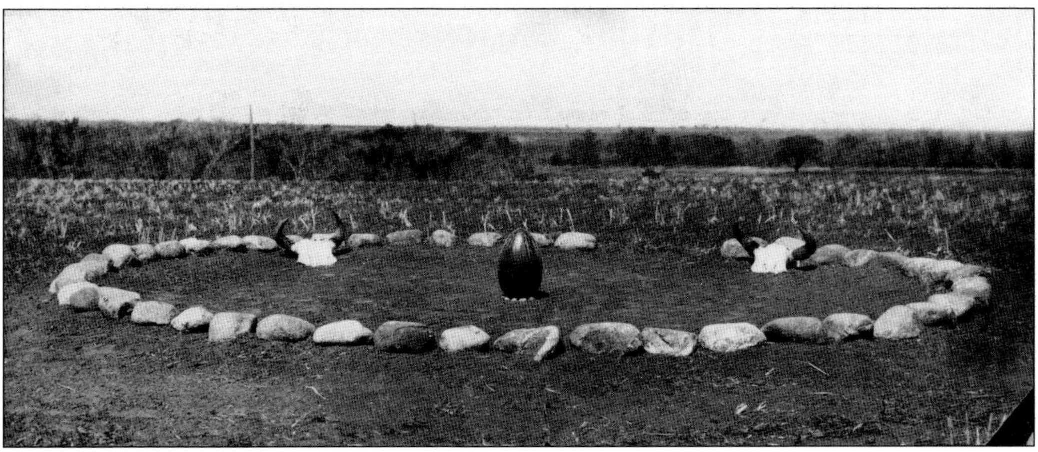

Pictured here is Council Rock. Originally, in southern Spink County, it was considered the Indian capital of the Dakotas. For decades, settlers would see many indigenous people stopping there as they passed through the area. An old burial ground is also in the vicinity, and for years one could follow an old Indian trail running through the pasture.

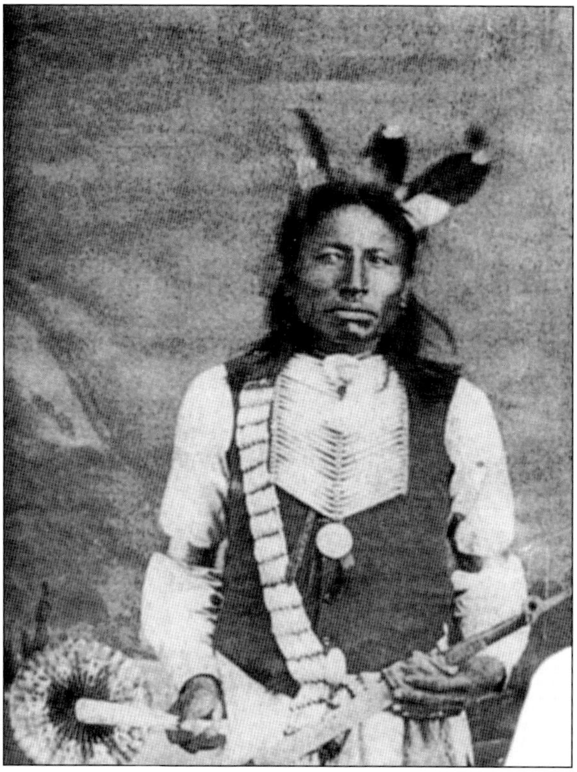

Drifting Goose is seen here as a young brave. Although he is often referred to as "Chief Drifting Goose," the title was not official. He did, however, lead a small band of about 130 Native Americans who called part of Spink County (Tetonka) home.

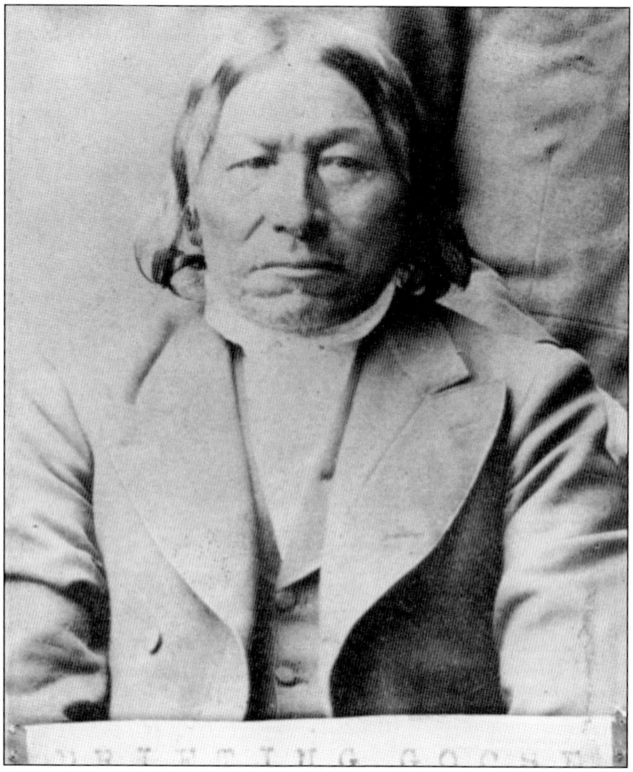

Here is Drifting Goose as he appeared in later years. A leader of a band of Yanktonais Sioux, he was sometimes referred to as Chief.

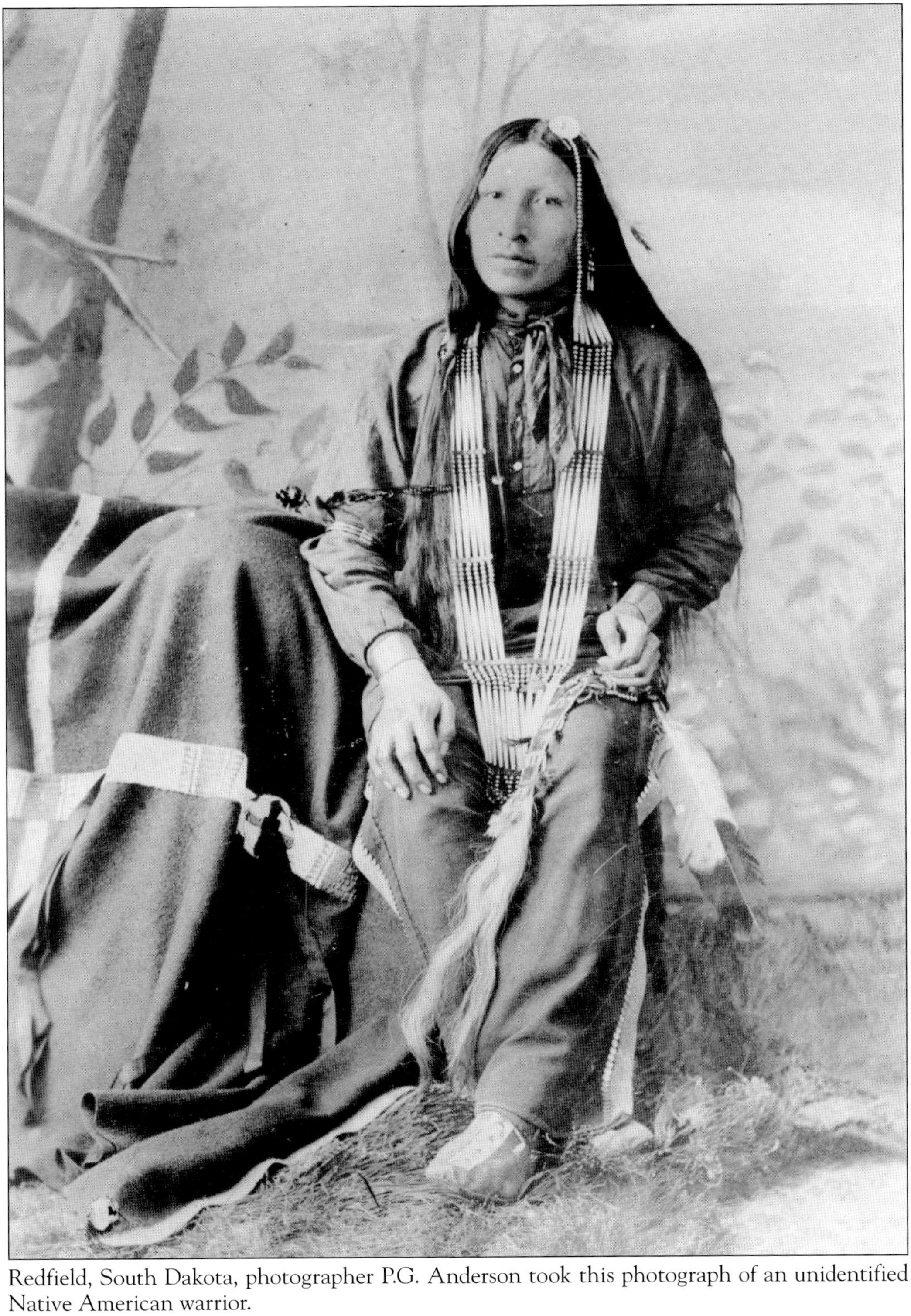

Redfield, South Dakota, photographer P.G. Anderson took this photograph of an unidentified Native American warrior.

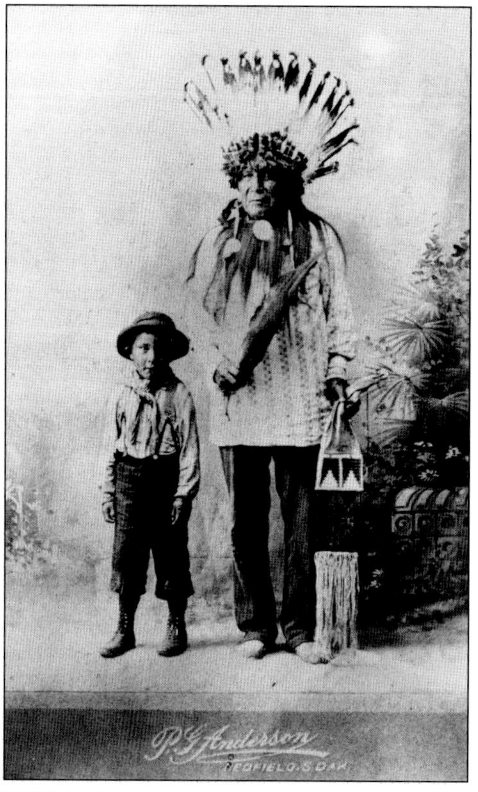

Anderson felt this portrait of Brother-of-All and a small boy captured the essence of a proud people.

This Native American group poses along the Jim River near Redfield. Their clothing shows the influence of the white culture.

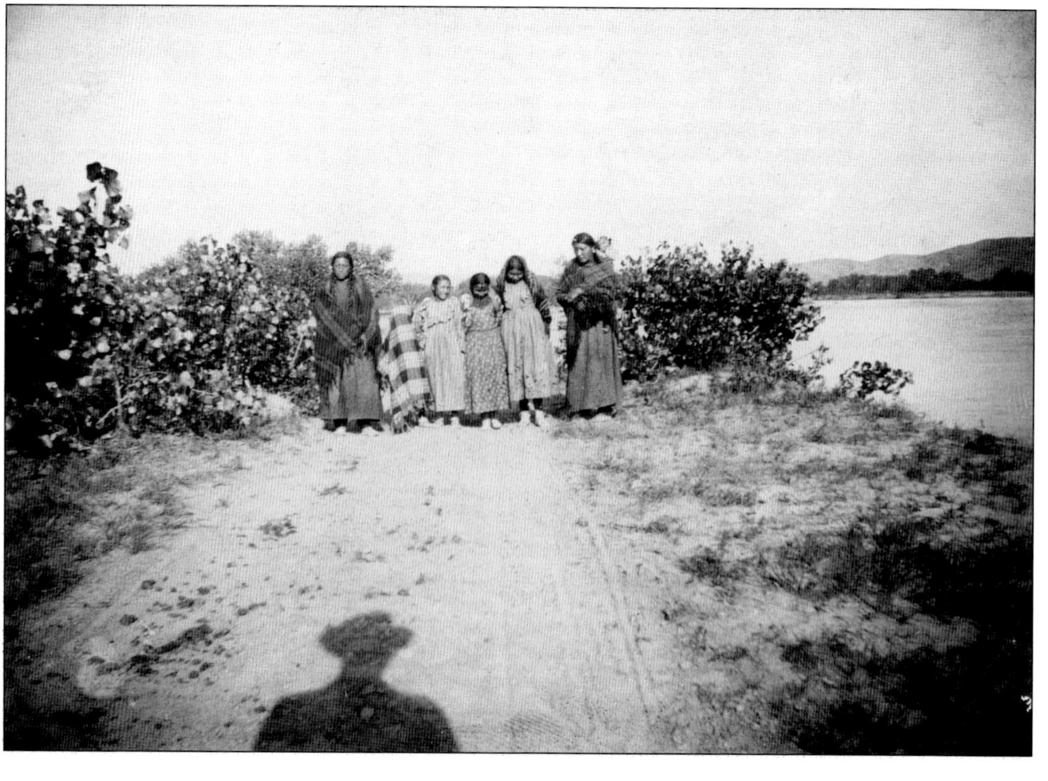

Anderson photographed this unidentified Indian twirler who traveled with Buffalo Bill's Wild West Show during the 1880s. (Courtesy of Norman Johnsen.)

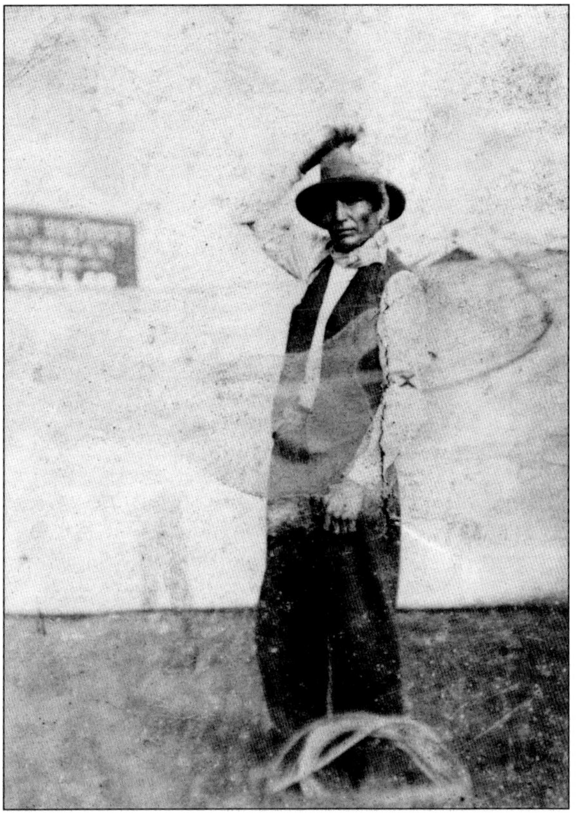

A man appears to be riding his bicycle over to watch the Native Americans put up a teepee during the late 1880s.

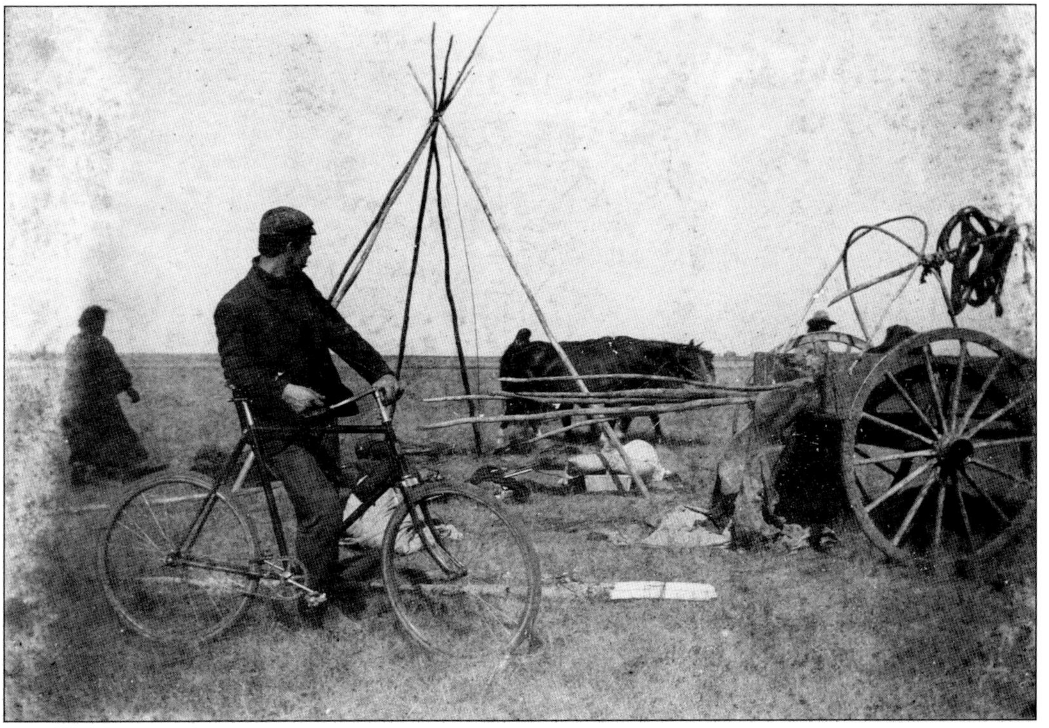

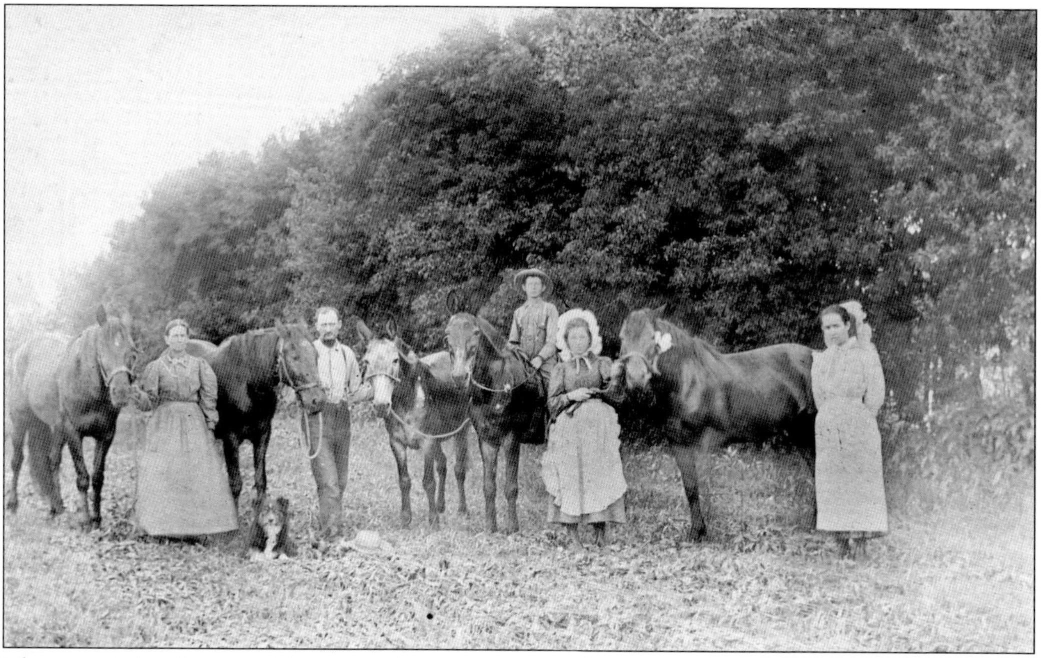

The Francis family arrived before the land was surveyed, filed a claim, worked it for a couple years, went south for the Oklahoma Land Rush to try their luck, and then returned later to Dakota Territory. They settled in Ashton. (Courtesy of Amber Overby Estate.)

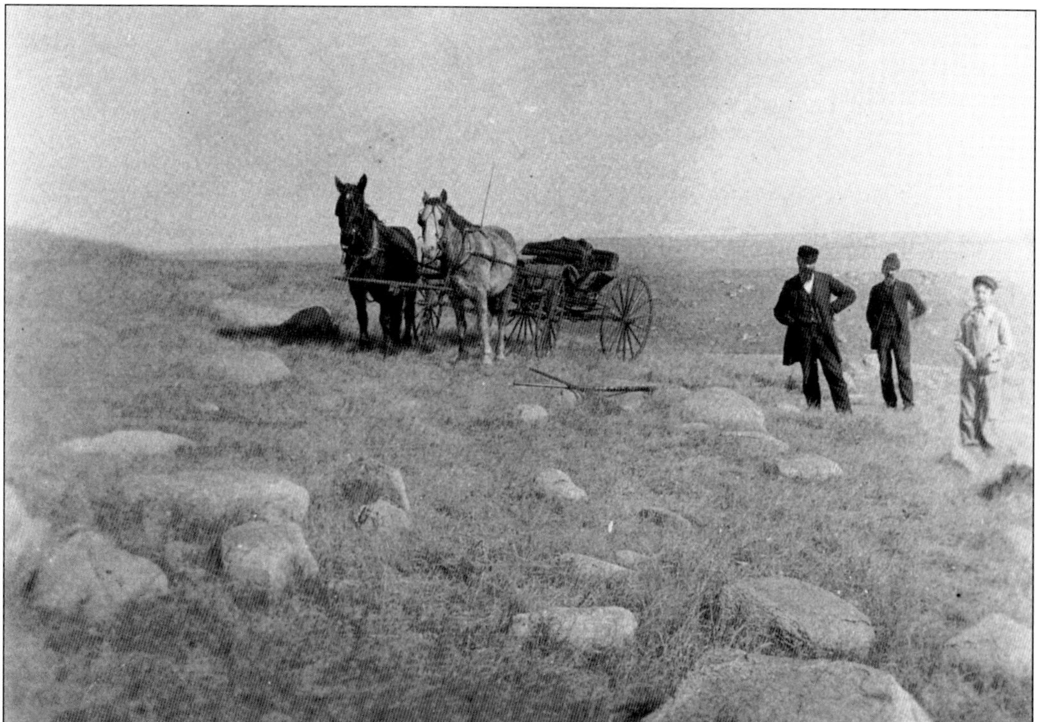

This group of two men, a boy, and two horses is out surveying the terrain for plowing obstacles. Huge boulders like those seen here dotted the plains and were a challenge for the early settlers.

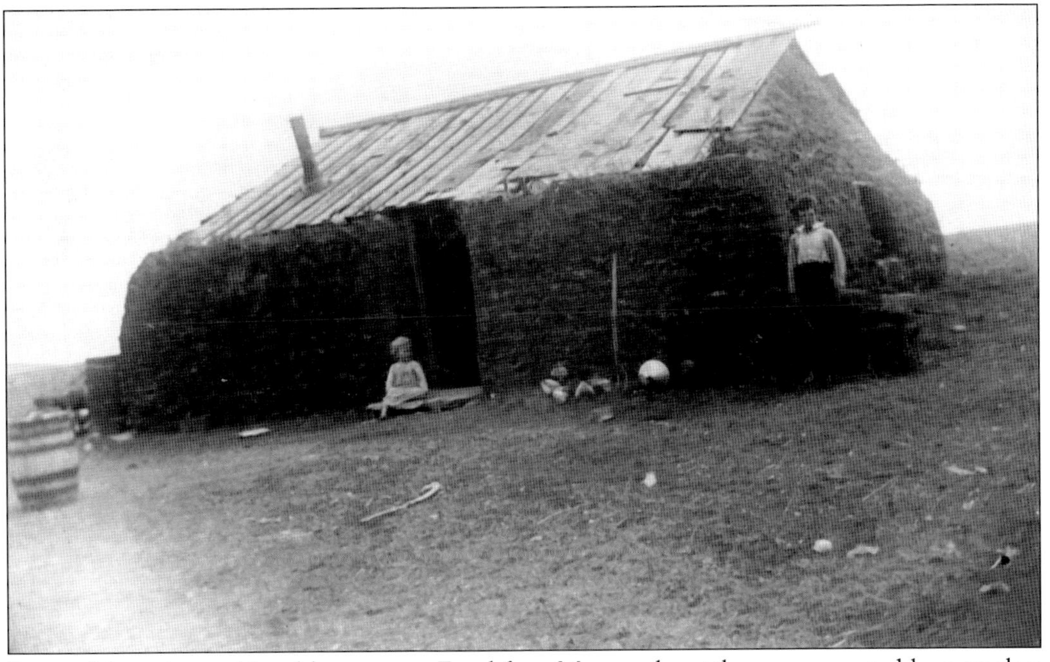

Pictured here is an old sod house near Frankfort. Most early settlers were greeted by a treeless plain, so they set about carving sod from the prairie to construct their homes. The children in this 1895 photograph are unidentified.

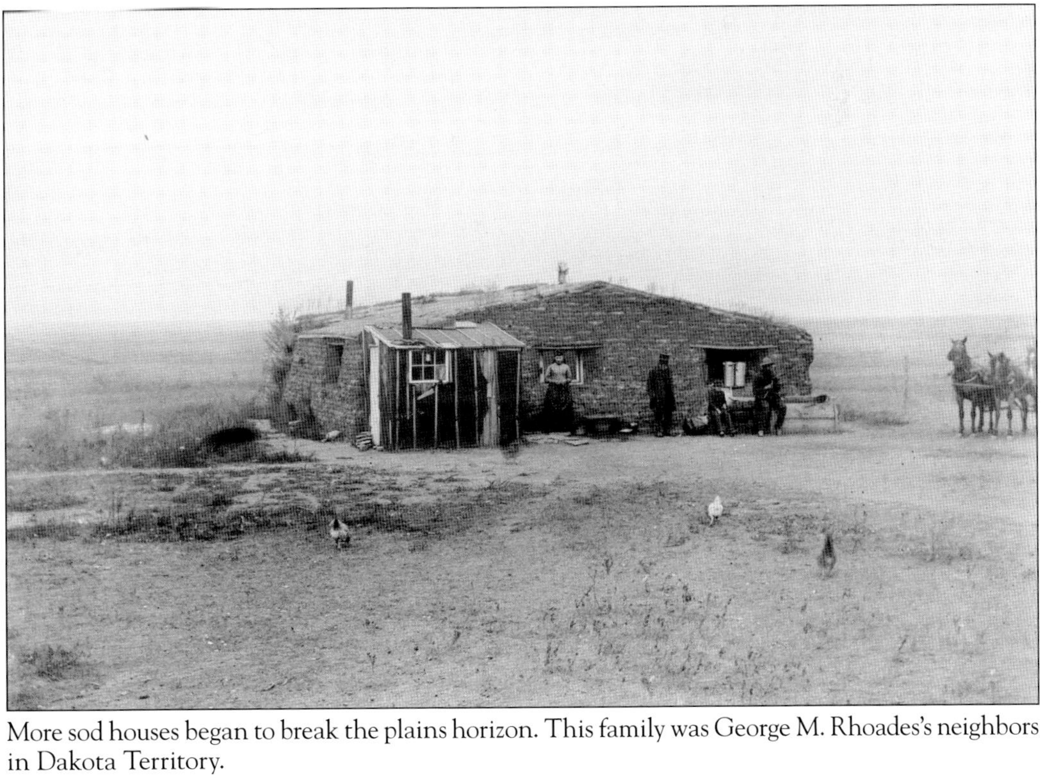

More sod houses began to break the plains horizon. This family was George M. Rhoades's neighbors in Dakota Territory.

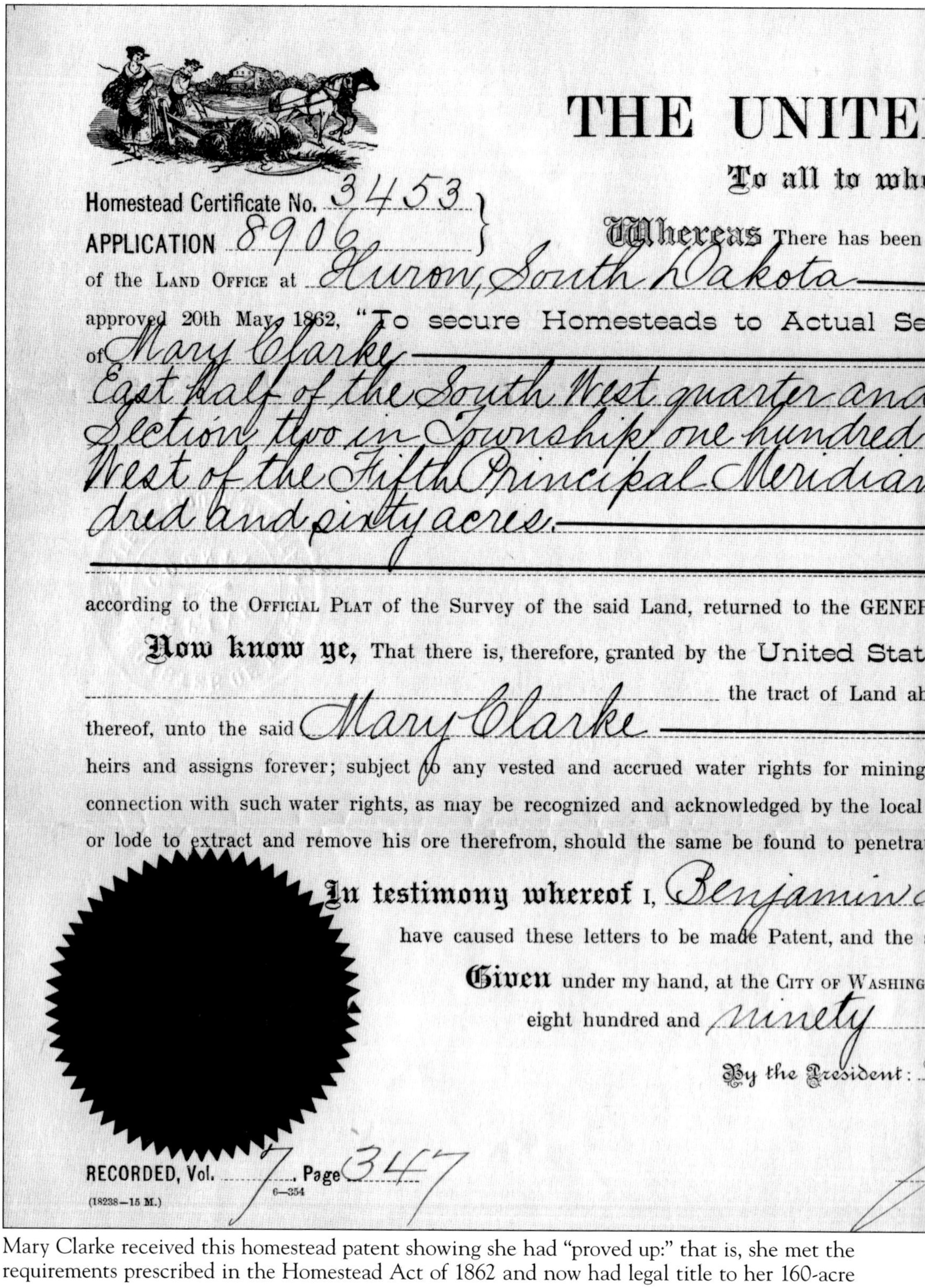

THE UNITE

To all to wh

Homestead Certificate No. 3453
APPLICATION 8906

Whereas There has been

of the Land Office at Huron, South Dakota

approved 20th May, 1862, "To secure Homesteads to Actual Se

of Mary Clarke

East half of the South West quarter and

Section two in Township one hundred

West of the Fifth Principal Meridian

dred and sixty acres.

according to the Official Plat of the Survey of the said Land, returned to the GENEF

Now know ye, That there is, therefore, granted by the United Stat

the tract of Land ab

thereof, unto the said Mary Clarke

heirs and assigns forever; subject to any vested and accrued water rights for mining

connection with such water rights, as may be recognized and acknowledged by the local

or lode to extract and remove his ore therefrom, should the same be found to penetra

In testimony whereof I, Benjamin

have caused these letters to be made Patent, and the

Given under my hand, at the City of Washing

eight hundred and ninety

By the President:

RECORDED, Vol. 7, Page 347

6—354

(18238—15 M.)

Mary Clarke received this homestead patent showing she had "proved up:" that is, she met the requirements prescribed in the Homestead Act of 1862 and now had legal title to her 160-acre

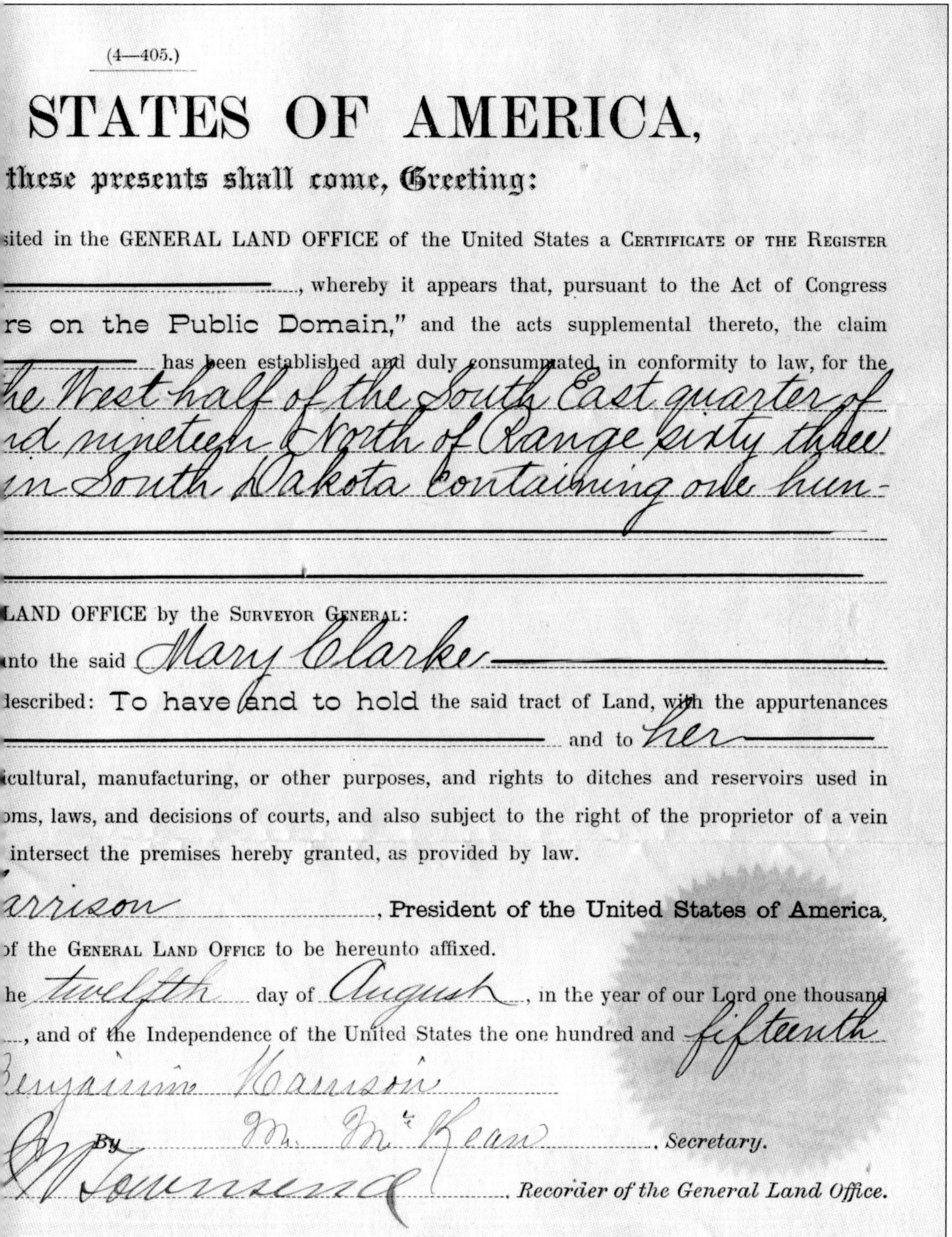

(4—405.)

STATES OF AMERICA,

these presents shall come, Greeting:

sited in the GENERAL LAND OFFICE of the United States a CERTIFICATE OF THE REGISTER

________________, whereby it appears that, pursuant to the Act of Congress

rs on the Public Domain," and the acts supplemental thereto, the claim

________ has been established and duly consummated, in conformity to law, for the

he West half of the South East quarter of

nd nineteen North of Range sixty three

in South Dakota containing one hun-

LAND OFFICE by the SURVEYOR GENERAL:

unto the said Mary Clarke

described: To have and to hold the said tract of Land, with the appurtenances

________________ and to her

icultural, manufacturing, or other purposes, and rights to ditches and reservoirs used in

oms, laws, and decisions of courts, and also subject to the right of the proprietor of a vein

intersect the premises hereby granted, as provided by law.

arrison ________, President of the United States of America,

of the GENERAL LAND OFFICE to be hereunto affixed.

he twelfth day of August, in the year of our Lord one thousand

, and of the Independence of the United States the one hundred and fifteenth

Benjamin Harrison

By M. McKean, Secretary.

Townsend, Recorder of the General Land Office.

claim. Pres. Benjamin Harrison signed the document in 1890. The document illustrates the equality of opportunity for women.

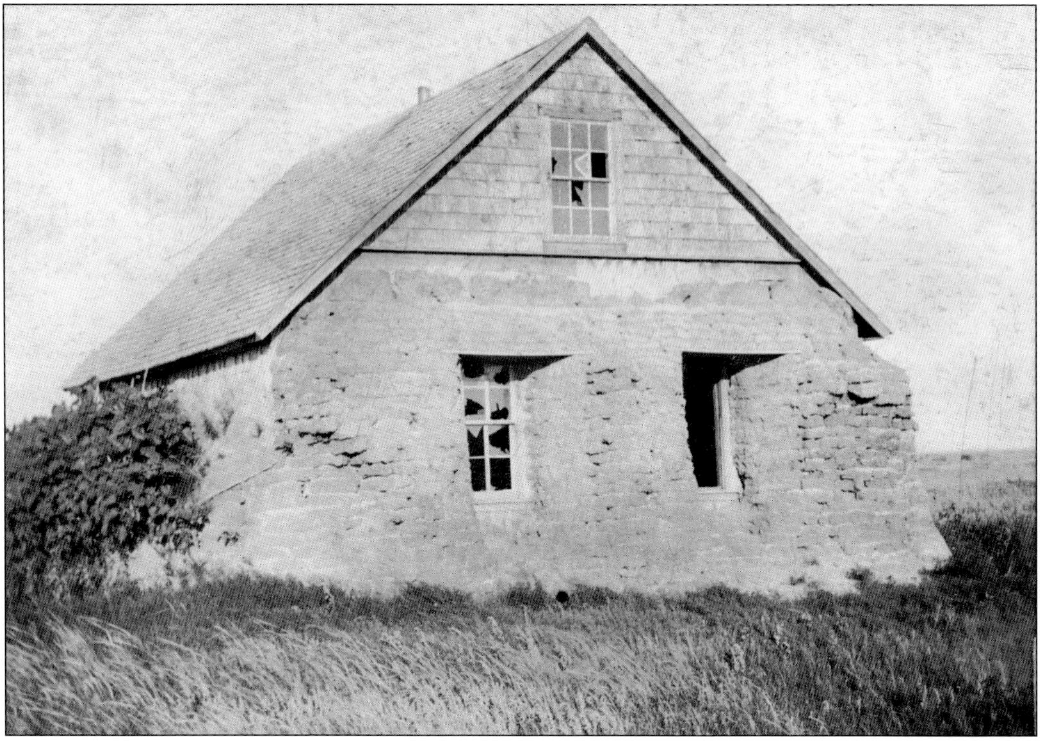

Pictured here is the last sod house in Spink County. Interestingly, this house, near Doland, had glass windows.

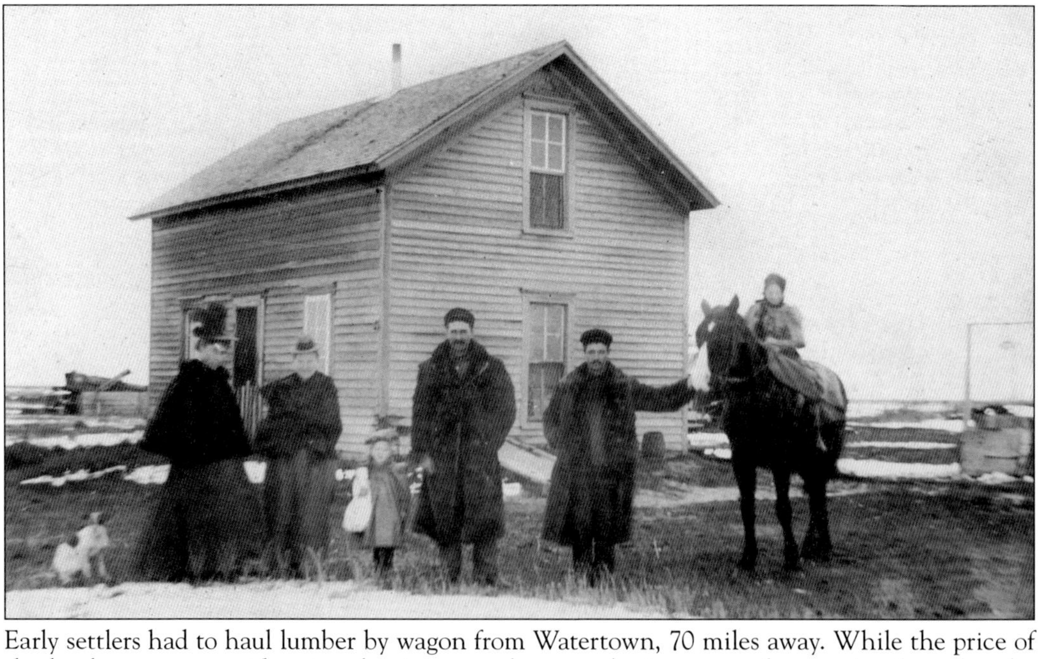

Early settlers had to haul lumber by wagon from Watertown, 70 miles away. While the price of the lumber was a consideration, having to make several trips across the prairie often played a greater role. Consequently, most of the early houses, like the A. Markham homestead seen here in 1897, met the owner's barest need. (Courtesy of Rod Evans.)

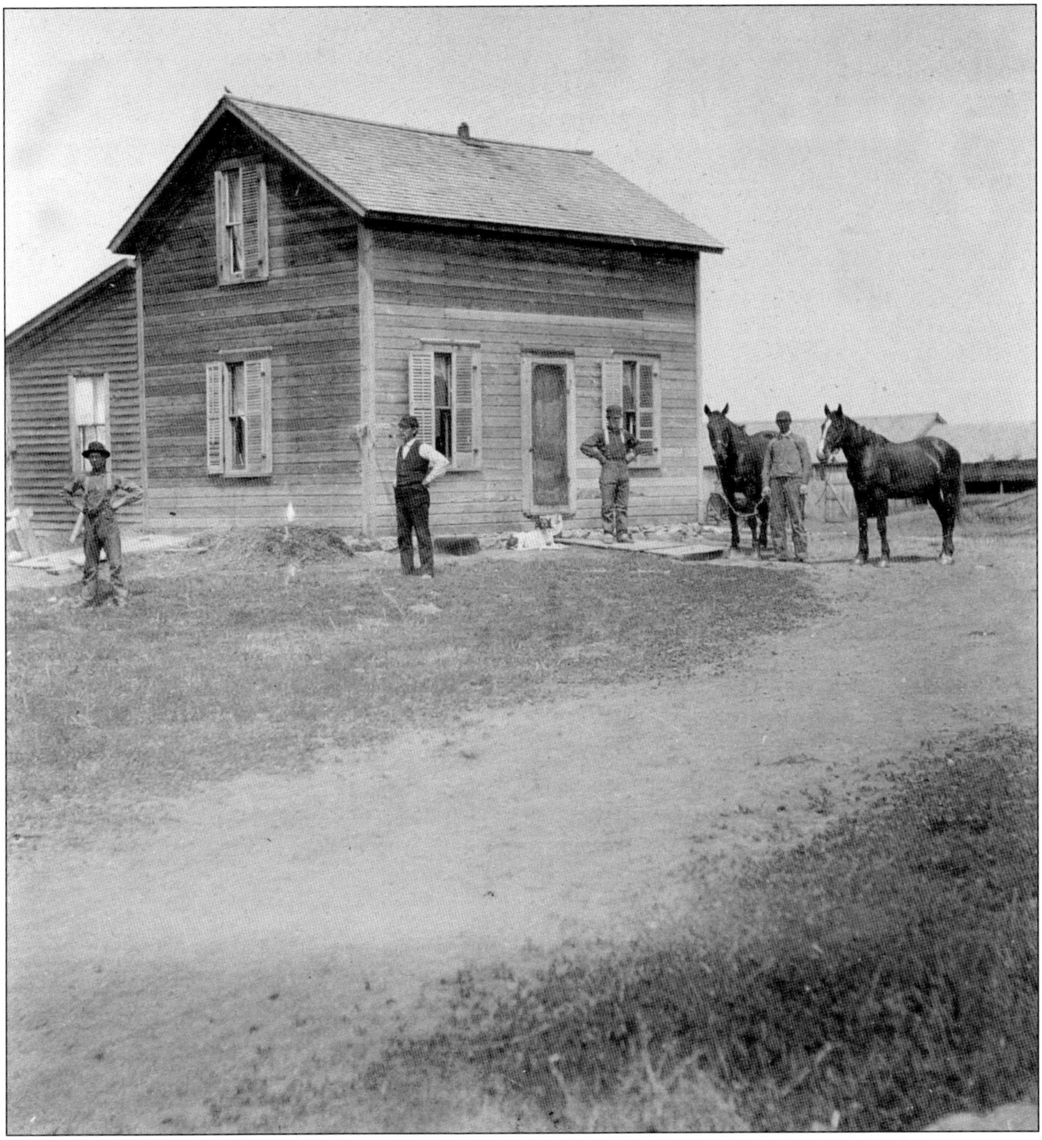

Pictured here is the C.L. Stutenroth farmhouse near Doland. Paint was not a high priority on the early houses.

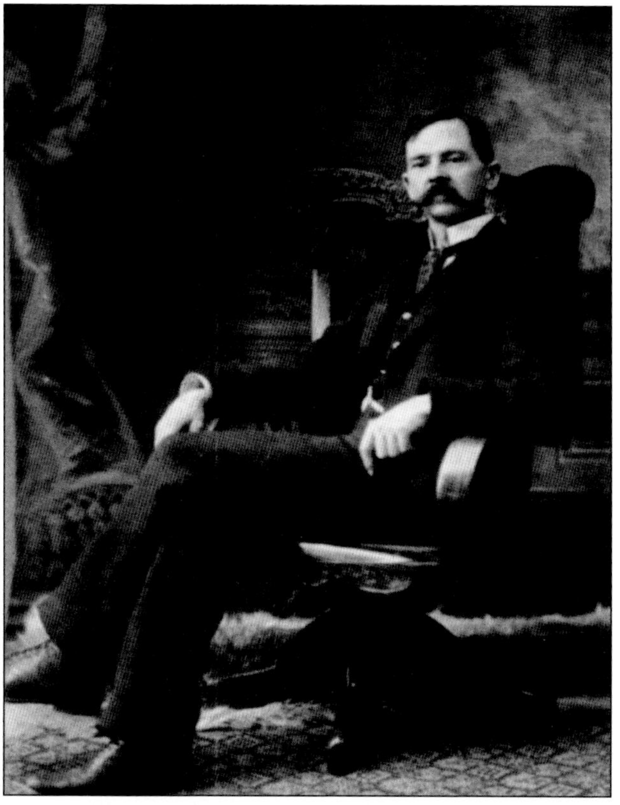

Posing in his chair is P.G. Anderson, Spink County's first photographer and the man credited for many of the images appearing in this book. This photograph was taken in 1883.

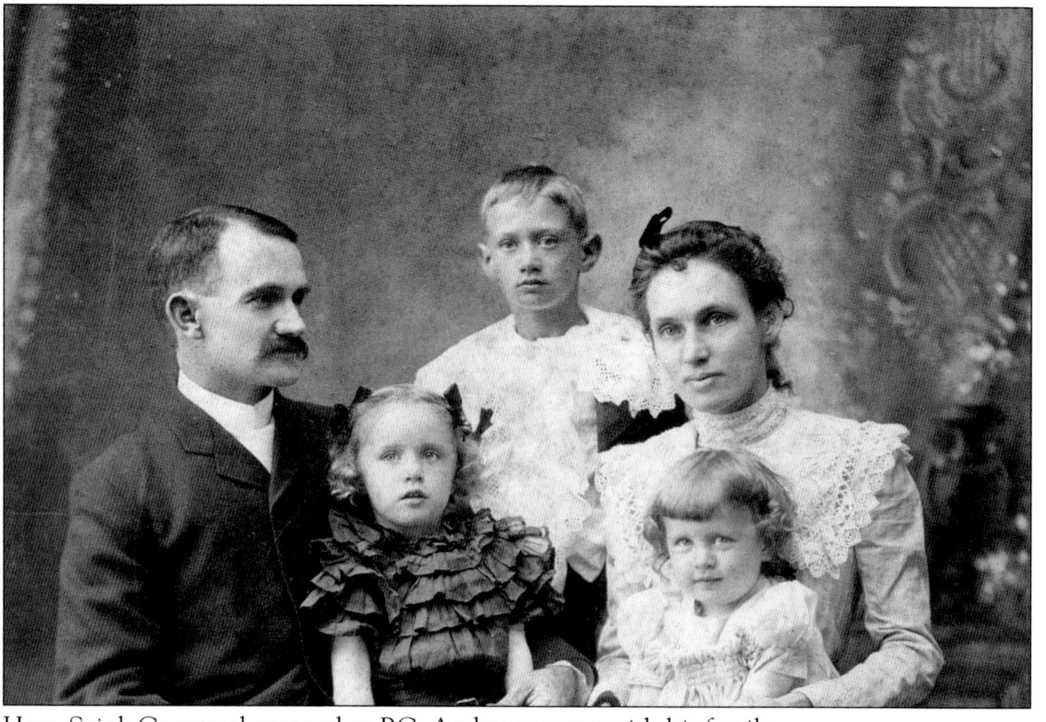

Here, Spink County photographer P.G. Anderson poses with his family.

Two

From Horses to Airplanes

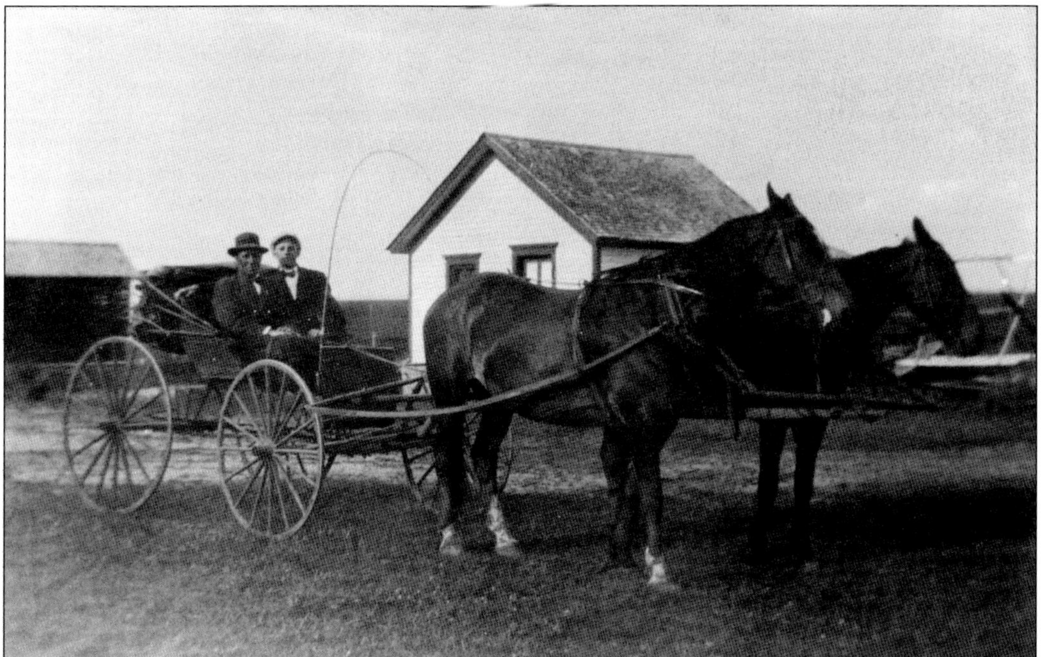

These two men are ready to go to town, with a nice looking pair of horses pulling a nice buggy. They would appear as good, solid citizens when they arrived on Main Street or at church.

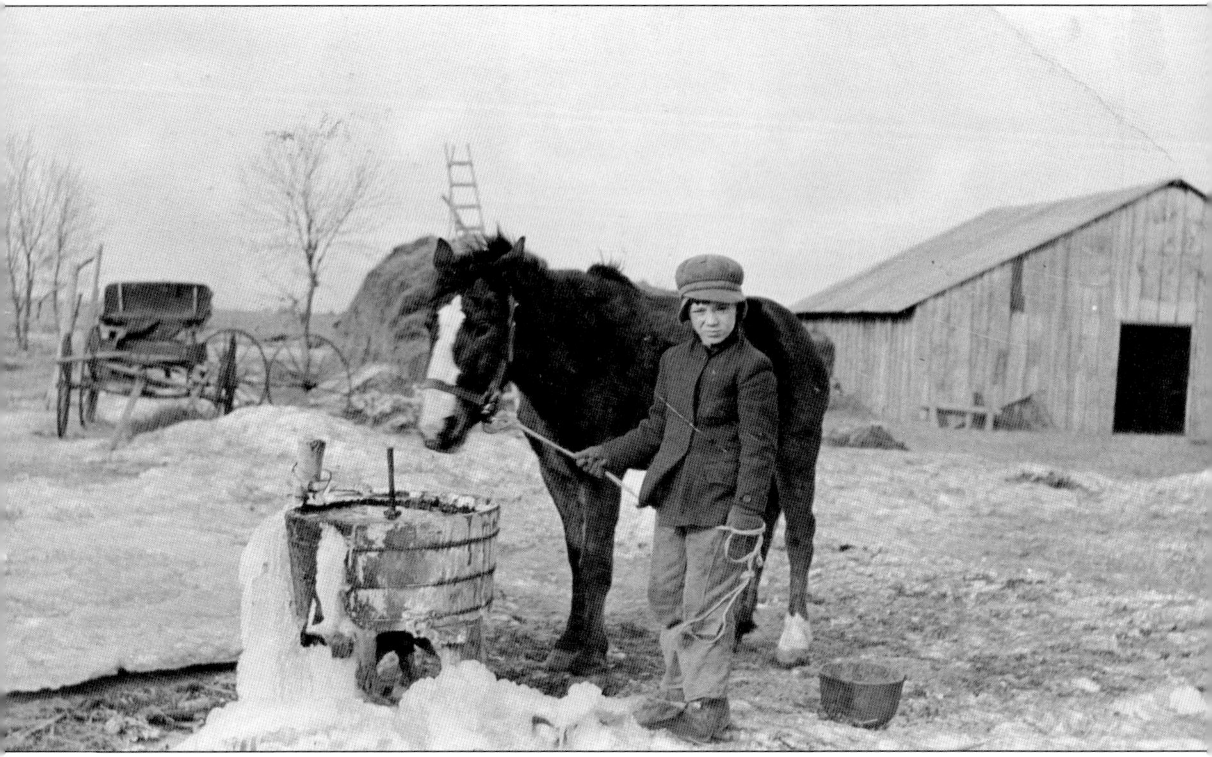

Here is Pete Ross and his horse. Many of the earliest homesteaders actually brought oxen rather than horses to break the sod. Oxen were slow but stronger. A sod-busting plow had a single blade; the accepted wisdom was that one man, a single-blade plow, and two oxen could "bust" one acre per day. A lack of photographs of oxen and many photographs of workhorses suggests that once the sod was broken up, workhorses shortly took the place of the oxen. In most barns, horses were kept beneath the hay mow on the main ground floor of the barn while the milk cows were left to the lean-to portion. In town, horses were kept in small stables on the property or at a livery stable. (Courtesy of Amber Overby Estate.)

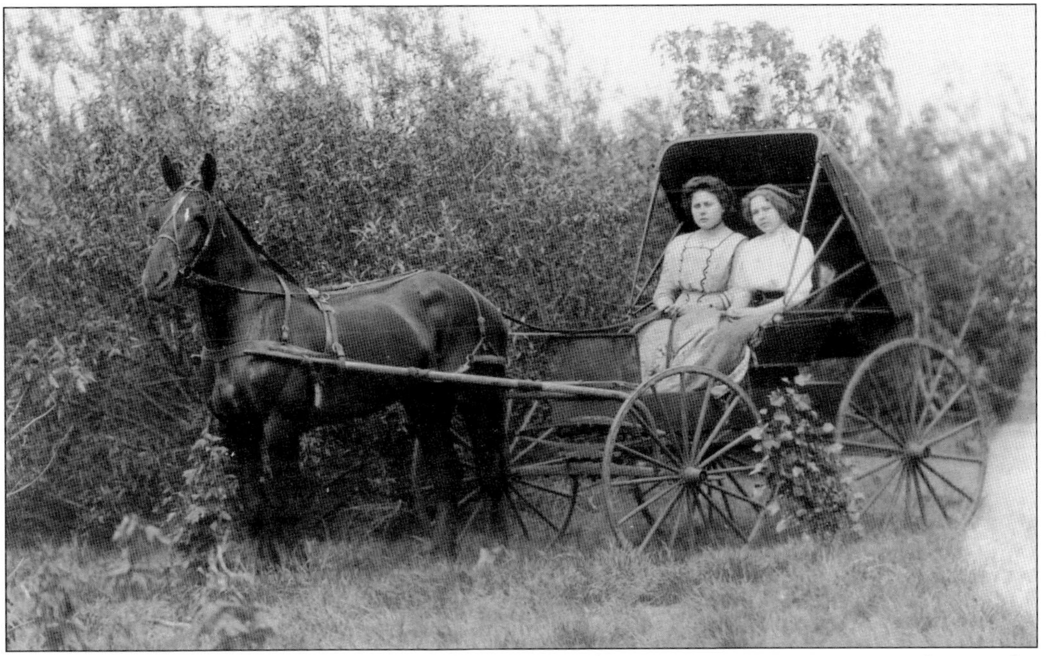

These two ladies are going for a ride in the countryside. Livery enterprises commonly rented a horse or team of horses; horse-drawn taxis were also part of the scene in larger towns. Then, as now, upscale hotels have their own taxis to pick up guests at the railroad station and return them to the platform after a stay.

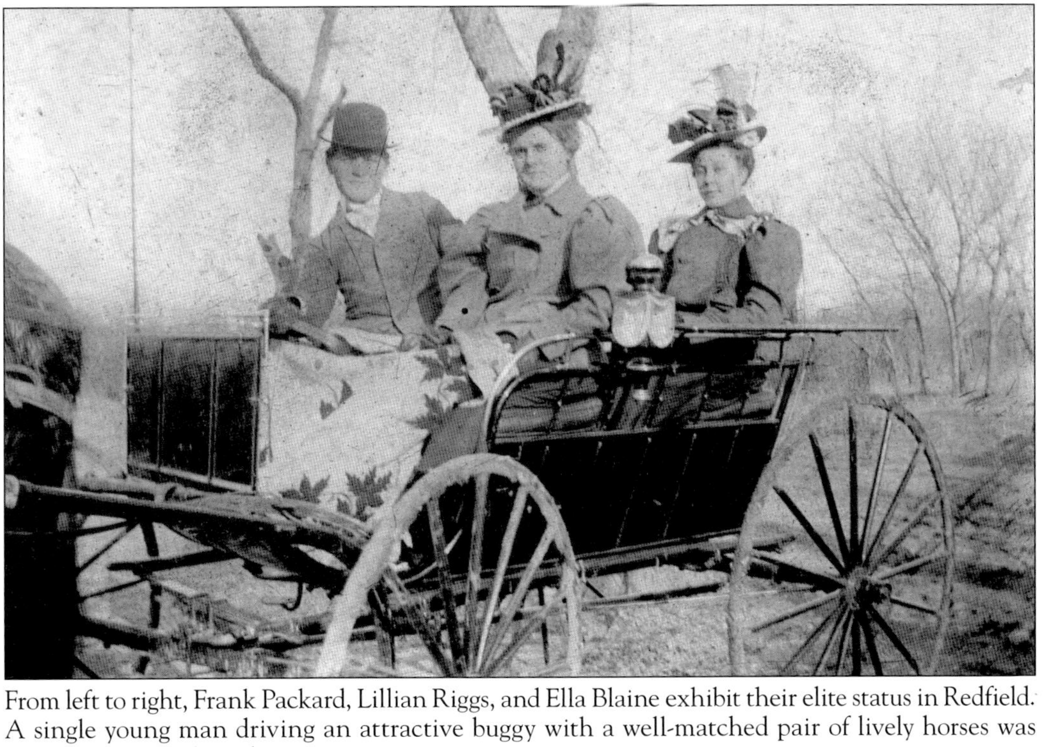

From left to right, Frank Packard, Lillian Riggs, and Ella Blaine exhibit their elite status in Redfield. A single young man driving an attractive buggy with a well-matched pair of lively horses was considered a good catch.

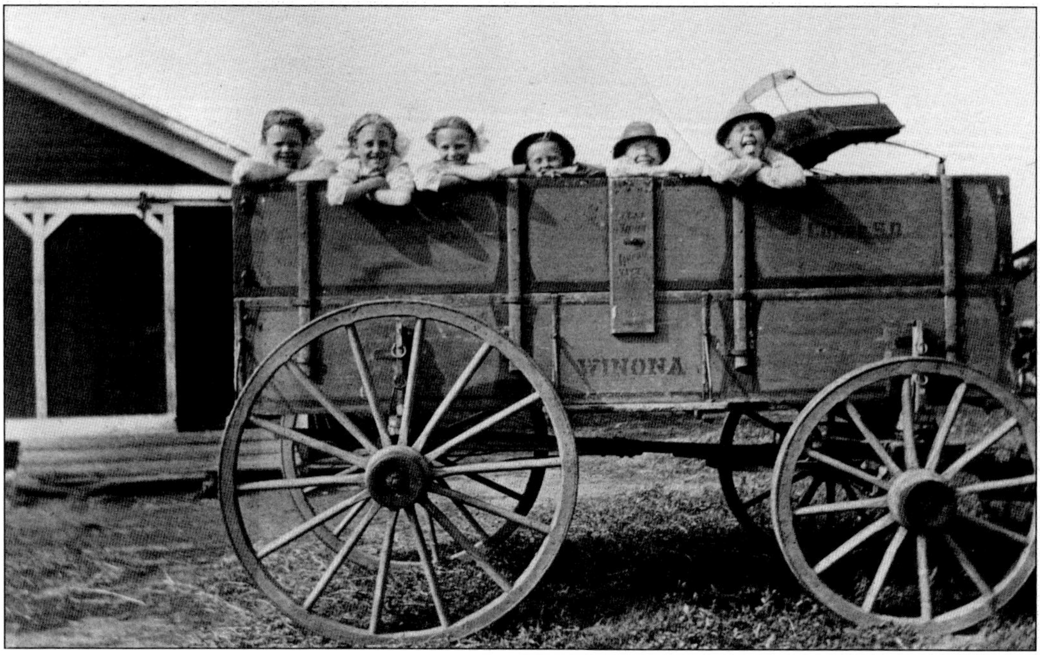

As evidenced above, Spink County frontier kids found their own time for fun, too, so long as the family wagon was not in service. Below, when it came time for work, every farm had a wagon like this, ready to go to town and stock up on much-needed supplies. This was the prevalent mode of transport for the rural majority.

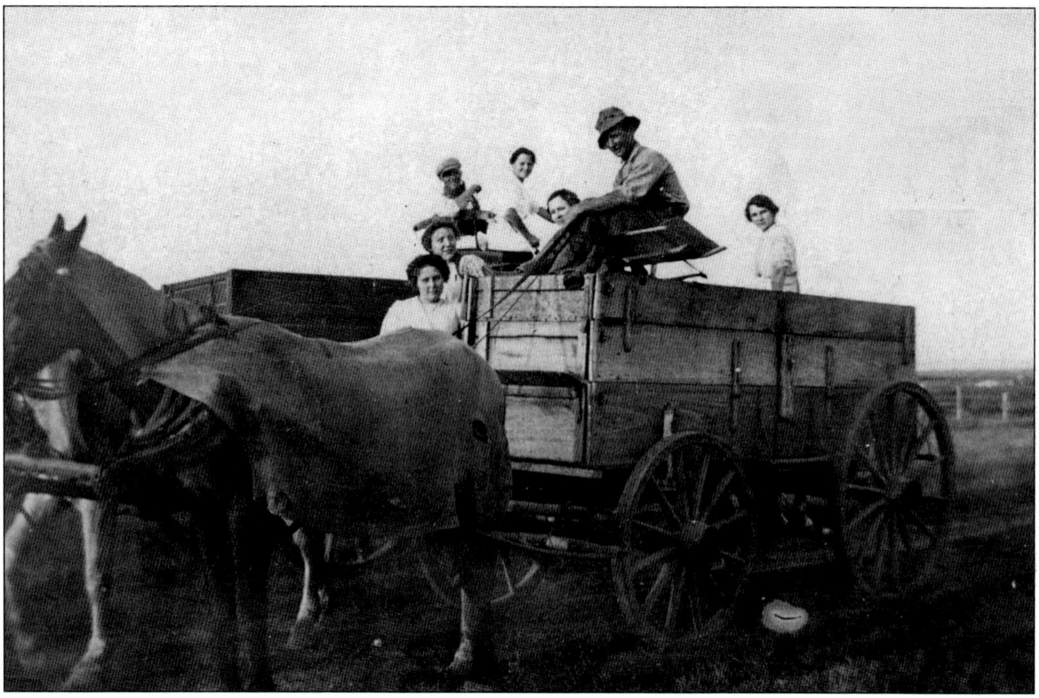

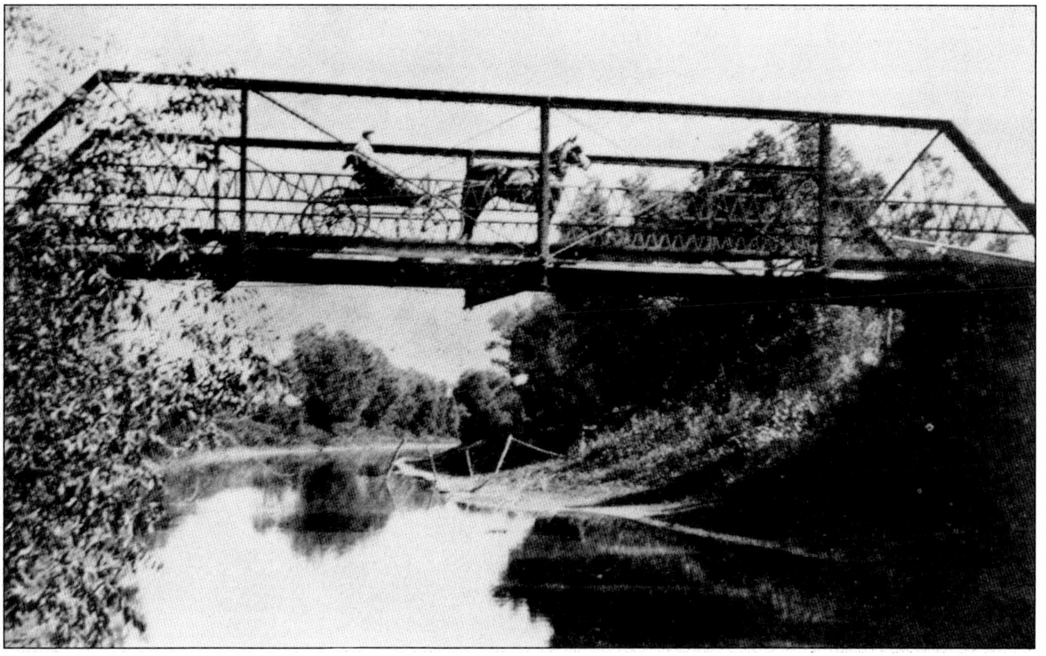

This rare photograph shows a man crossing the bridge over the James River on a horse and buggy. The spot is likely near Mellette. (Courtesy of Rod Evans.)

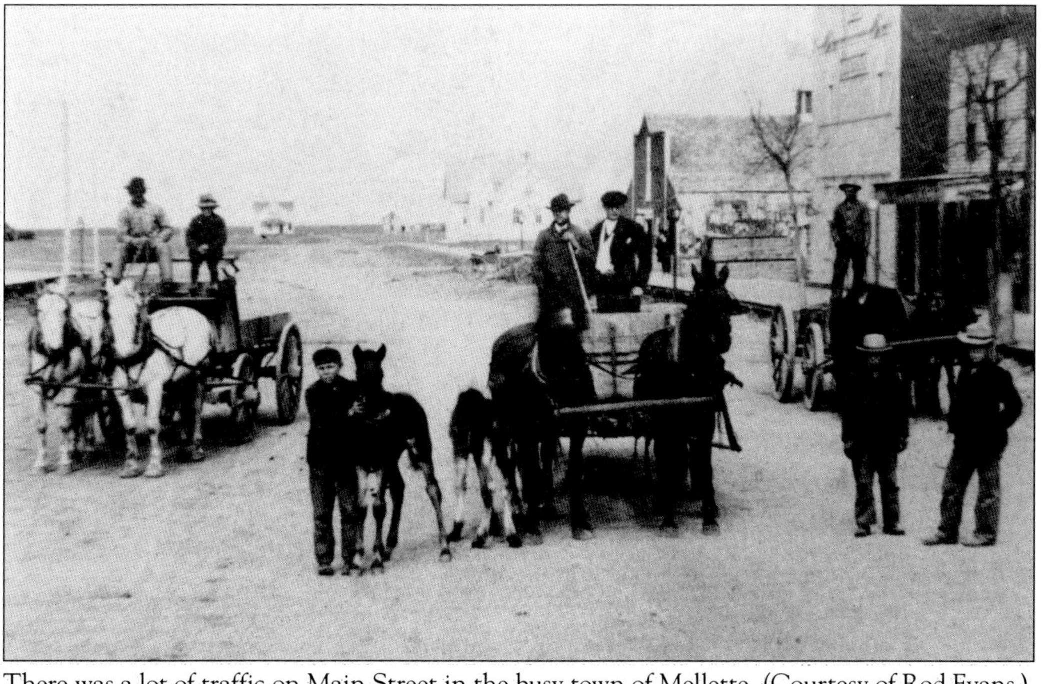

There was a lot of traffic on Main Street in the busy town of Mellette. (Courtesy of Rod Evans.)

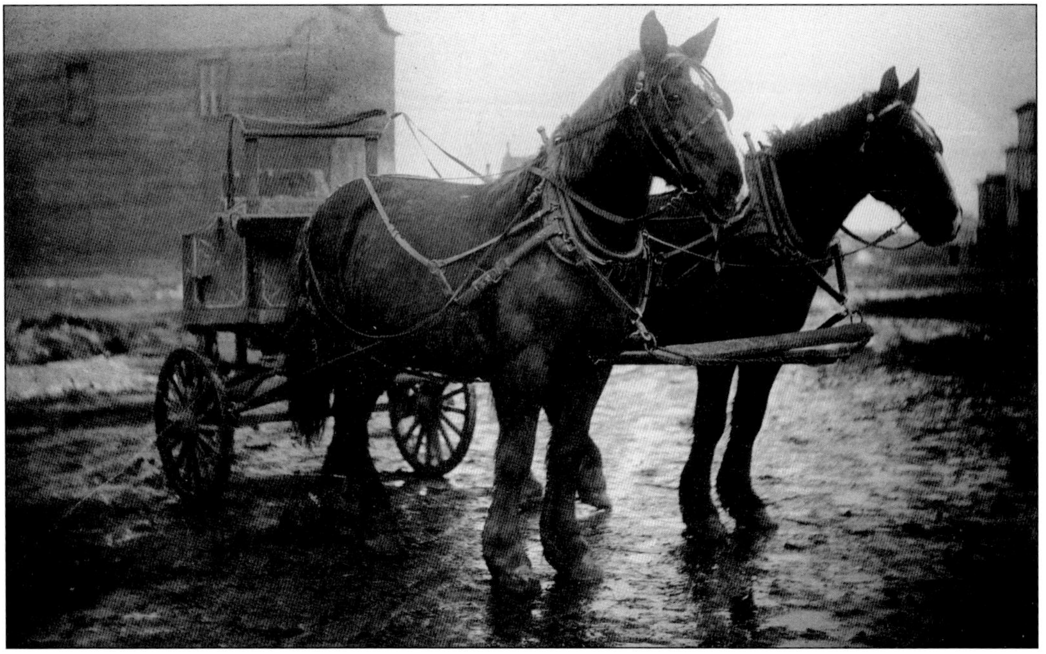

This pair of work- or draft horses is ready for or has just completed hauling a heavy load. (Courtesy of Marion Jensen and Earl Grandpre.)

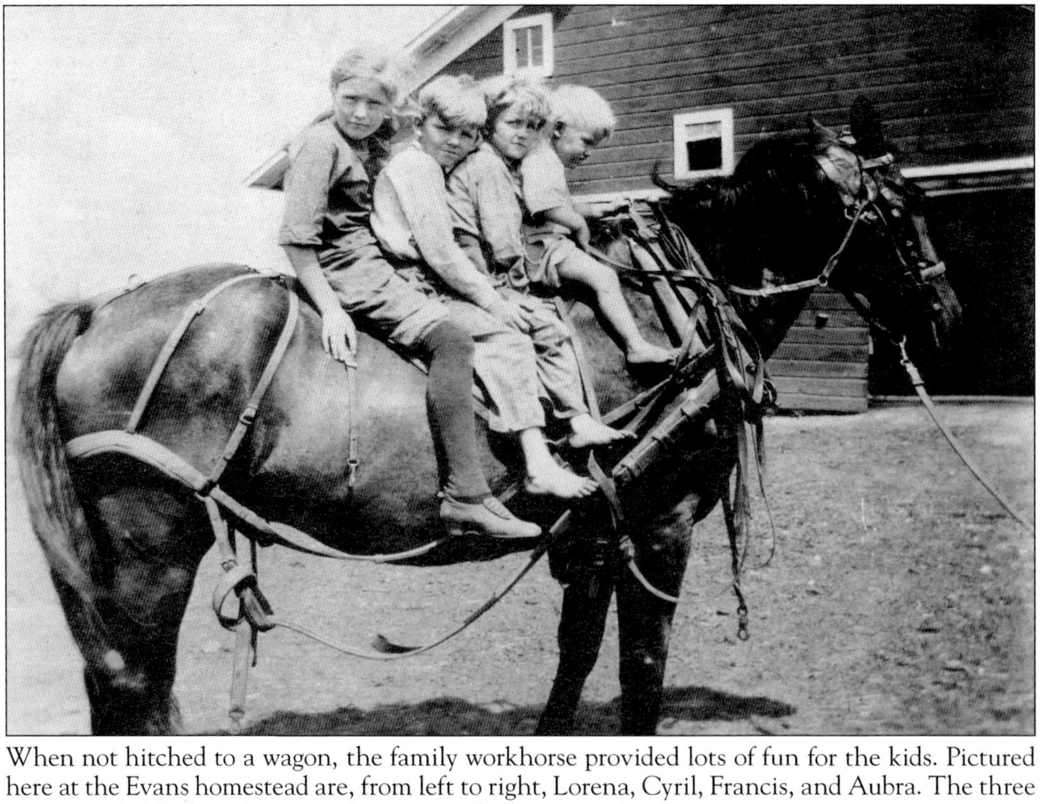

When not hitched to a wagon, the family workhorse provided lots of fun for the kids. Pictured here at the Evans homestead are, from left to right, Lorena, Cyril, Francis, and Aubra. The three youngest children are barefoot. (Courtesy of Alan Evans.)

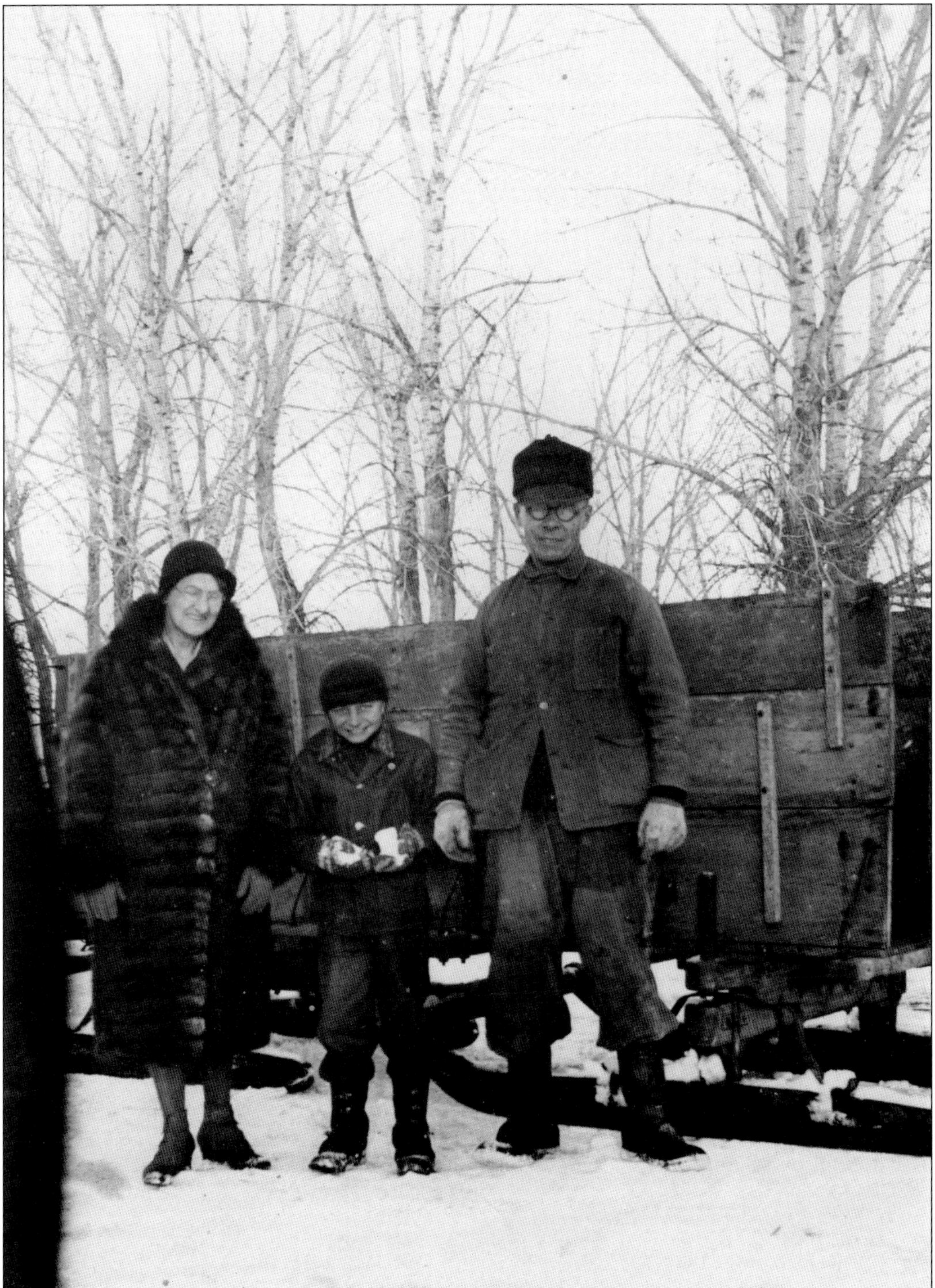

Early settlers had to adapt to the changing seasons. Emil and Maude Overby and son Buddy are ready for travel; Emil took the wheels off the wagon and substituted sleigh runners. (Courtesy of Amber Overby estate.)

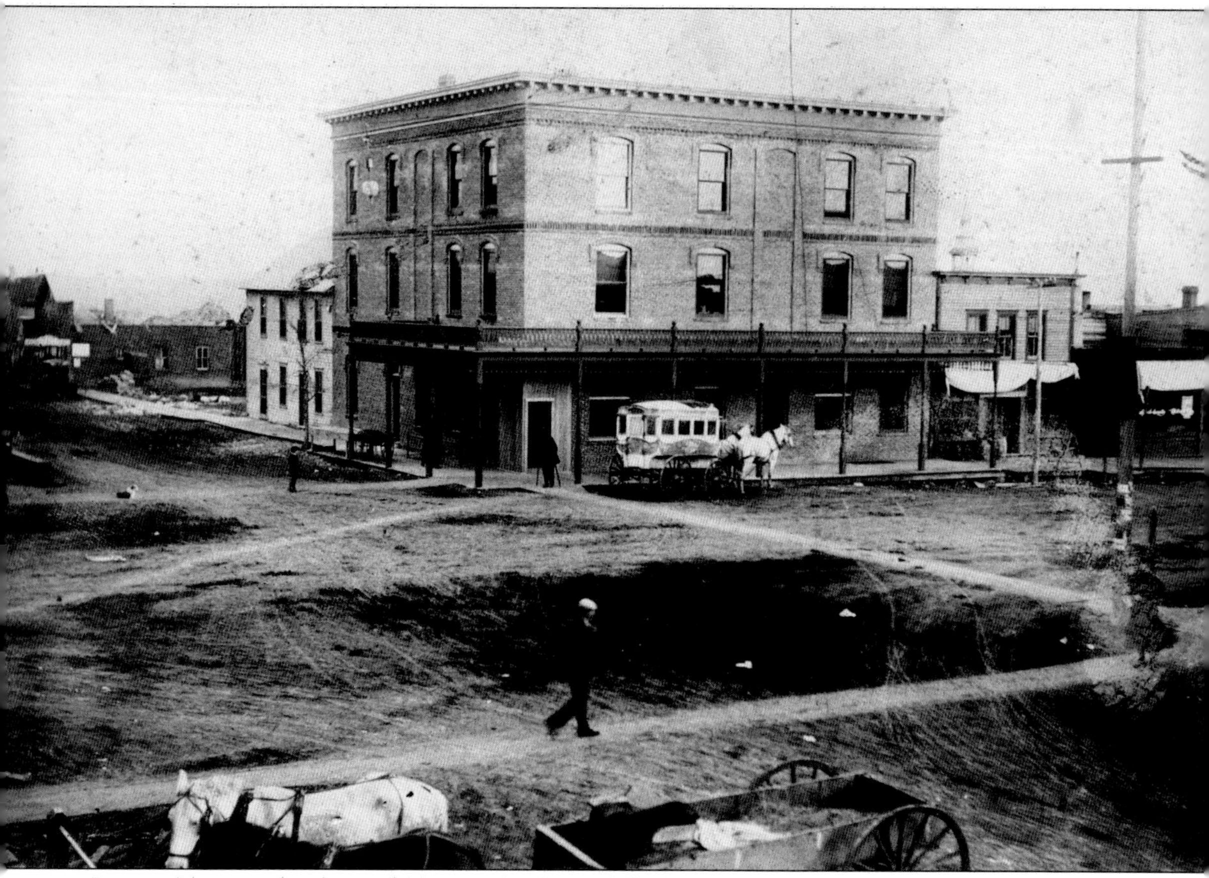

Pictured here is the Central House Hotel taxi. The horse-drawn, enclosed carriage has likely brought passengers from the Milwaukee depot and now is ready to take departing guests to their railroad platform of choice.

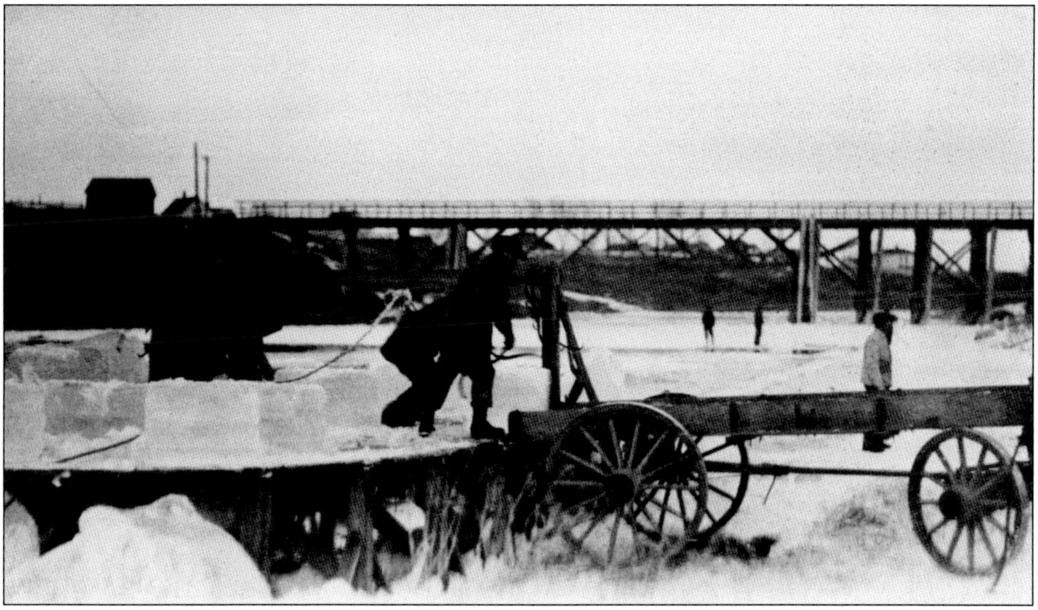

The photograph above captures men loading blocks of ice, cut from the river, onto wagons. The ice would be hauled off to town and stored away in ice houses for use in the summer months. Below, an Arns Ice Co. delivery wagon makes its rounds to replenish the iceboxes in Redfield's homes and businesses in 1904.

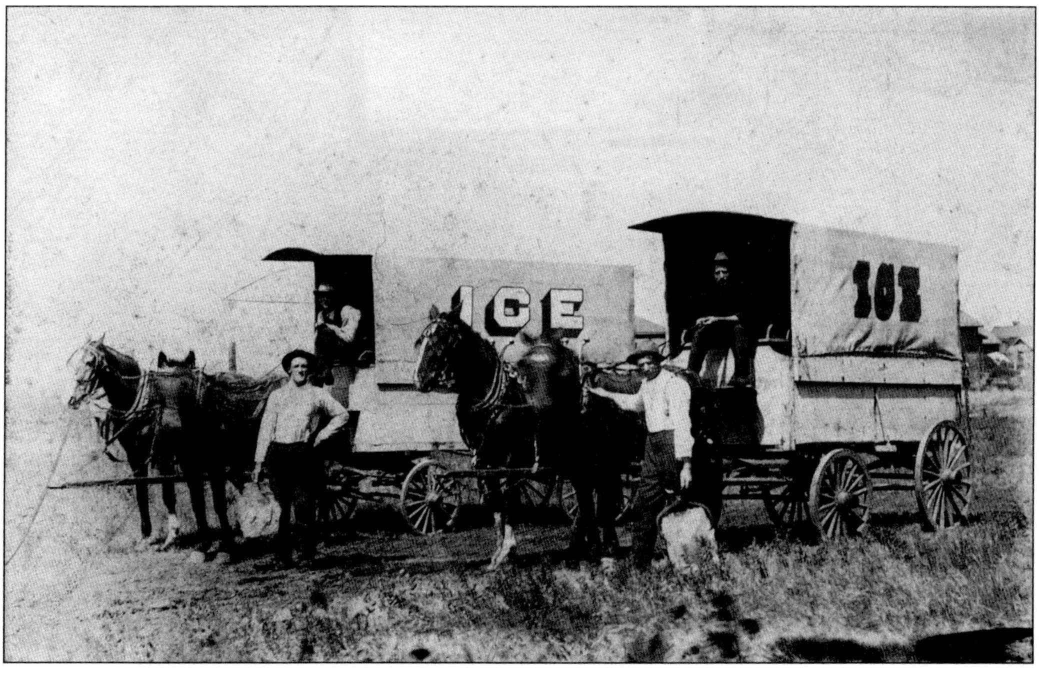

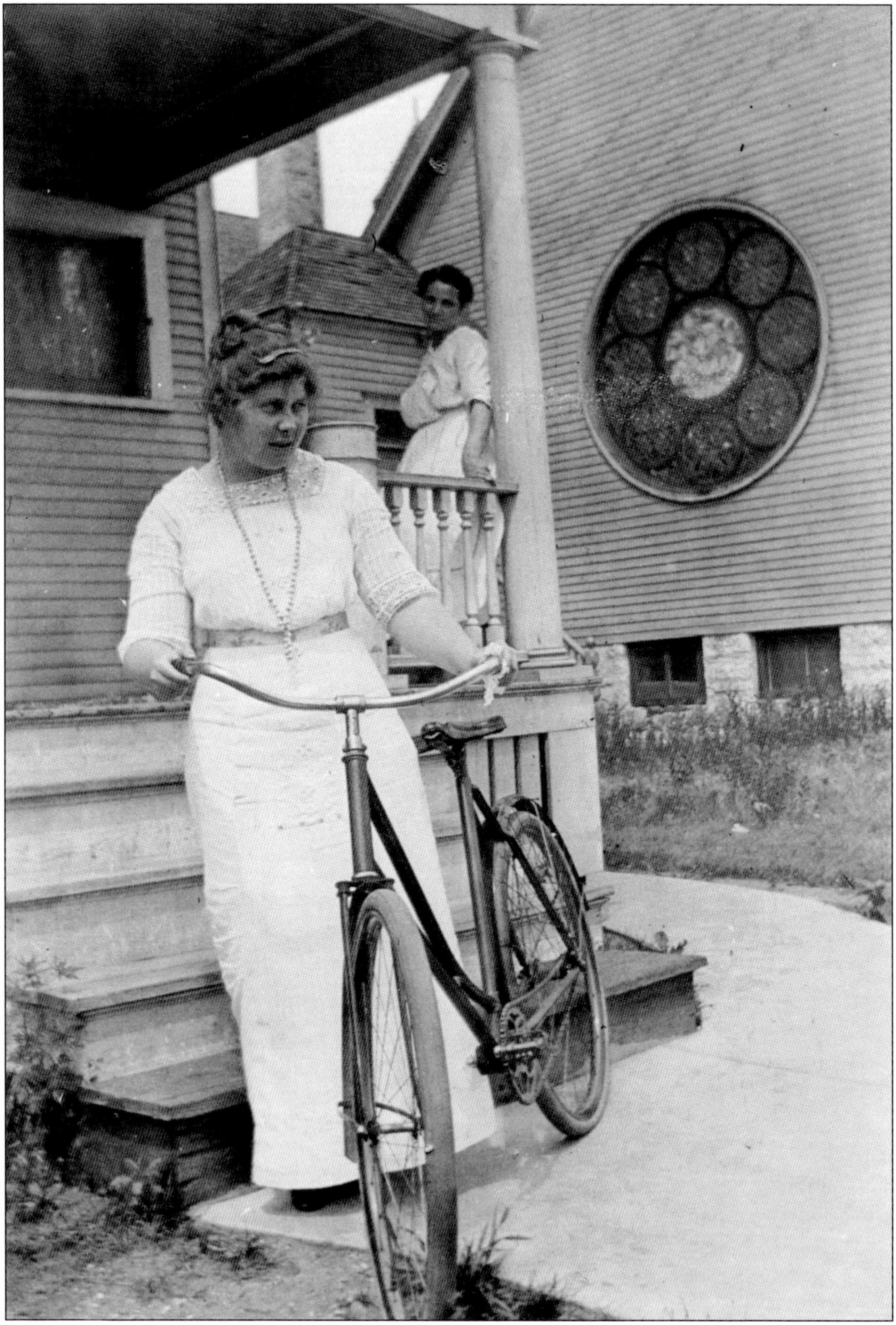

Bicycles were handy for the ladies. They were a relatively popular form of transportation. Most roads were dirt rather than gravel, so the ride was smoother, a definite plus when riding a high-wheeled "bone-crusher" bicycle.

Dr. Kutnewsky paused for this photograph while making his rounds. A bicycle was certainly the quickest way to tend to Redfield's in-town patients.

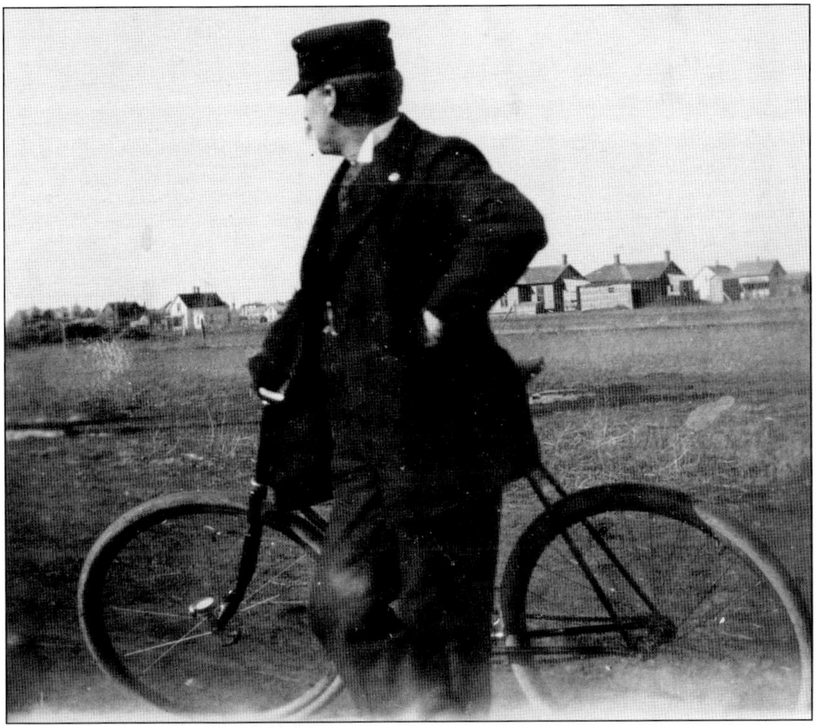

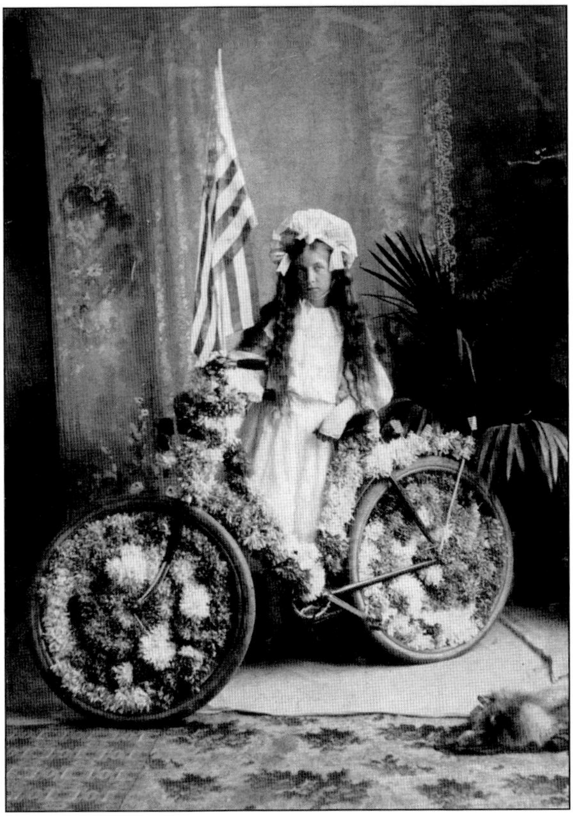

Young Florence Ouimet poses with her bicycle in Floyd O'Brian's studio. This patriotic themed bicycle must have made a colorful statement in Redfield sometime around the Fourth of July.

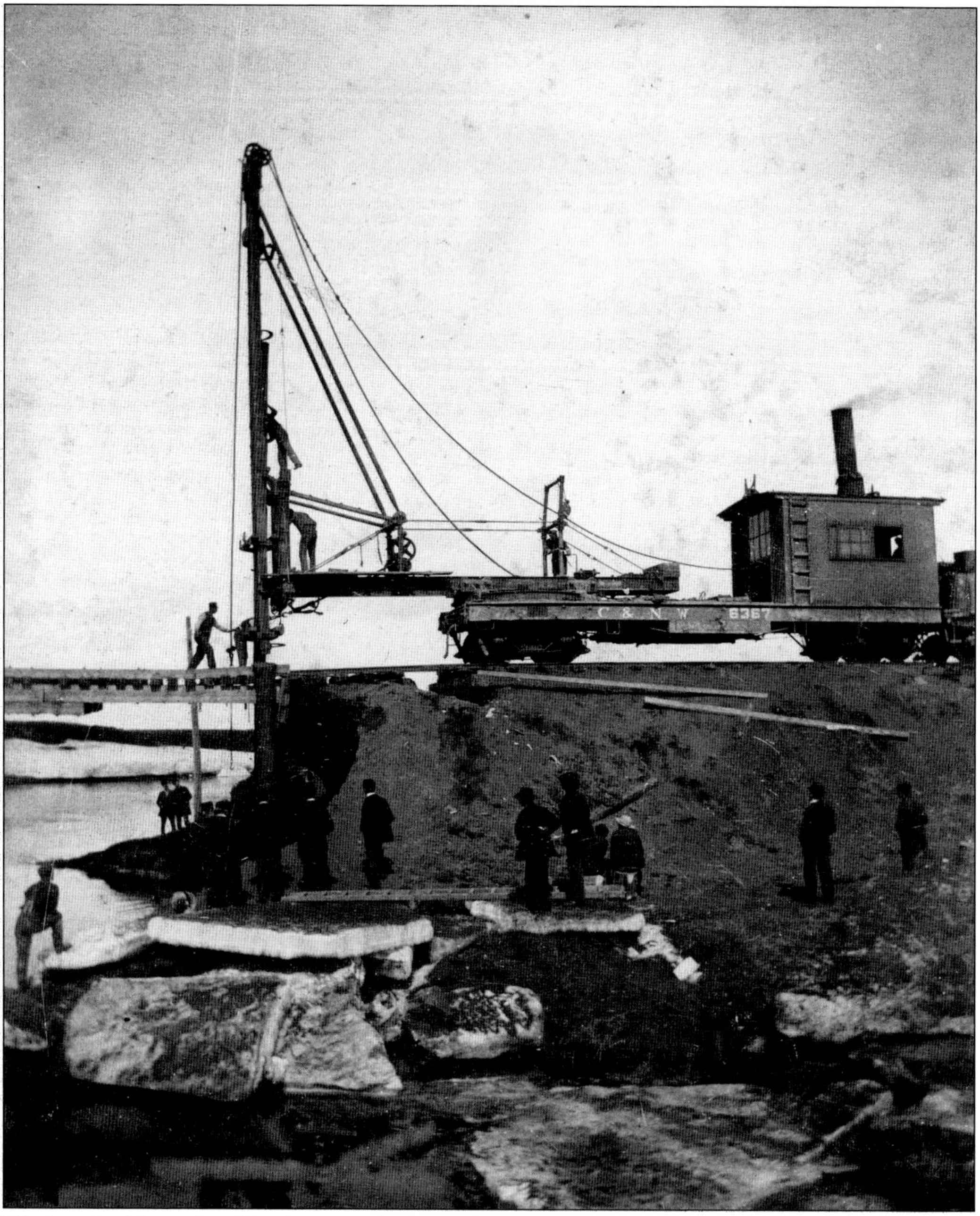

Workers build a railroad bridge over the James River in 1897. To move greater distances required faster transportation. The homesteaders arriving in Spink County in the mid-1880s could get to Mellette and Redfield by railroad and then had to "hoof it" the rest of the way to their claim. Lumber had to be purchased from as far away as Watertown, a four day round trip with oxen or work horses. When railroads reached into the small but booming towns, it still was expensive to have it hauled closer by rail. That is almost certainly why many initially settled for dugouts and sod houses. The still standing claim shanties are single story or story-and-a-half structures, bearing witness to the challenge of obtaining lumber on the then treeless prairie. It was wagons as well that brought the grain to the rail head.

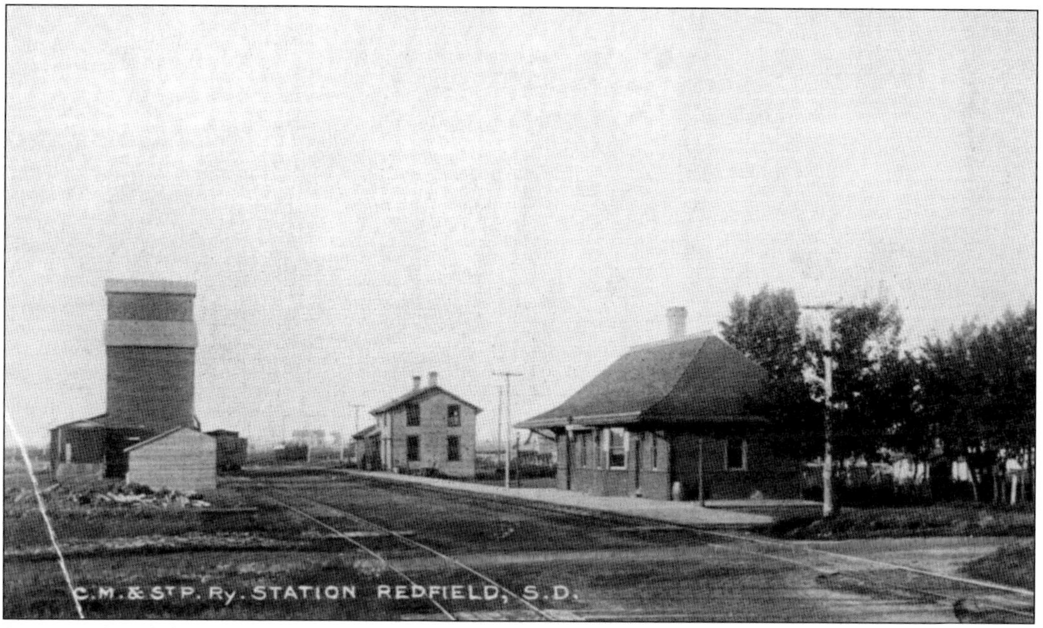

Soon, railroads blossomed in Spink County. Seen here is the Redfield depot as it appeared prior to 1914. The Minneapolis & St. Louis and the Chicago & North Western were the two major railroads in the county.

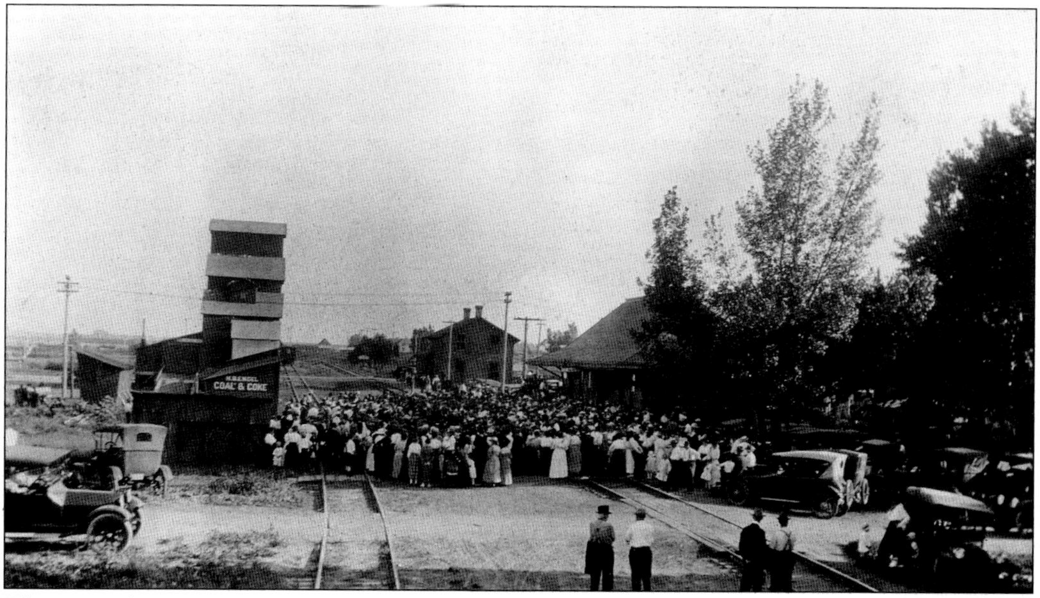

The same depot is pictured here several years later. Railroads liked to have their own towns to themselves—they made money by buying up homesteads, laying out a town, hauling in the materials needed to build a town, and creating a long-term customer base for hauling in needed merchandise and hauling out cream, grains, and cattle. Before there were dining cars on even long-distance trains, trains would stop in a town and passengers would have their choice of restaurants and boarding houses for meals.

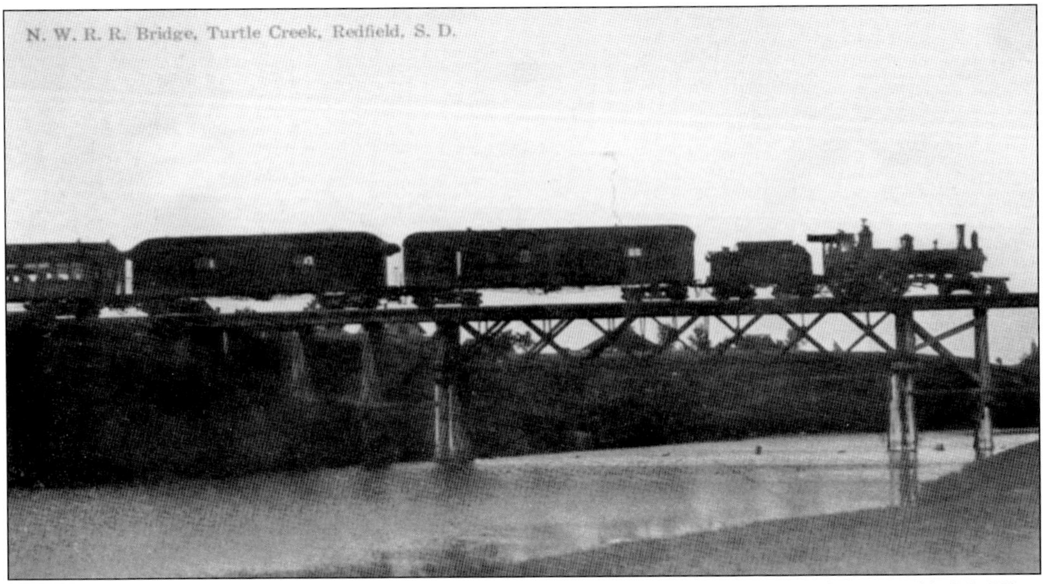

The Chicago & North Western railroad bridge crossed over Turtle Creek in Redfield. This photograph, a rather blurry image on a postcard, is still exciting for railroad buffs. A 4-4-0 is the quintessential locomotive of the 19th century; since they were mostly phased out by the late 1890s, this must be an image of a very early time in Spink County history. The baggage cars and passenger car appear to be wood-sided, also phased out along with the 4-4-0s. The "American" locomotive, a 4-4-0 needed water for its boiler about every 15 miles.

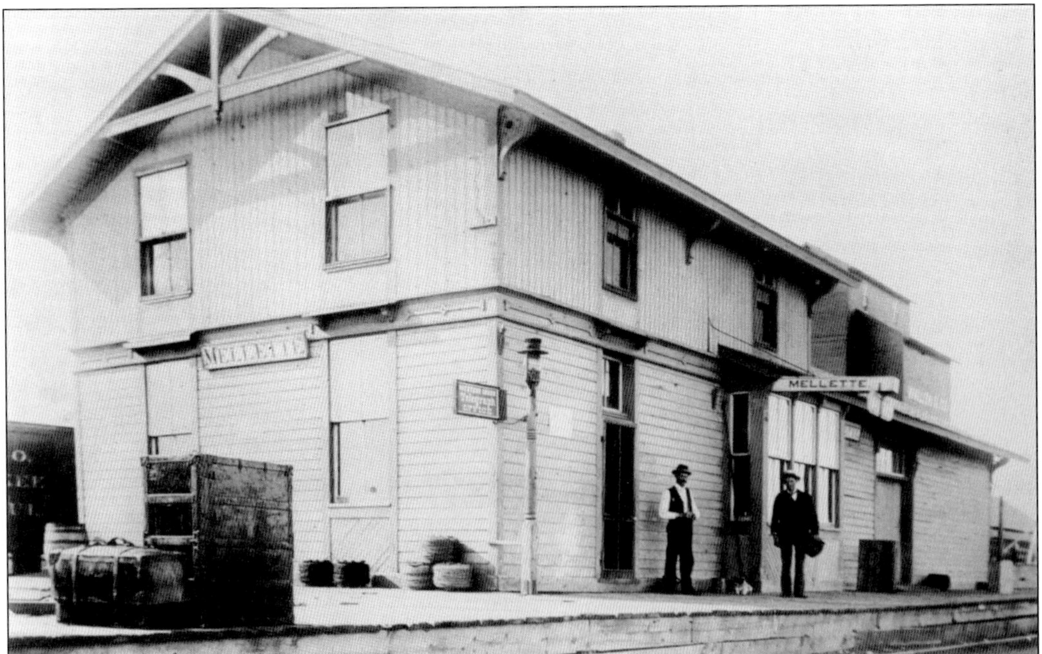

This Chicago, Milwaukee and St. Paul (generally referred to as the Milwaukee Road) depot was built in Mellette in 1881. Spink County was very sparsely settled by that year, the rush was 1883 to 1885. Many homesteaders unloaded their immigrant cars at this station. (Courtesy of Rod Evans.)

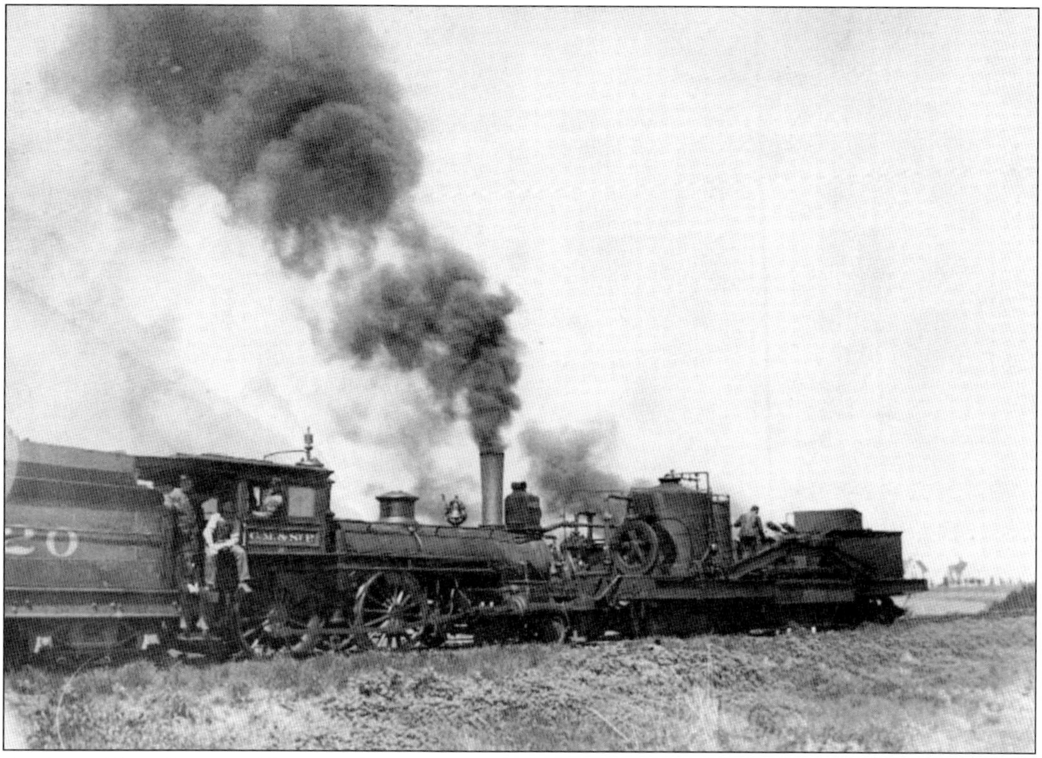

As this Milwaukee weed burner shows, in an era before many herbicides, railroads had to control weeds along and among the tracks by burning.

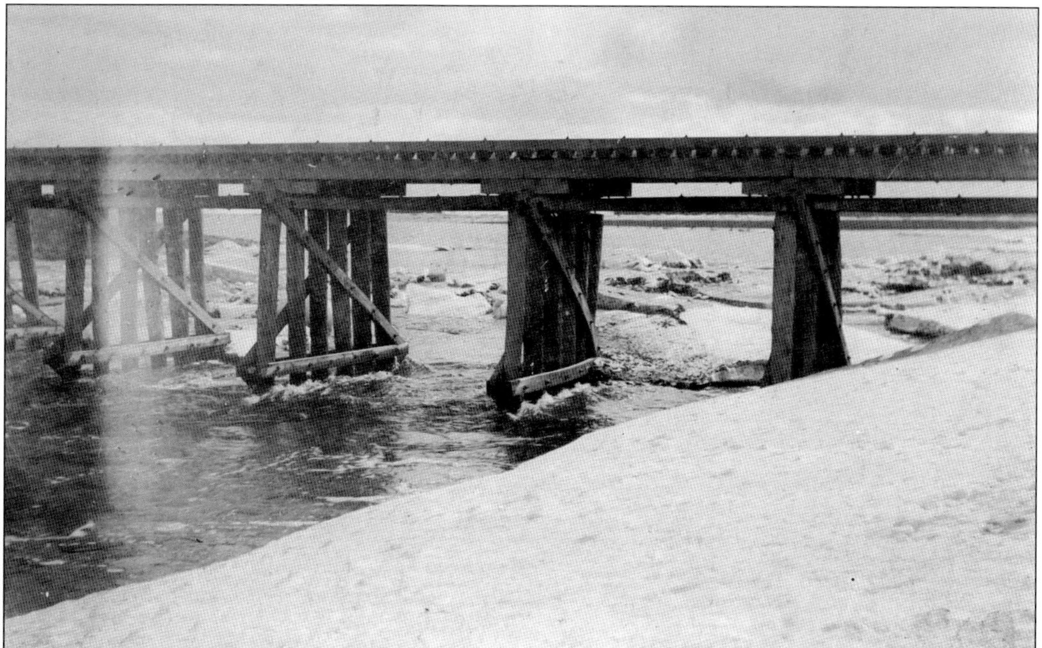

Winter posed its own challenges. As seen here in the late 1890s, quite a bit of ice has formed on this newly built trestle, threatening to jam the railroad bridge.

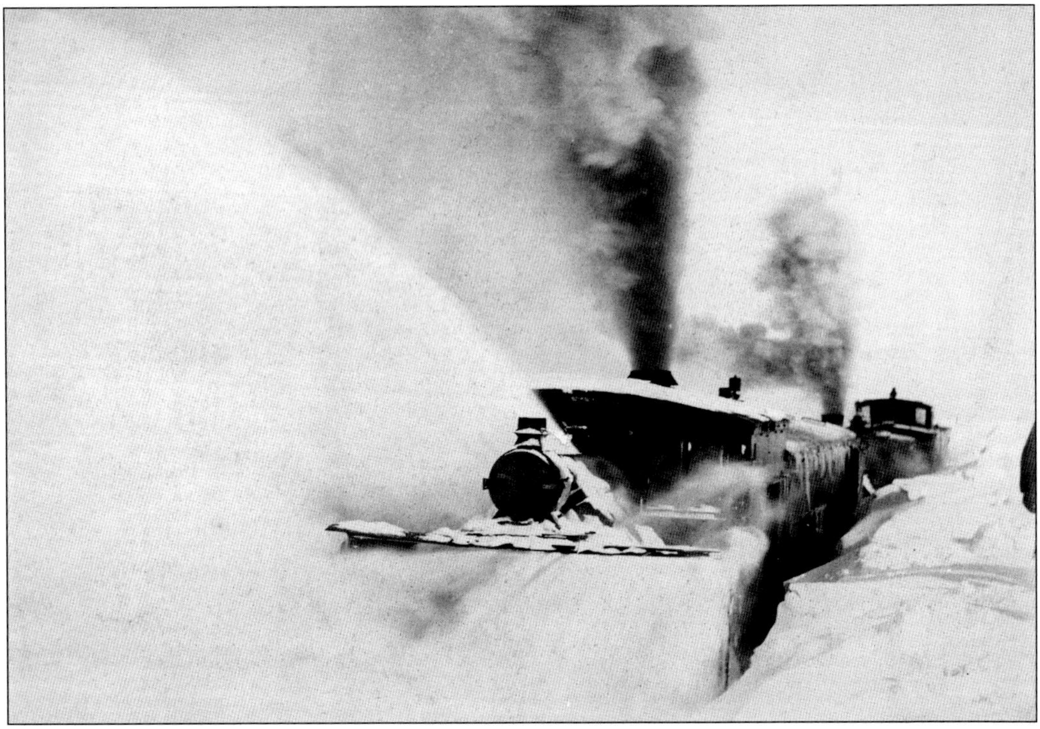

Pictured here in 1897 is a steam-operated snowplow. Steam powered the engine, but the plow itself was not self-propelled. It had to be pushed by one or two steam locomotives, and then it would throw the snow into the air and away from the tracks.

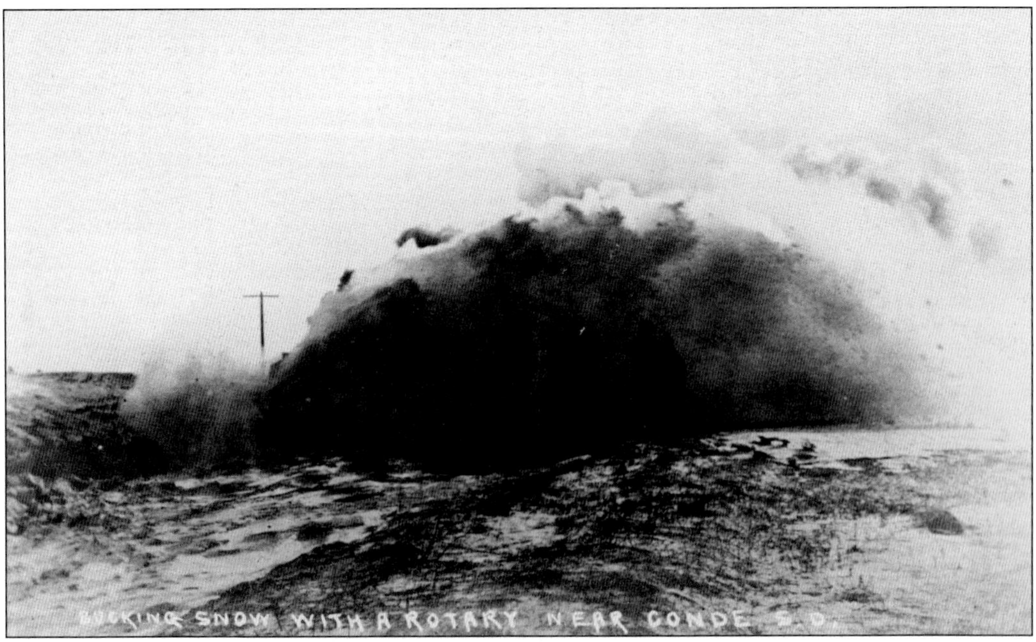

Workers break snow with a steam-powered rotary snow plow. Big snowdrifts have always been a major challenge for keeping the trains running, let alone on time. This scene was photographed near Conde during the winter of 1897.

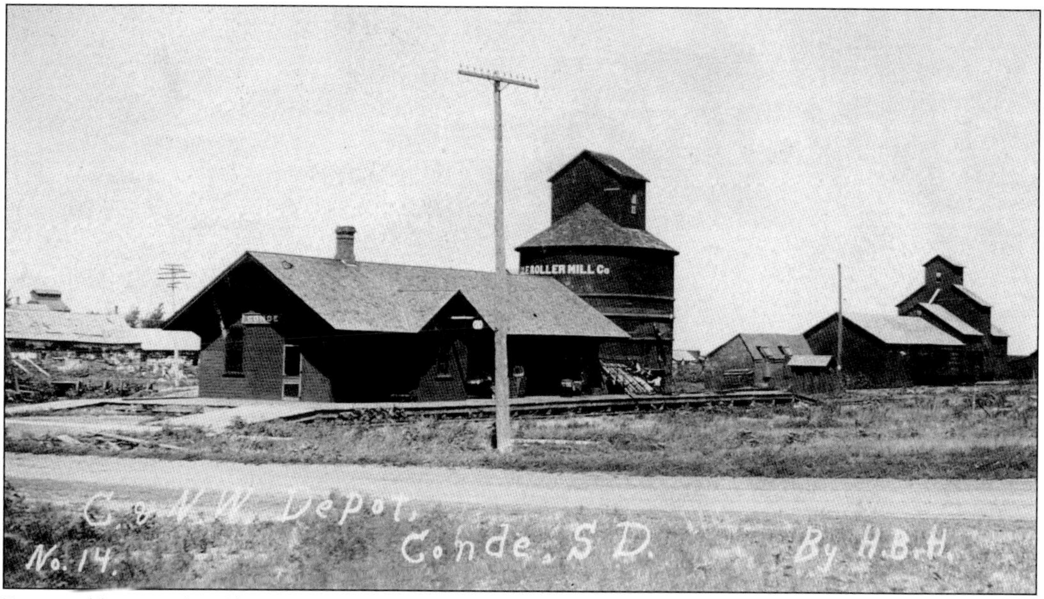

Pictured here is the Chicago & North Western depot in Conde. The C&NW was one of two rail lines serving Conde. The other was the Minneapolis and St. Louis. Visible in the background is the elevated coal ramp and a wooden grain elevator. (Courtesy of Doug Jensen.)

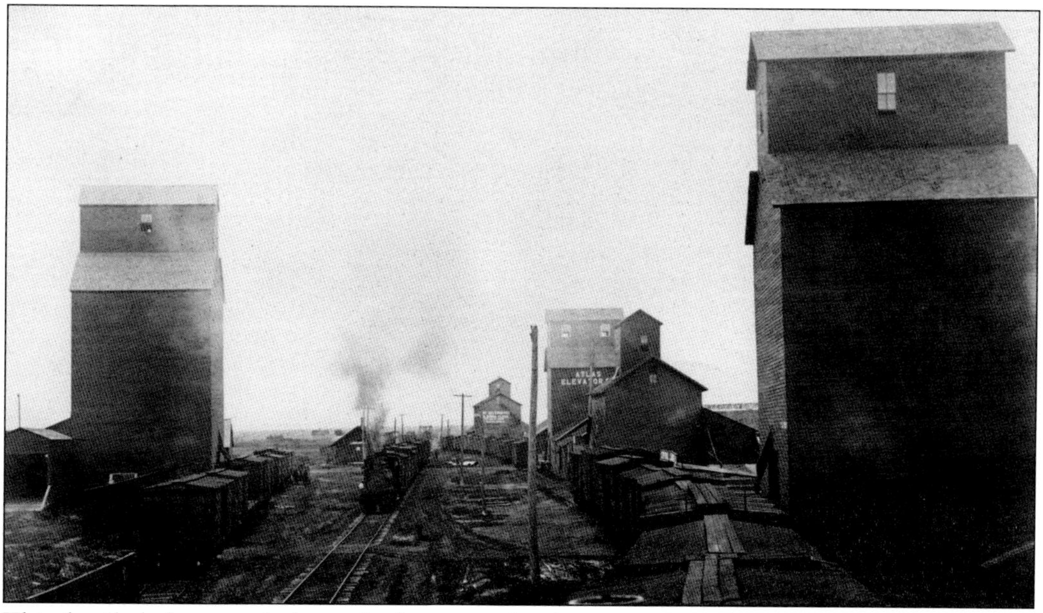

This detailed photograph shows the busy interface between grain elevators and train consists of grain hoppers at harvest time in Doland.

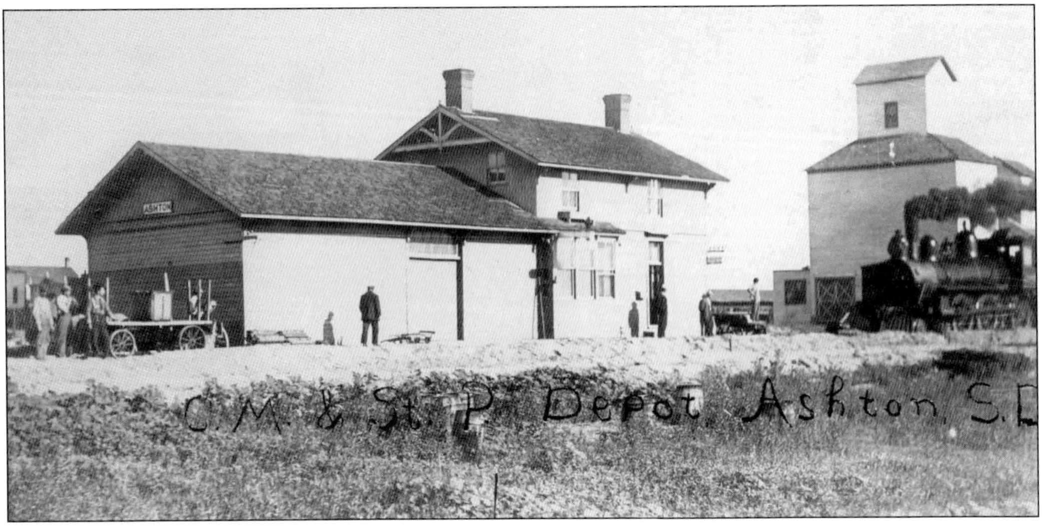

The train is approaching and baggage is ready to load. All appears in order as the train pulls into the Milwaukee station at Ashton.

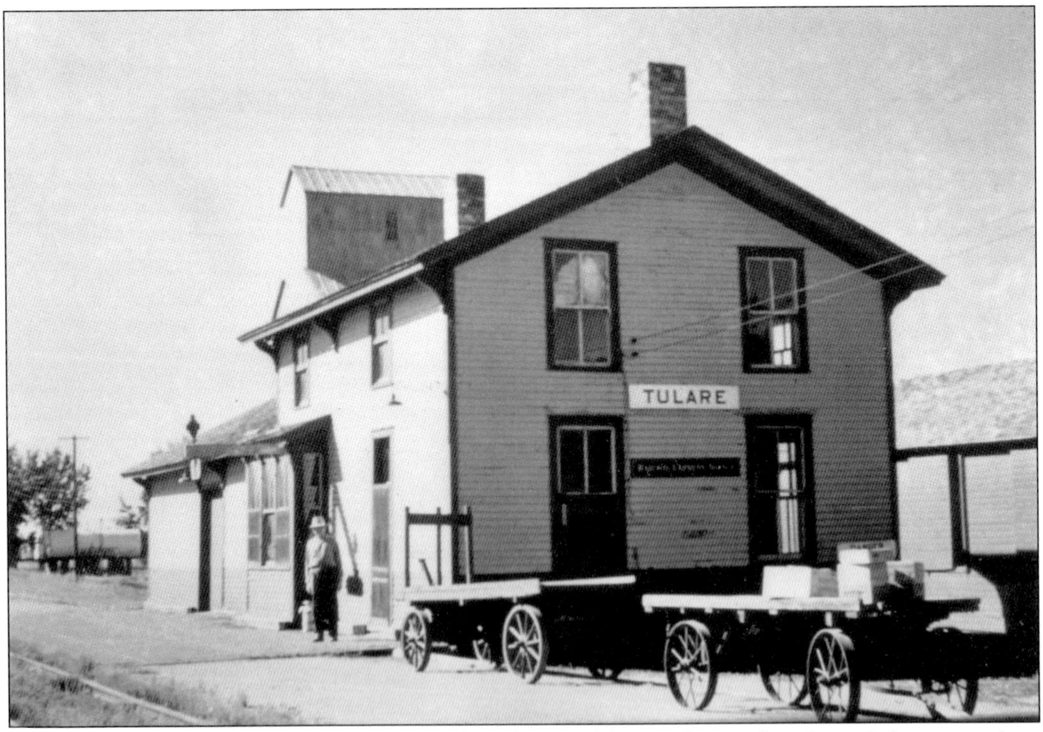

Railroads, wanting to populate the area so that they could grow their railroads made homesteading somewhat easier by providing "immigrant cars"—flat cars with railing. Since the railcar could only go to the railhead, the homesteading family had to bring a covered wagon to make the rest of the trip. An immigrant car would be loaded with the wagon, a "sodbuster" single-blade plow for breaking up the root-choked prairie, a milk cow, some chickens, and maybe a pair of hogs. If at all affordable, the women would ride coach while the men would ride on the flat car with the animals and equipment. The earliest railhead in Spink County was at Mellette, South Dakota, in 1881.

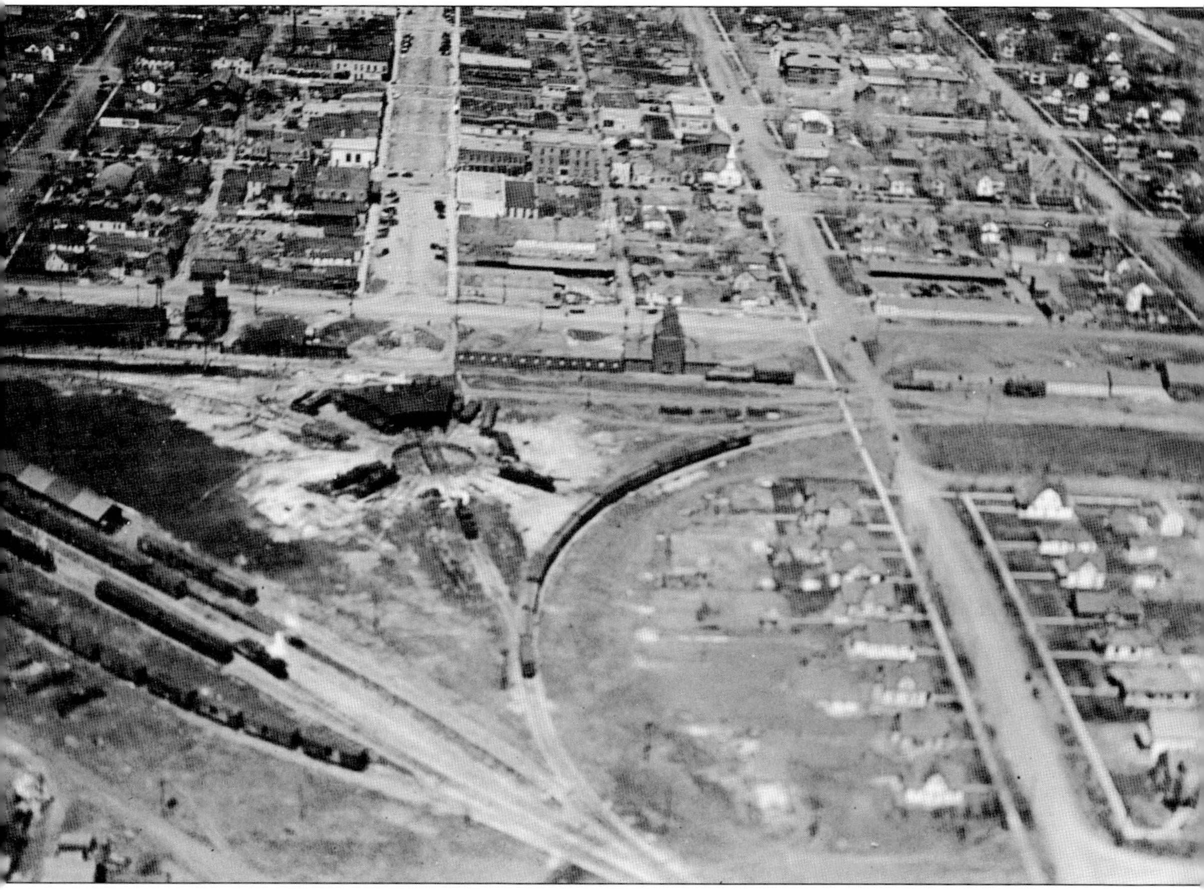

This aerial view shows the rare combination of a roundhouse inside a "wye." A locomotive could be turned around on a turntable, but a wye, laid out over a mile or so, enabled changing the direction of an entire train. The site of this rail yard surrounds the present historic Redfield Chicago & North Western depot.

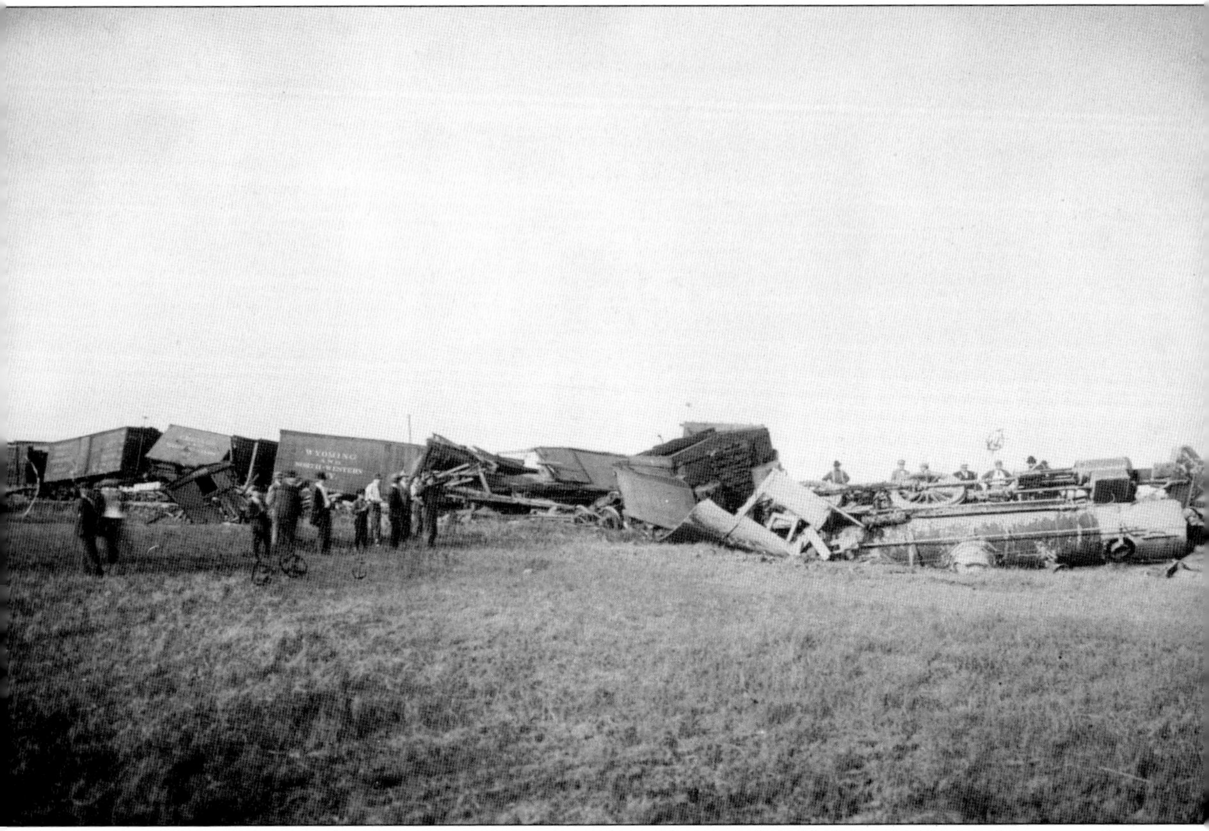

This Chicago & North Western wreck occurred northwest of Redfield in 1910. At the time, the first cars were making their entrance into Spink County, and the automobile would supplant passenger trains within 50 years. Cars were a novelty at first, not relied on considerably until the late 1910s and early 1920s. The newly arrived immigrants to Spink County saw quite a remarkable series of changes in transportation within a relatively few short years.

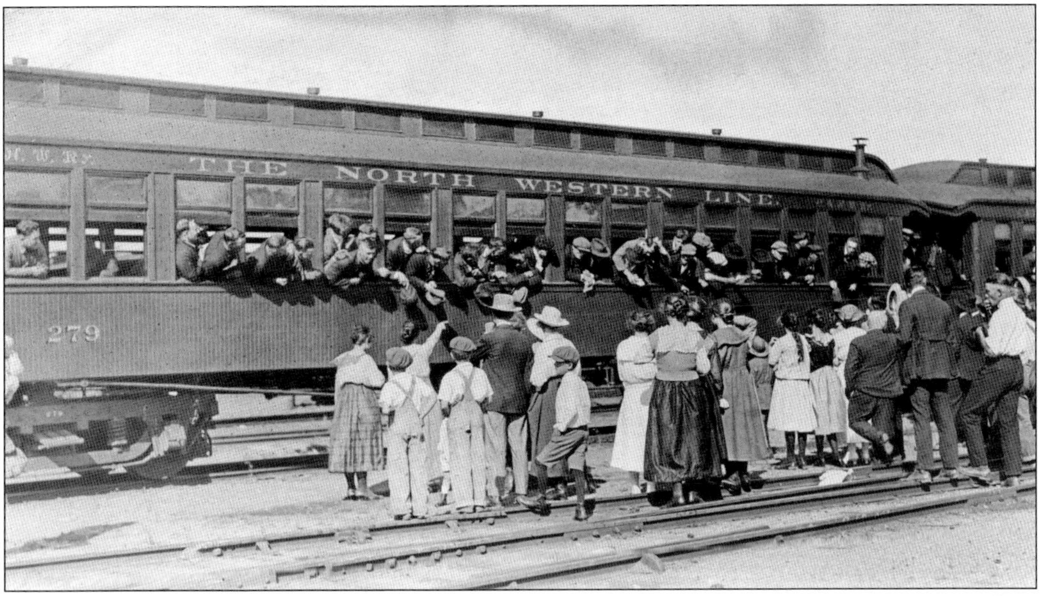

Spink County soldiers and civilians are saying good-bye. Few scenes are more poignant than saying farewell to loved ones as they go off to war. This World War I troop train is ready to pull out from Redfield in 1916. The lists of Spink County men who went off to fight in the "War to End all Wars" are long.

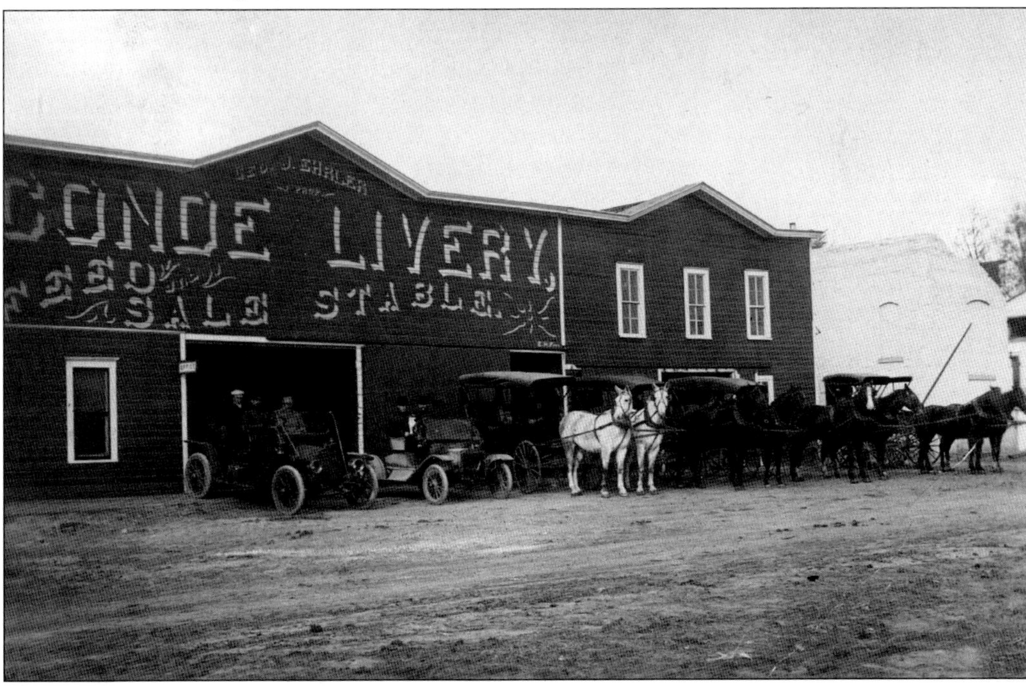

This image captures the end of one era and the beginning of another. Rarely does a photograph so vividly illustrate change. This is the last livery stable in Conde. Autos are on the left; the horses and buggies on the right are about to pass from the scene. This livery stable burned in 1917. Two of the people in the photograph are identified as George J. Ehler and Pete Lesley. (Courtesy of Earl Grandpre.)

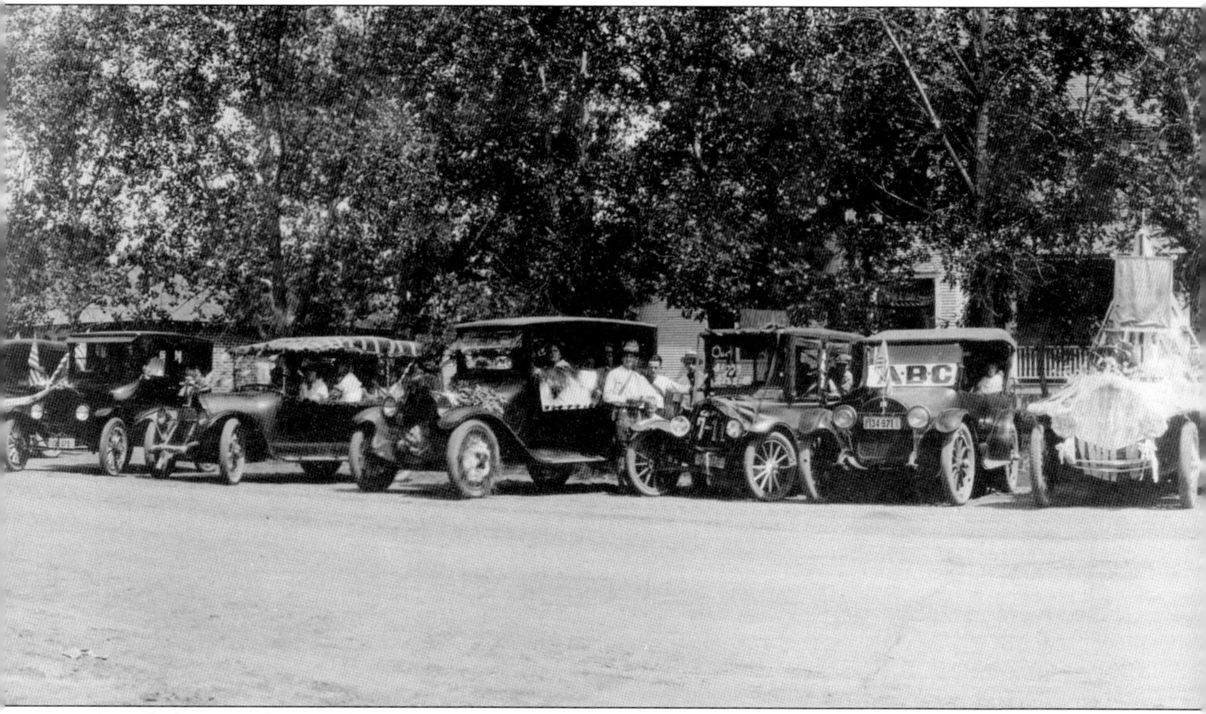

Locals line up their early model cars, perhaps for a parade. Autos from this era were shipped in double-door boxcars, three autos to a boxcar. The touring cars (open or canvas top) had their

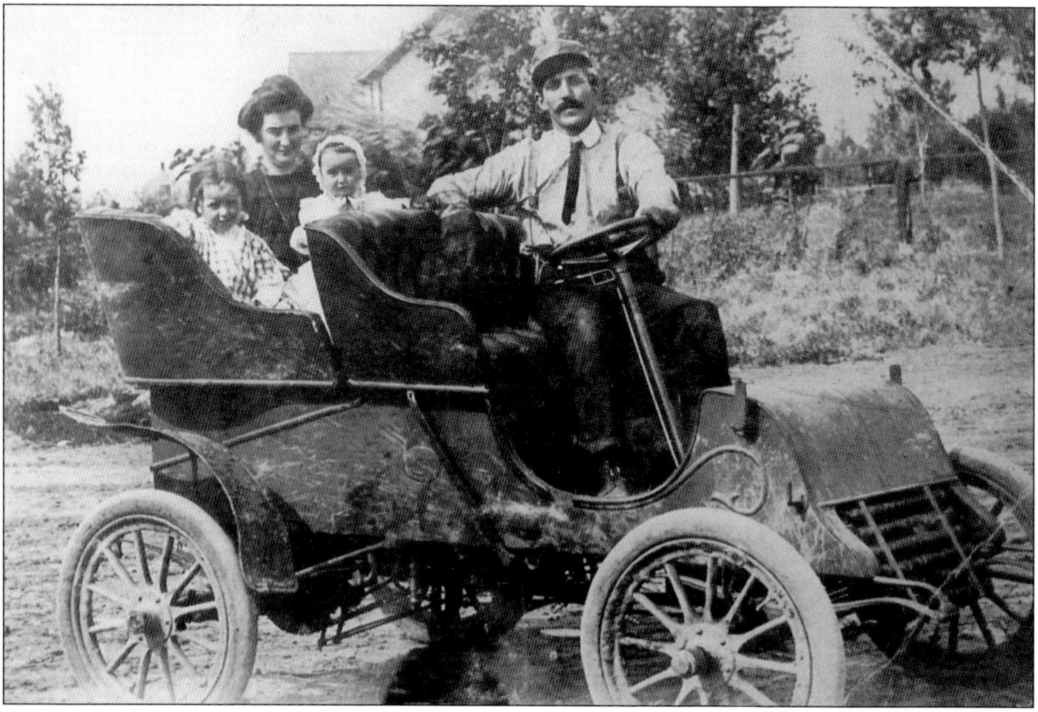

Dominic St. Peter, wife Kate, and daughters Hazel and Mavyen Turton pose in the first car purchased in Spink County. This auto was typical of the cars built during the first 10 years of the 1900s.

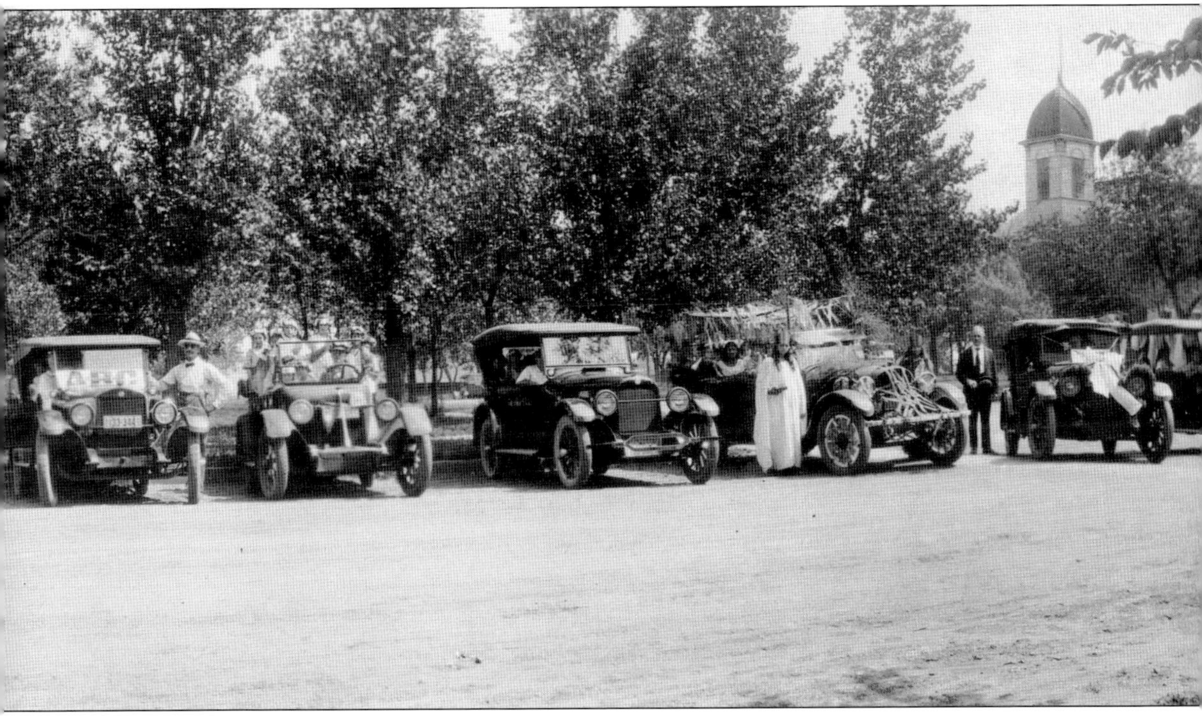

fenders removed; the fenders were then bound together and placed in the rear seat for the duration of shipment.

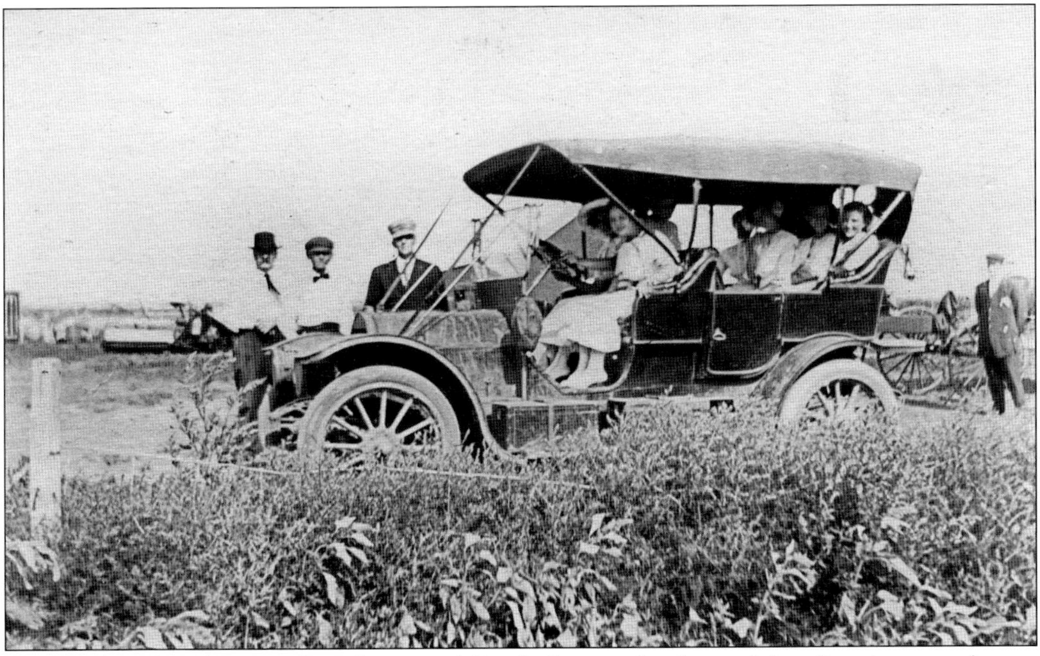

Captured in this photograph is the typical Spink County family car. Most first-time auto buyers bought a car into which the whole family might be squeezed, known as a touring car. It had an open top with a retractable canvas roof and attachable side curtains with glass window inserts to offer some protection from rain, wind, and cold.

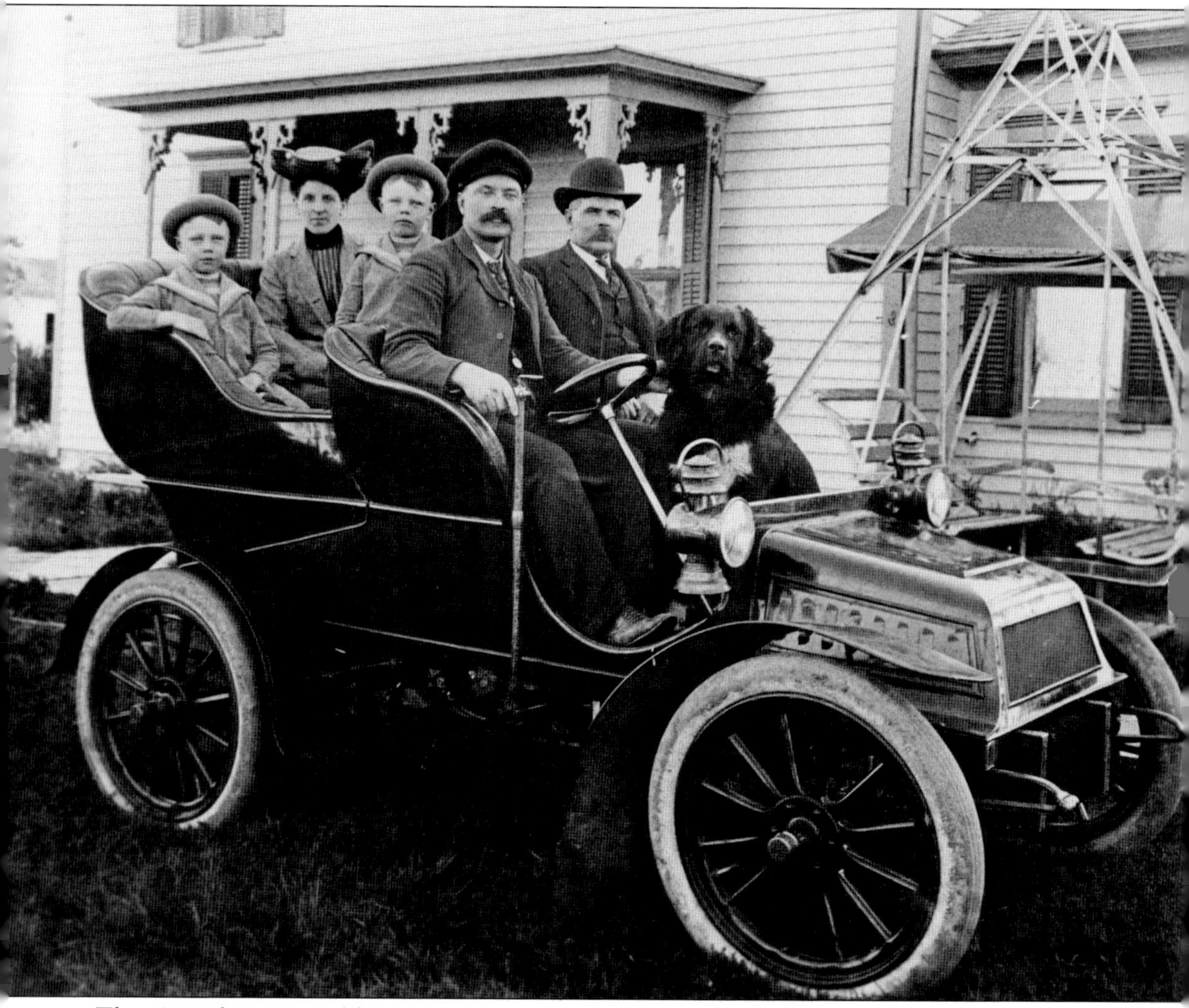

There's nothing quite like a Sunday outing with the family. The occupants of this auto are unknown, but the location was in front of the then Emil Overby farm home, now owned by the Stuck family. The location is several miles south and west of Brentford. The auto featured headlamps powered by kerosene.

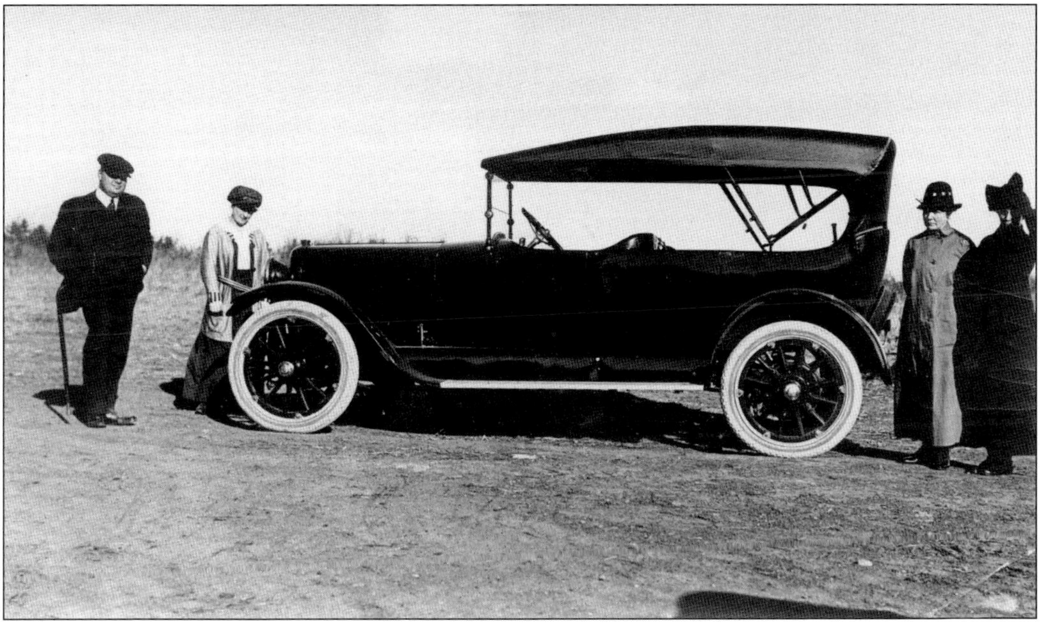

The car is the star in this photograph. The white tires, not uncommon, were certainly impractical on muddy or dusty Spink County roads.

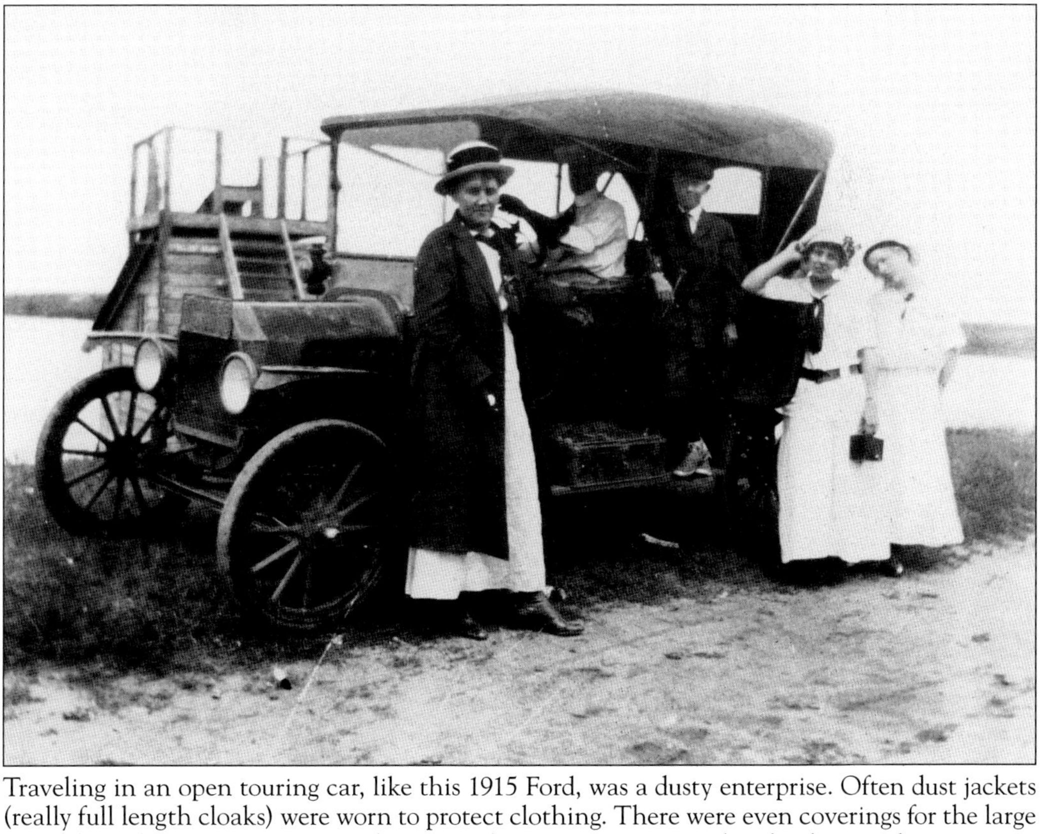

Traveling in an open touring car, like this 1915 Ford, was a dusty enterprise. Often dust jackets (really full length cloaks) were worn to protect clothing. There were even coverings for the large ladies' hats that were in vogue at the time. This auto was equipped with a brass radiator.

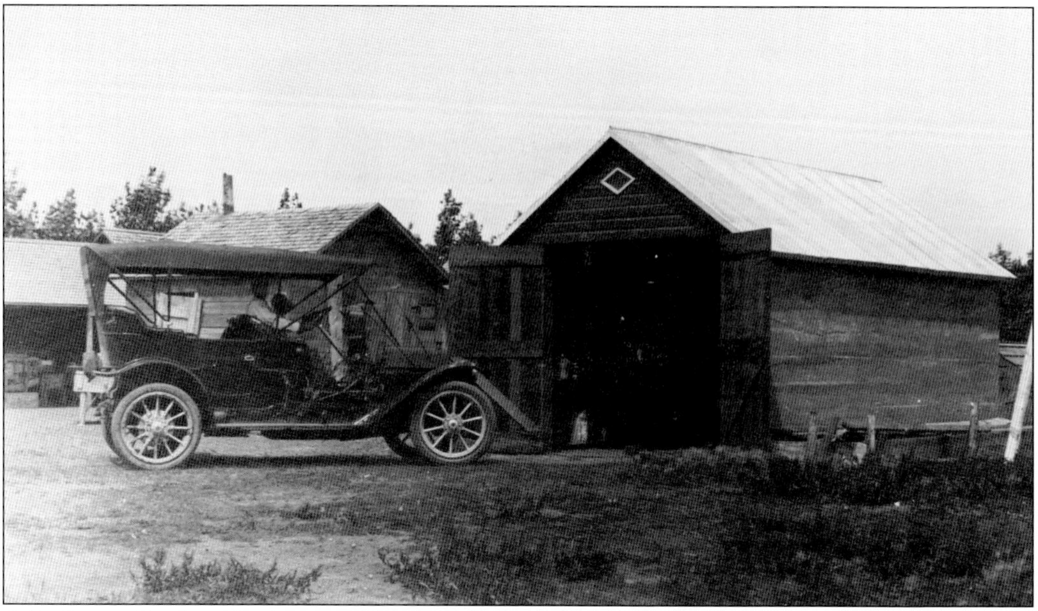

A.R. Fryer of Doland had a garage built for his new car, a 1911 Cadillac.

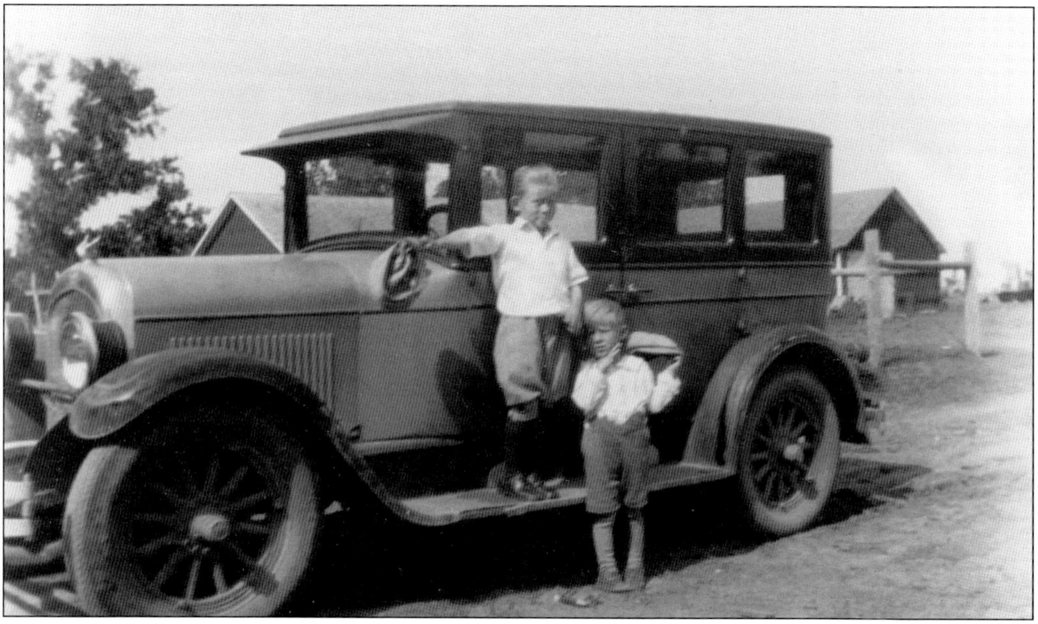

By 1925, enclosed cars became the norm. Glenn and Jack Overby pose with the family's 1925 Chrysler. (Courtesy of Glenn Overby.)

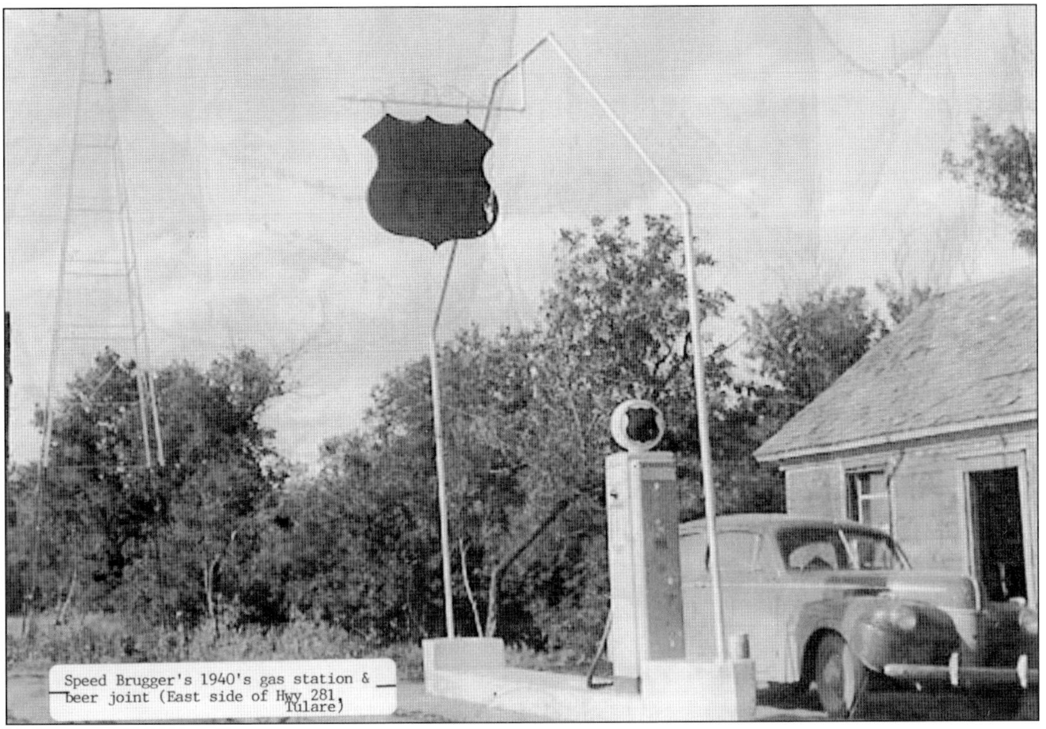

Pictured here in the 1940s is Speed Brugger's gas station. This was a mainstay in Tulare, providing fuel for the area farmers. Located on the east side of Highway 281, it was also a beer joint.

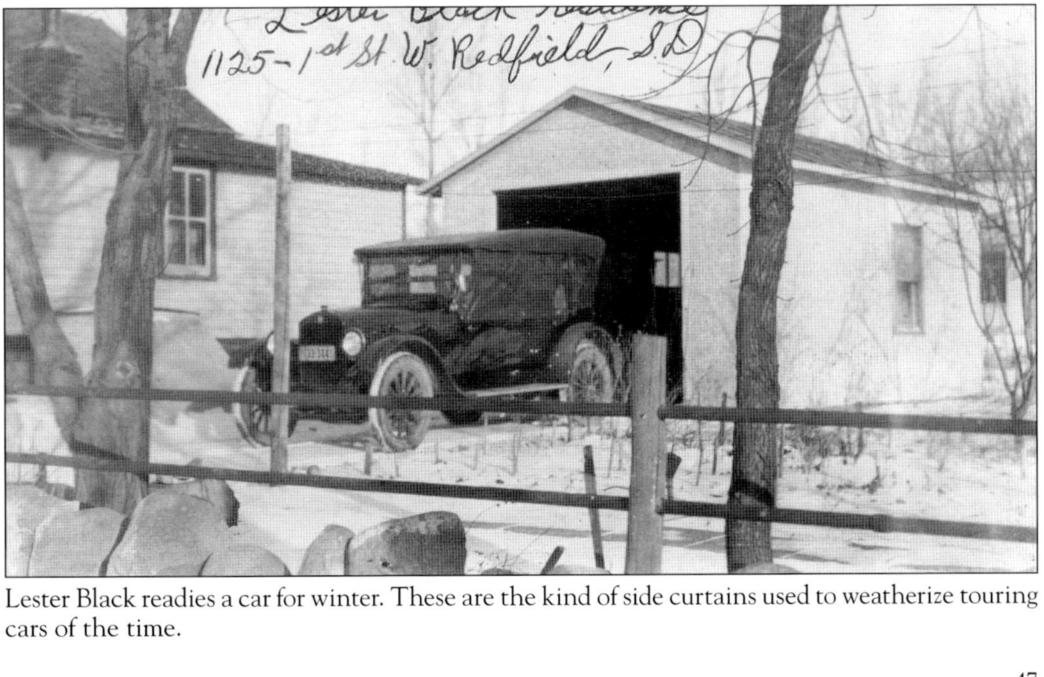

Lester Black readies a car for winter. These are the kind of side curtains used to weatherize touring cars of the time.

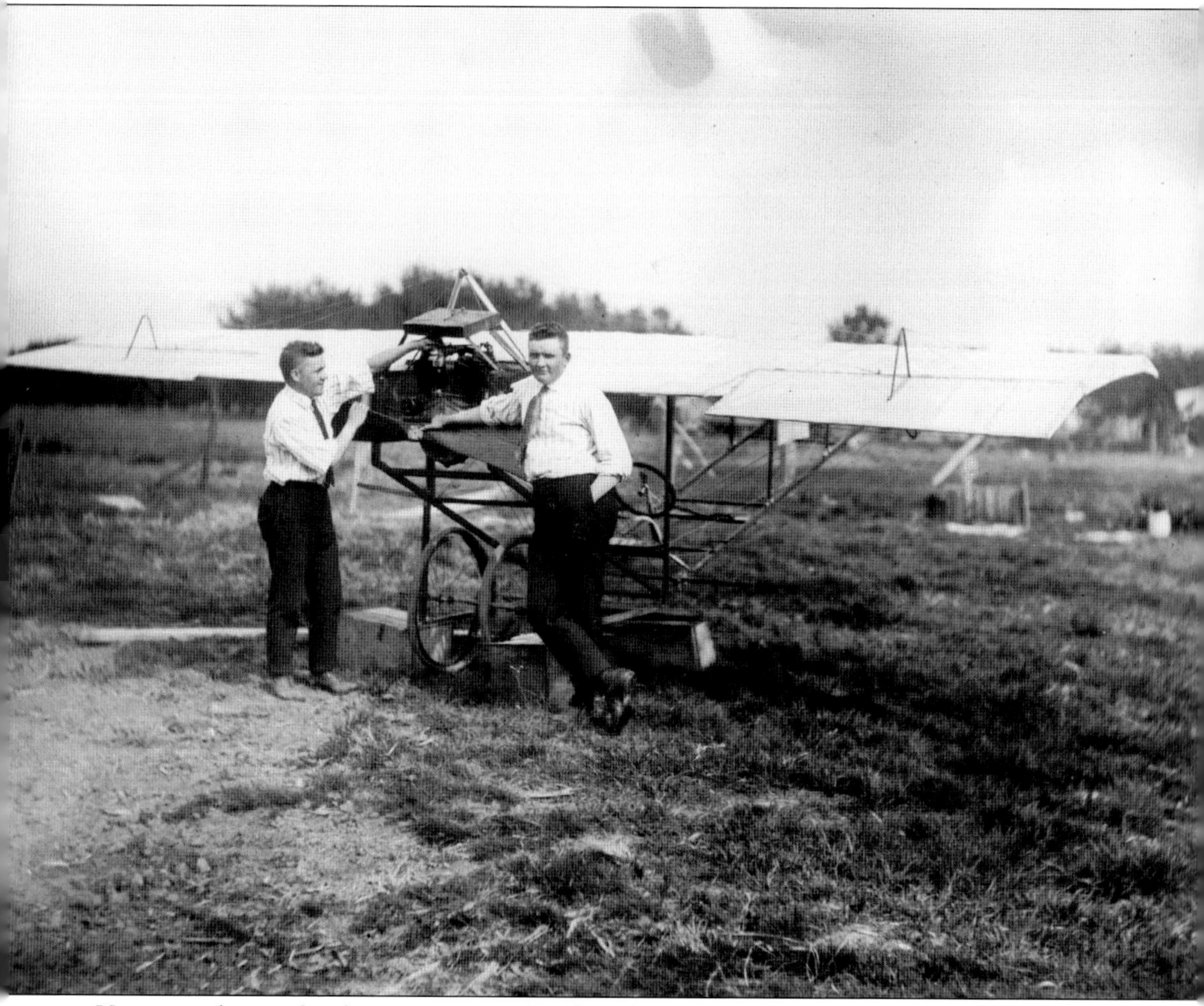

Here is evidence of early aviation near Conde. It has proven difficult to date this and the next photograph. They were taken by a camera using glass plate negatives. It is assumed that the Lenz brothers are in the photograph and that it may have been the first instance of aviation in Spink County. The airplane started out as an amusement, a spectacle. These early photographs of small, single engine, single passenger aircraft are surprising. Apparently between the 1906 first flight and the beginning of World War I, planes were available to citizens of Spink County, presumably arriving in the form of kits or at least partially built. (Courtesy of Alan Evans.)

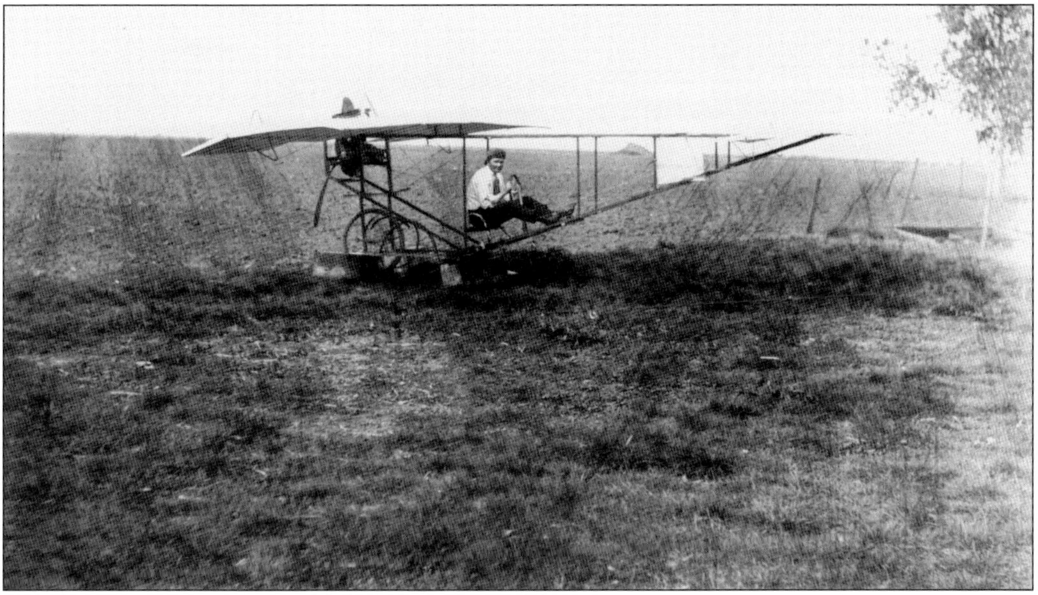

Did it fly? These Lenz photographs ask many questions and provide very few answers. (Courtesy of Alan Evans.)

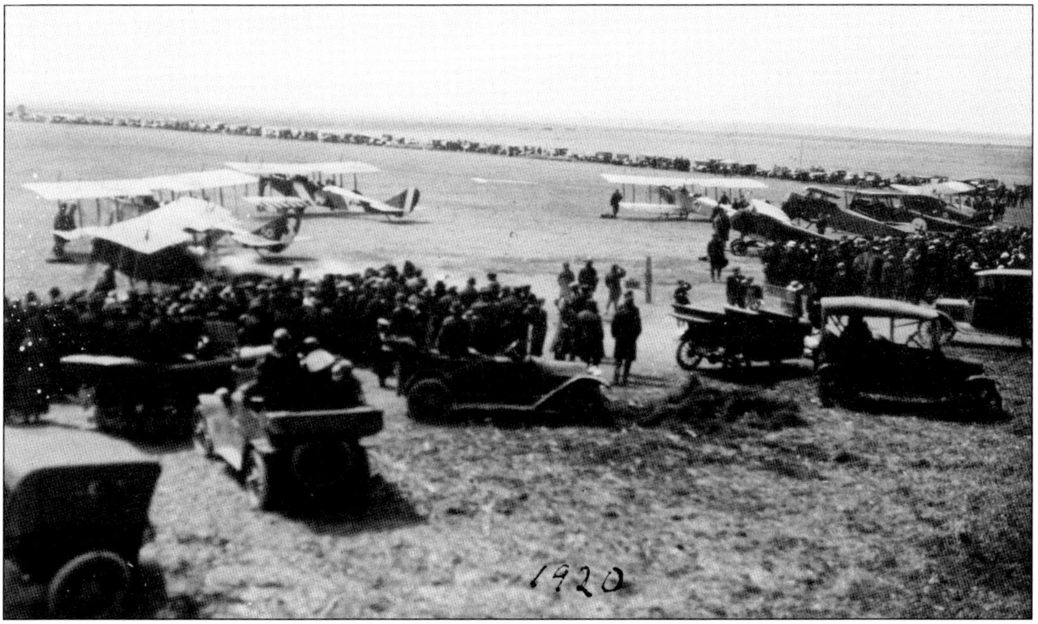

Whistles all over town announced the Flying Circus as it descended on Redfield on Thursday, April 24, 1919. Led by Harry C. Roberts and Capt. William Spain, a son-in-law of Redfield's first mayor, Daniel H. Hunt, it was the only overland flight in the United States at the time. Later, 10 more planes arrived, including Curtiss JN-4H planes and scout planes including the German Fokker, an English SE-5, and a French Spad. The local paper surmised that 18,000 people gathered the following day just south of Redfield to view sham battles, scout and bombing formations, and crowd strafing. Interestingly, Mayor Stutenroth reported it "a success without any drunks or unpleasantness connected to the event." The city also paid Phil Tyrell $109 for policing the event; the sheriff's monthly salary was only $45 per month.

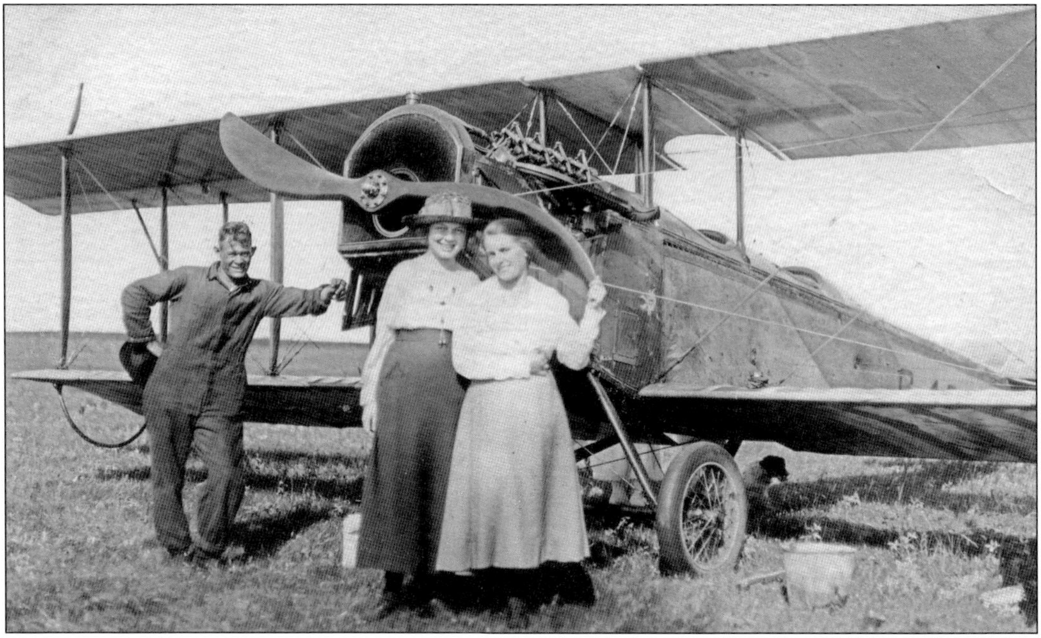

Katherine Fargo and Irene Labrie pose before taking a flight. Those who bought Victory loan bonds (issued to pay World War I debts) were treated to a plane ride.

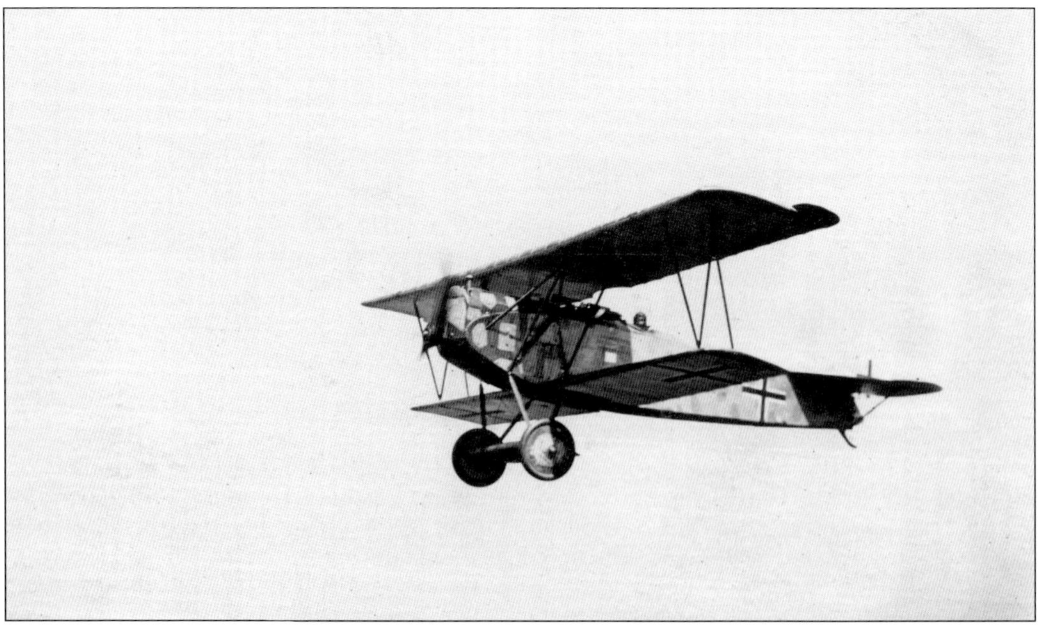

Referred to as "Jenny," this Curtiss biplane could move through the sky at speeds of 75 miles per hour. The air show was only part of the city's celebration. Bands from Mitchell and Watertown provided music; Gov. Peter Norbeck and Sen. Thomas Sterling addressed the crowds.

Three

FARMING

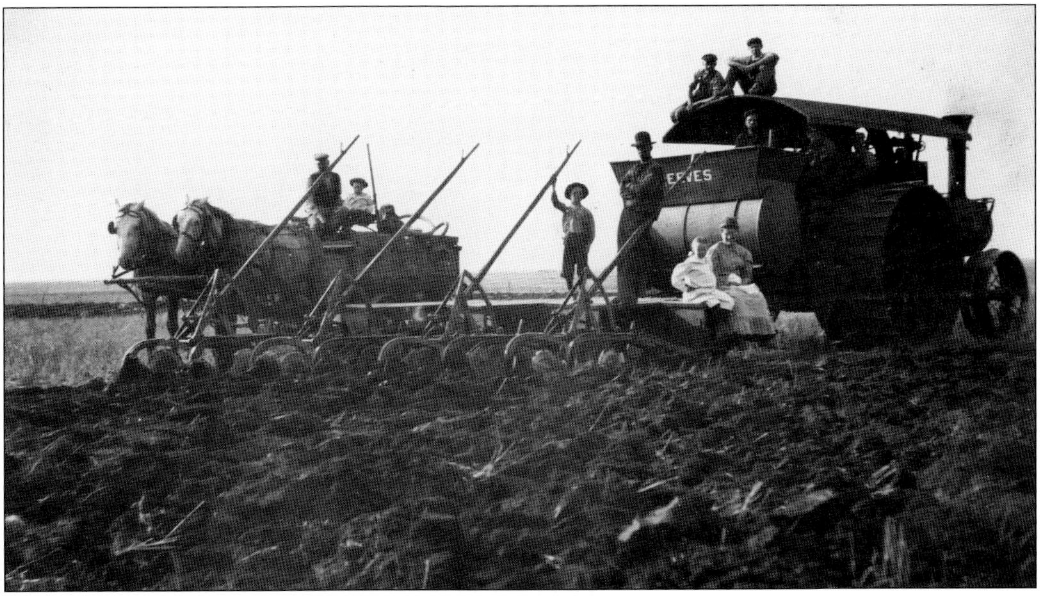

Taking a break! It was farm tradition to eat dinner at noon in the house, and then the wife brought a lunch to the crew about 4:00 p.m. Supper was eaten towards sundown. (Courtesy of Alan Evans.)

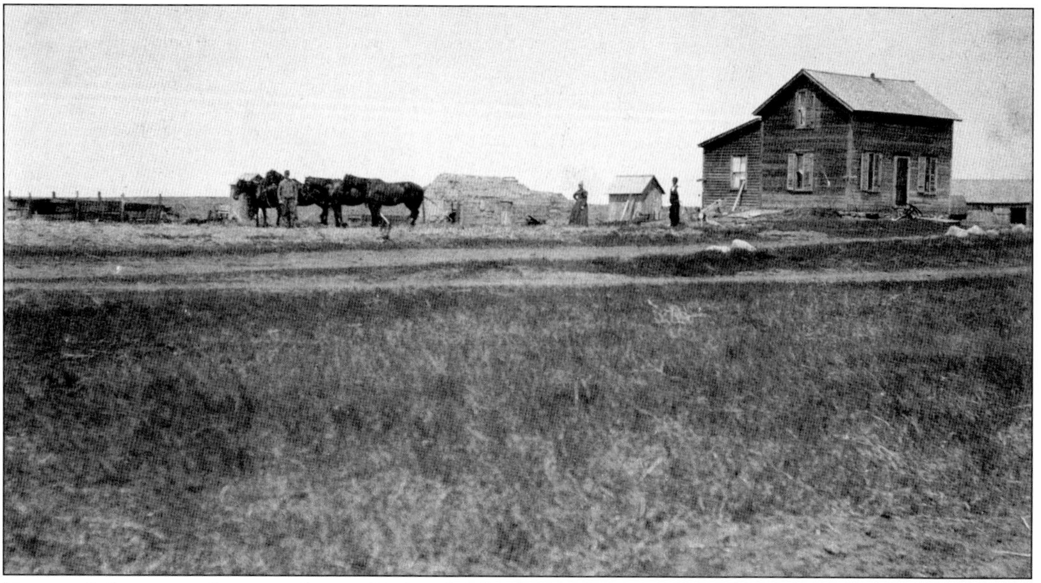

Pictured above is a farmstead near Doland. The lack of trees and outbuildings indicates that this is very early farming activity, likely in the early 1890s. The business of Spink County is farming and ranching. From the earliest farmstead through the 1950s, the traditional family farm was the norm. Farming two or three quarters, a family could live well during wet years when stock and grain prices were high, and get by during dry years and low commodity prices. Below is a steam tractor with an eight bottom plow.

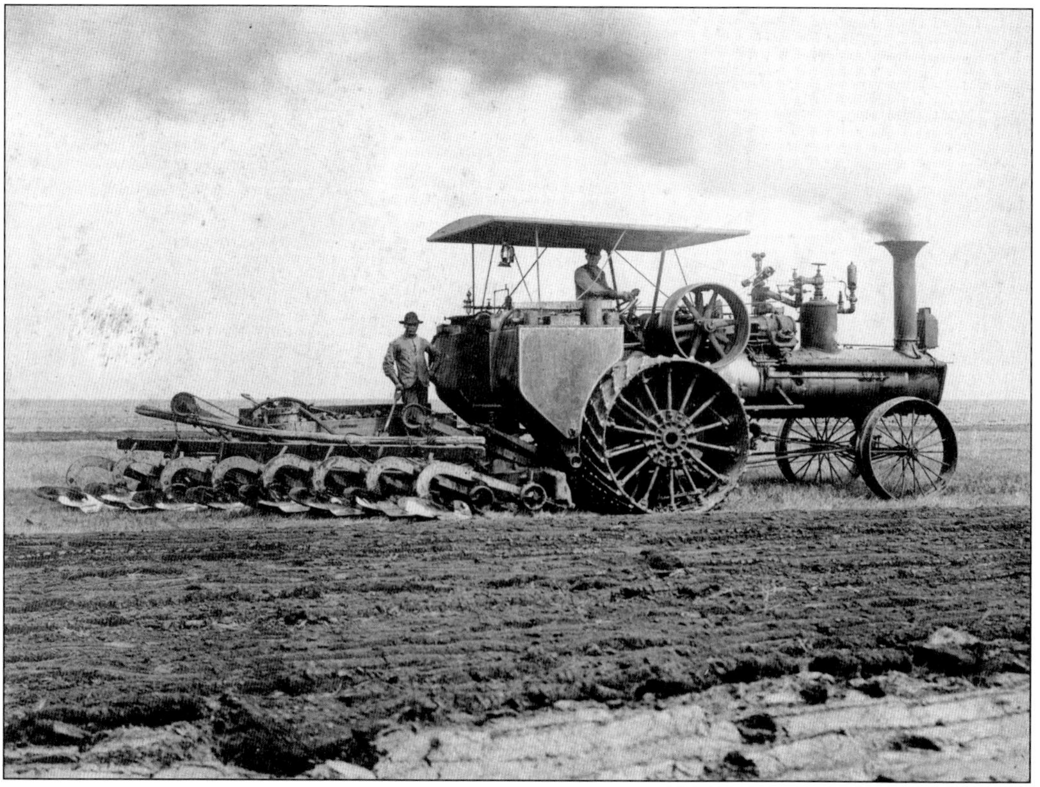

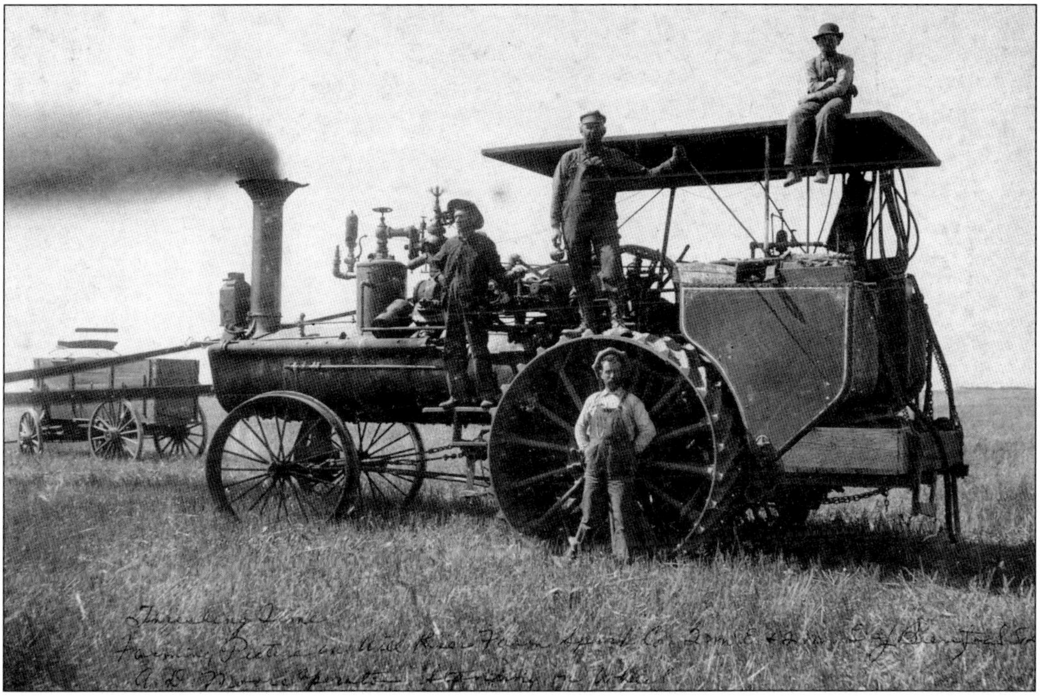

The boss and his crew cease for a photograph in the midst of plowing and seeding. That is A.D. Moore standing on the tractor wheel.

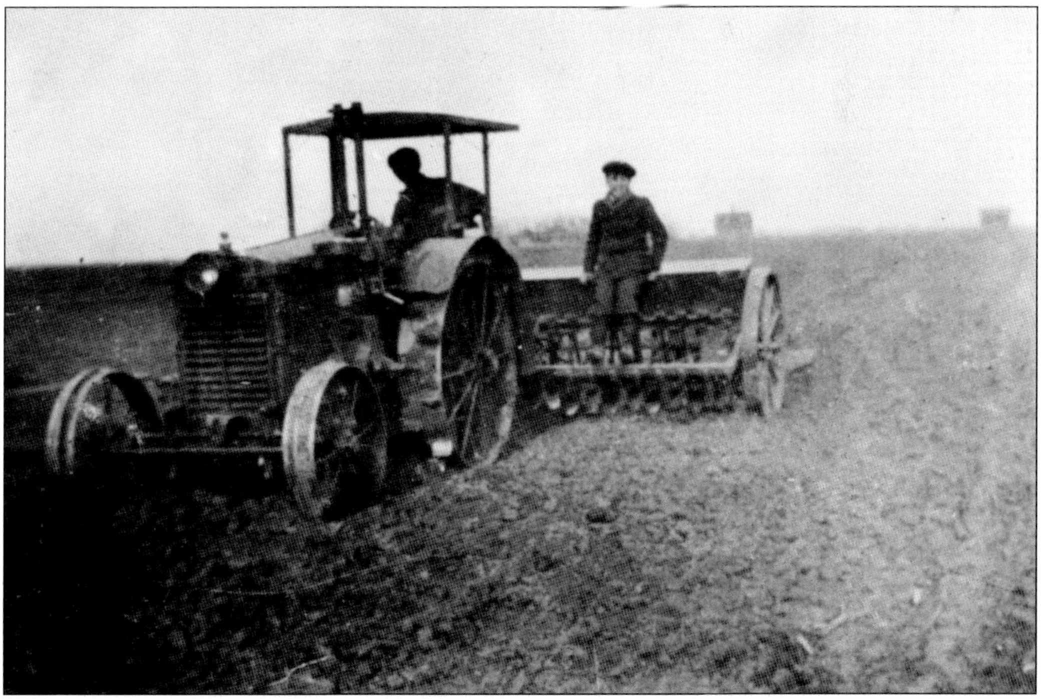

Because steam-powered tractors were expensive to purchase, extremely cumbersome, and required a crew to operate, the 1920s saw the development of fuel-powered tractors such as this kerosene operated iron-wheeled tractor. Gasoline powered tractors replaced them within a few years.

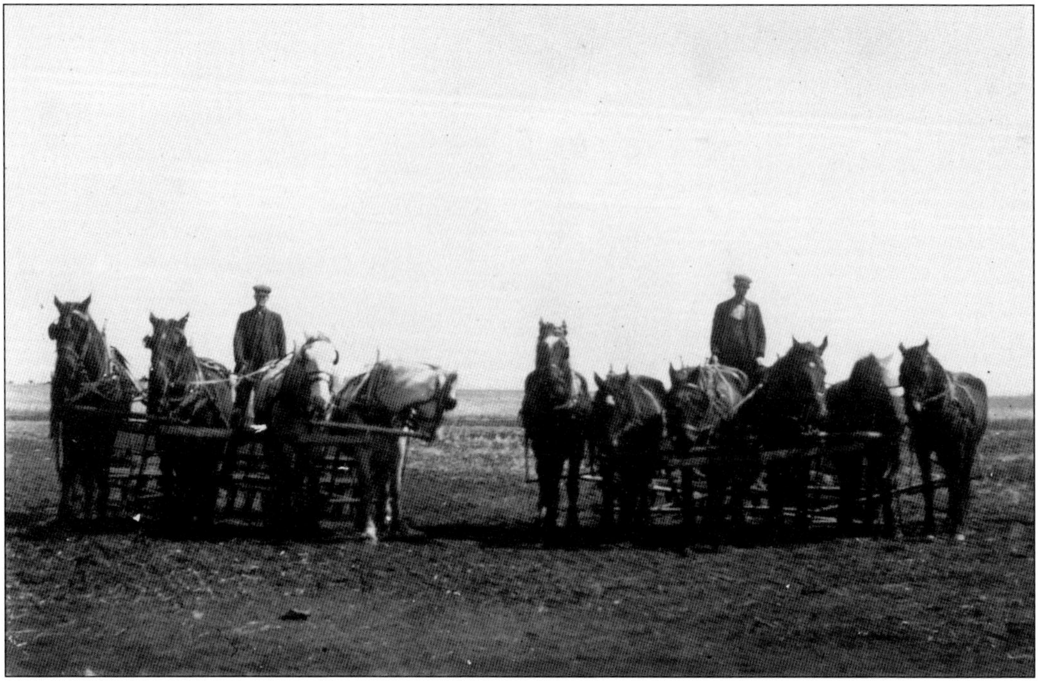

These two teams of horses are disking. This evens out the soil after it has been furrowed by plowing, leaving the ground fallow with no stubble covering. This farming practice set the stage for the terrific dust storms of the "Dirty Thirties." (Courtesy of Alan Evans.)

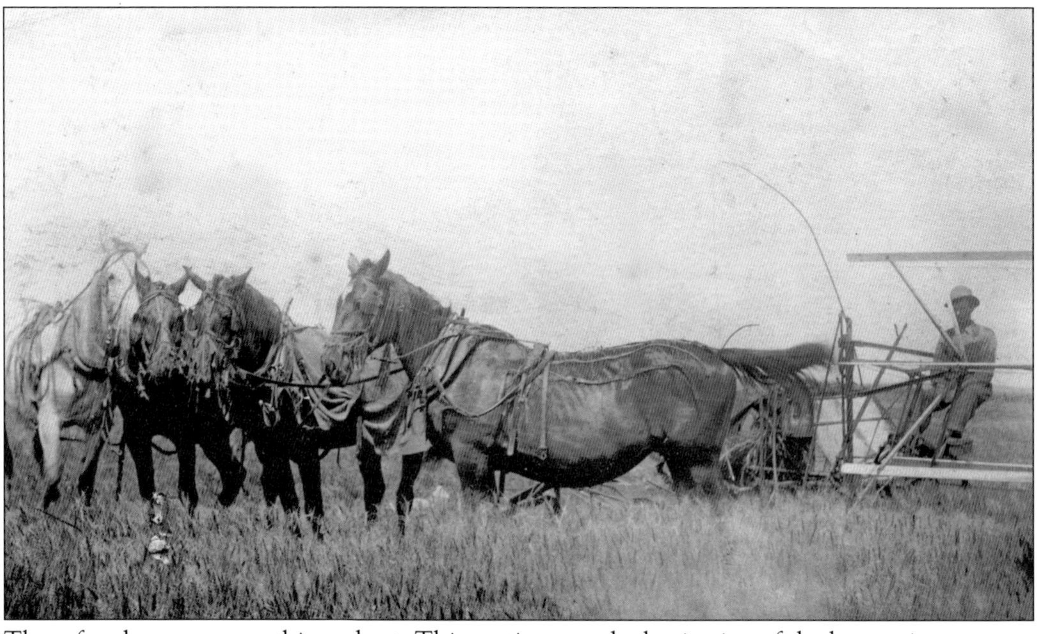

These four horses are swathing wheat. This cutting was the beginning of the harvesting process. Farmers would then bundle the wheat and make it into shocks to dry. Then they would manually feed the bundles into a steam operated threshing machine.

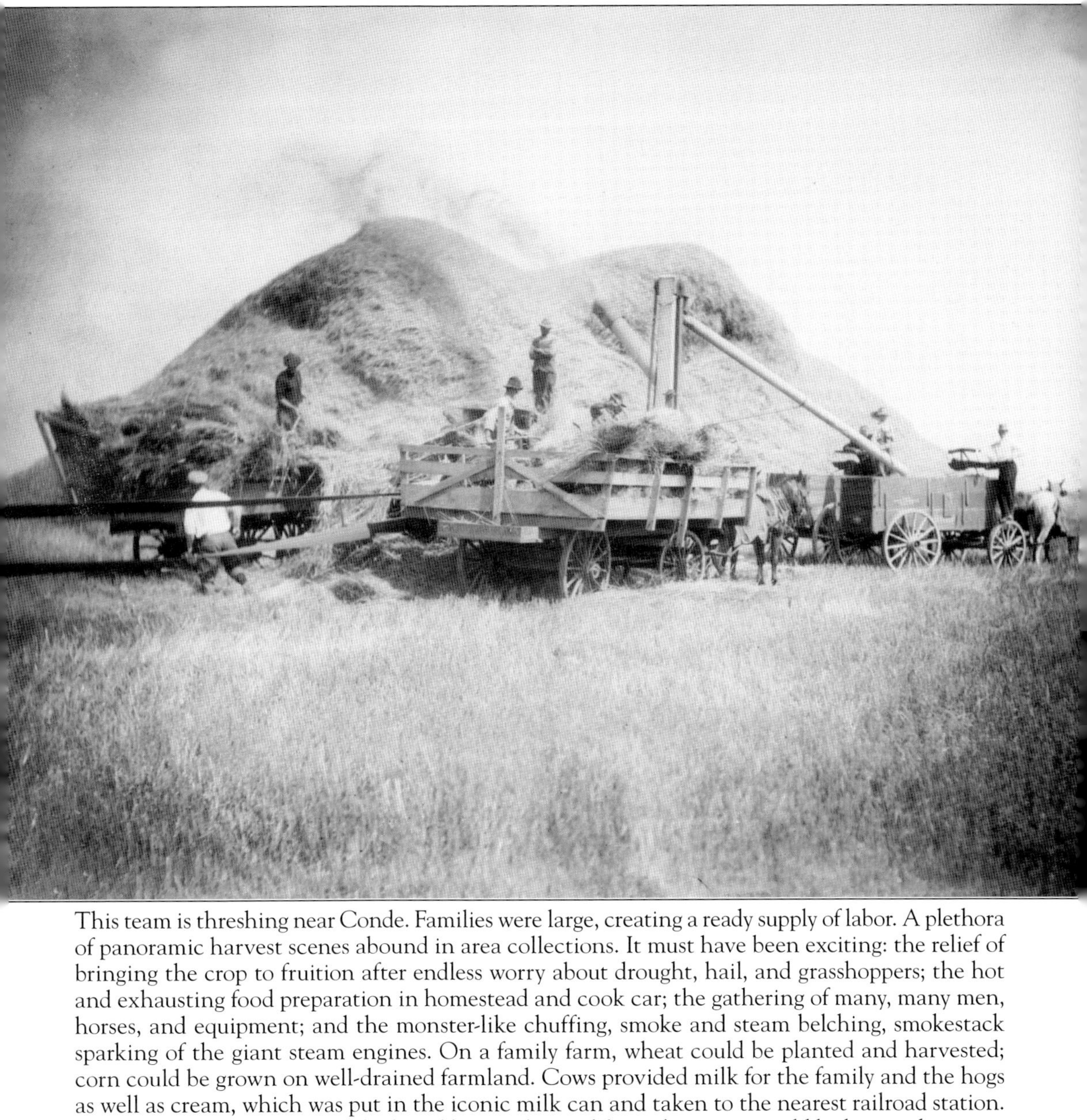

This team is threshing near Conde. Families were large, creating a ready supply of labor. A plethora of panoramic harvest scenes abound in area collections. It must have been exciting: the relief of bringing the crop to fruition after endless worry about drought, hail, and grasshoppers; the hot and exhausting food preparation in homestead and cook car; the gathering of many, many men, horses, and equipment; and the monster-like chuffing, smoke and steam belching, smokestack sparking of the giant steam engines. On a family farm, wheat could be planted and harvested; corn could be grown on well-drained farmland. Cows provided milk for the family and the hogs as well as cream, which was put in the iconic milk can and taken to the nearest railroad station. Eggs from the wife's chicken flock and butter churned from the cream could be bartered in town at the local grocery and general store. Cattle and hogs could be sold at market, with a few held back and butchered for the family needs. Gardens provided fresh fruits and vegetables in summer; produce and meat could be canned to get through the winter. Potatoes and root vegetables, stored in root cellars that stayed cool in summer and frost-free in winter, would last through the winter, Firewood was cut and along with corn cobs, burned in the kitchen cook stove and parlor stove for winter warmth and year-round cooking. (Courtesy of Alan Evans.)

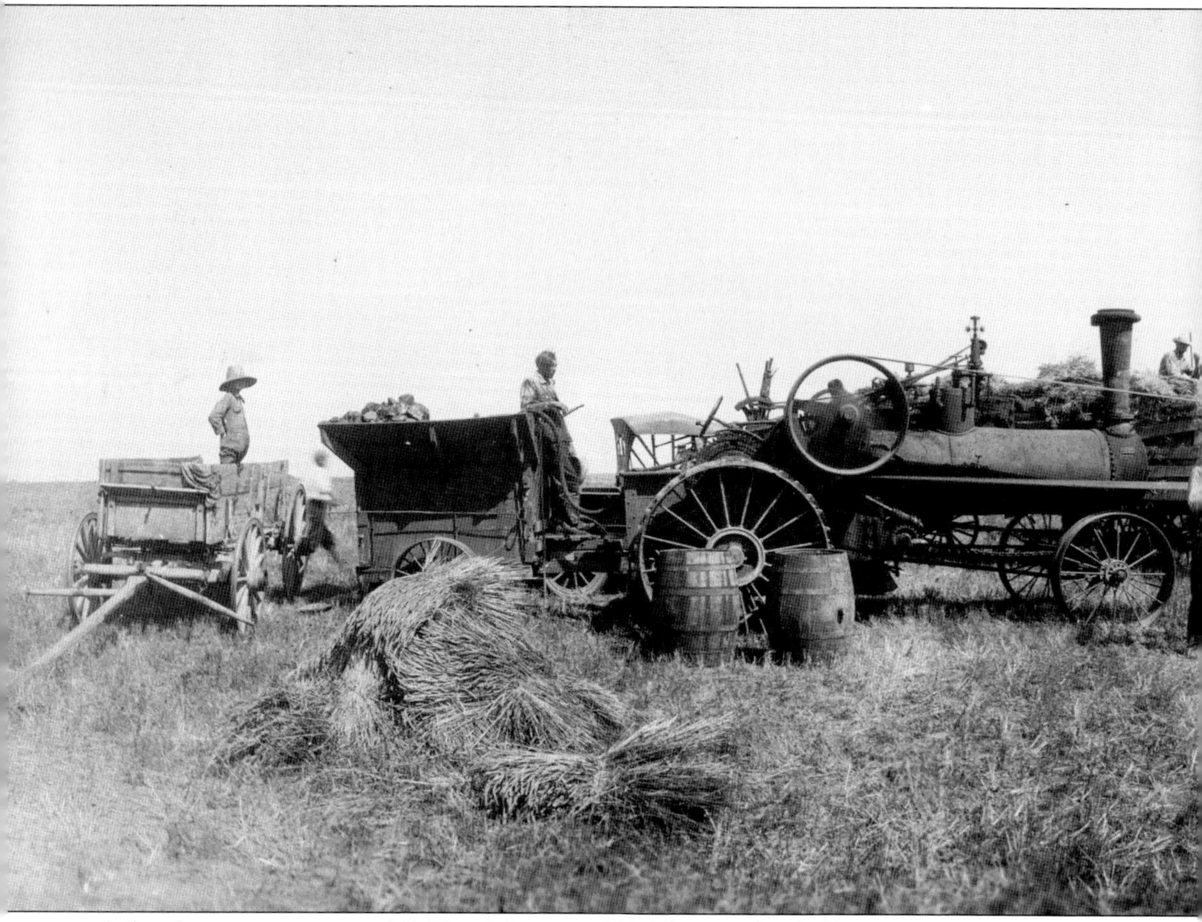

A threshing crew poses on A.B. Fryer's farm in 1922. The crew loaded bundles of grain and hauled them to the threshing machine, and tossed them onto the conveyor belt powered by a steam tractor-operated tractor. A rotating knife cut the twine holding the bundles together. These grain

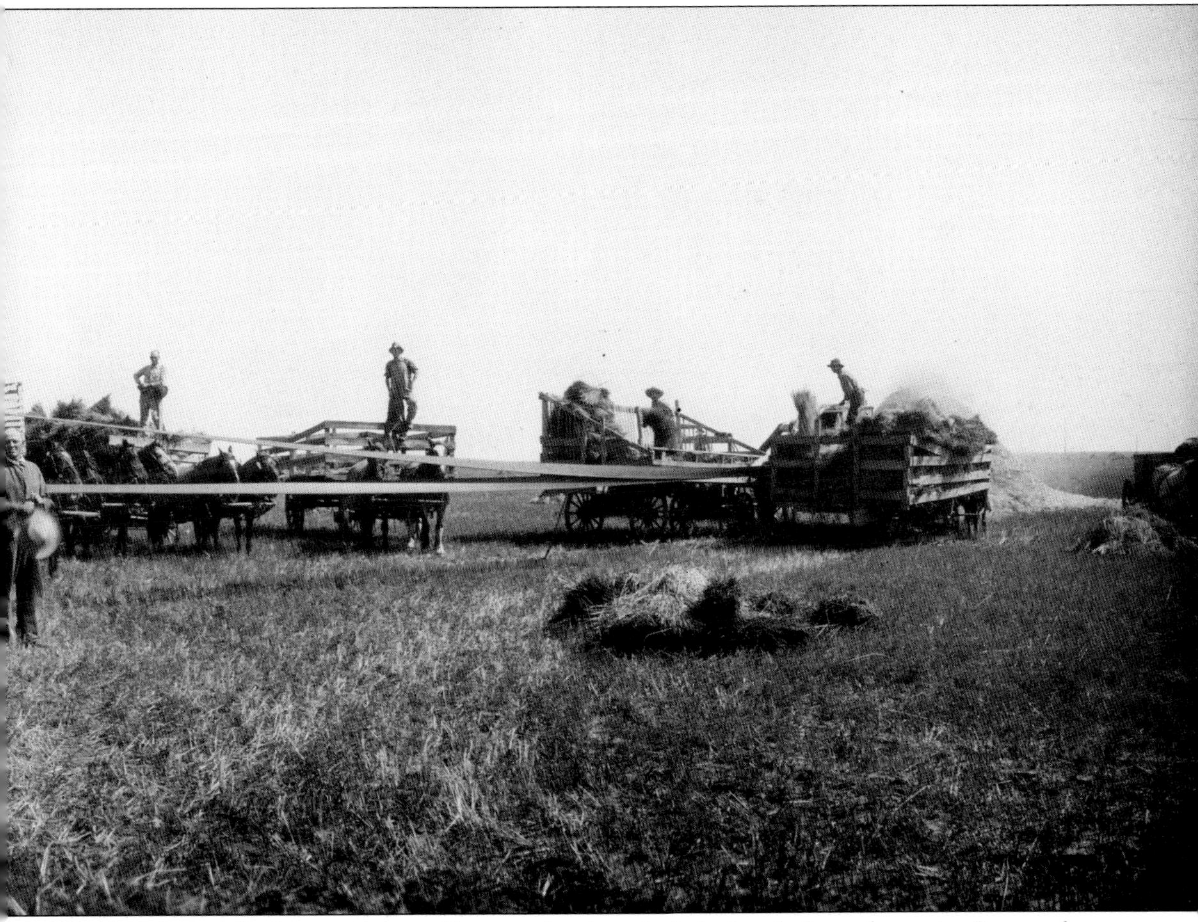

stalks were pitched into a series of beaters that knocked the heads from the grain. Breezes from the operation threw the grain up into the air with the chaff settling into a pile, and the clean grain dropping into a waiting wagon.

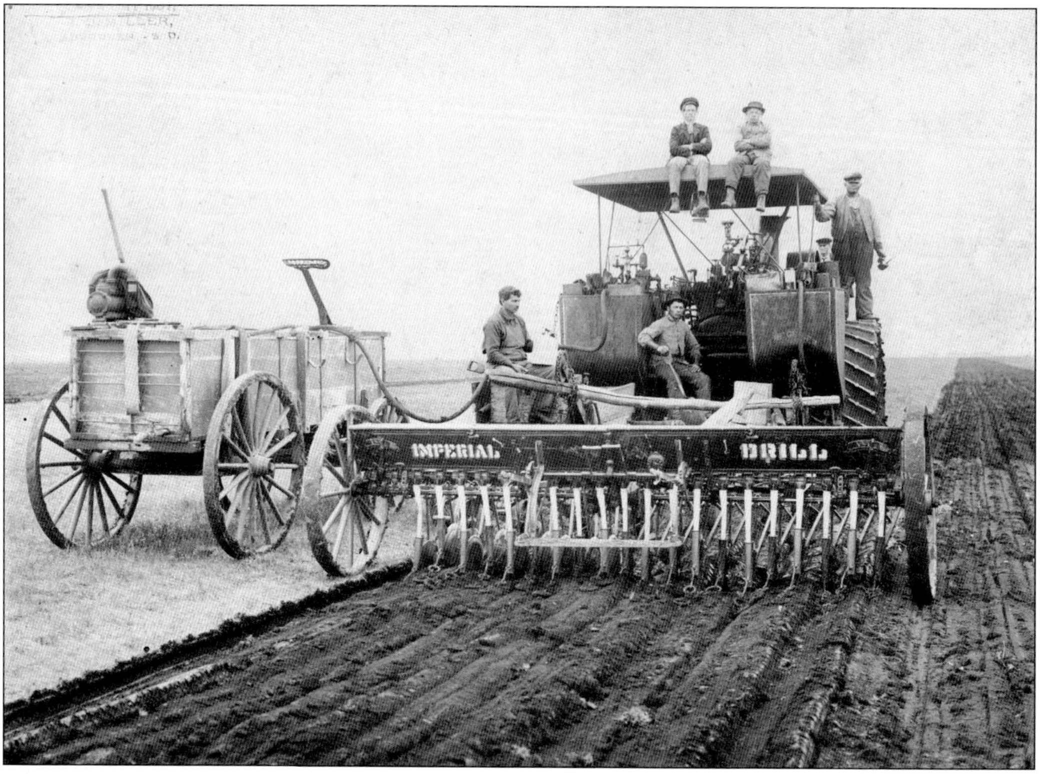

This crew pauses from plowing and seeding work to pose on their Imperial Drill machine.

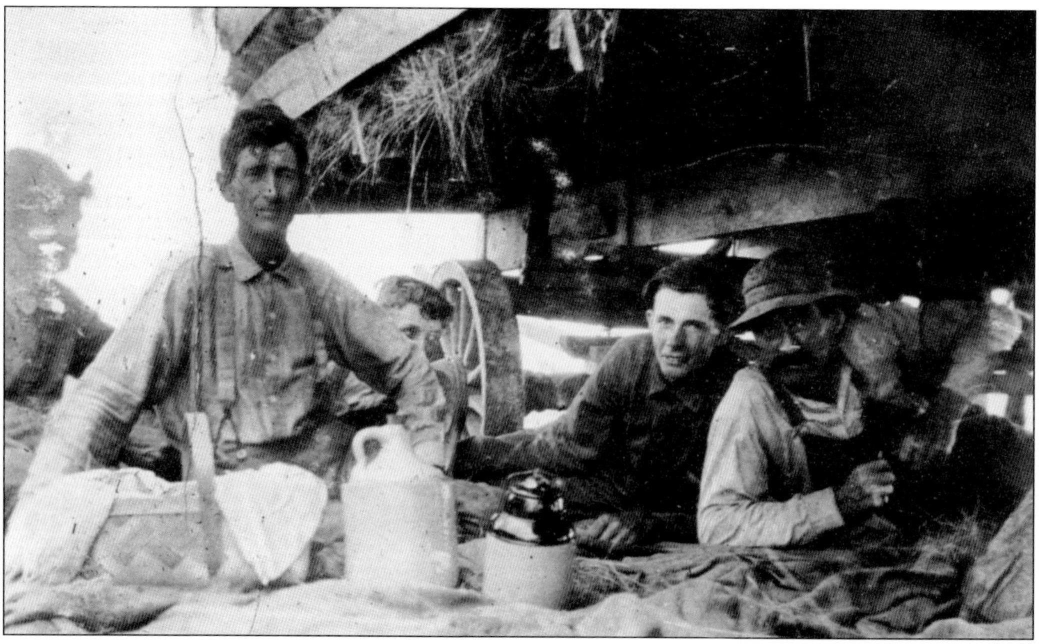

Making hay while the sun shone often meant eating meals in the field, picnic style. This photograph shows Luxton farmers taking advantage of shade offered by the hay wagon.

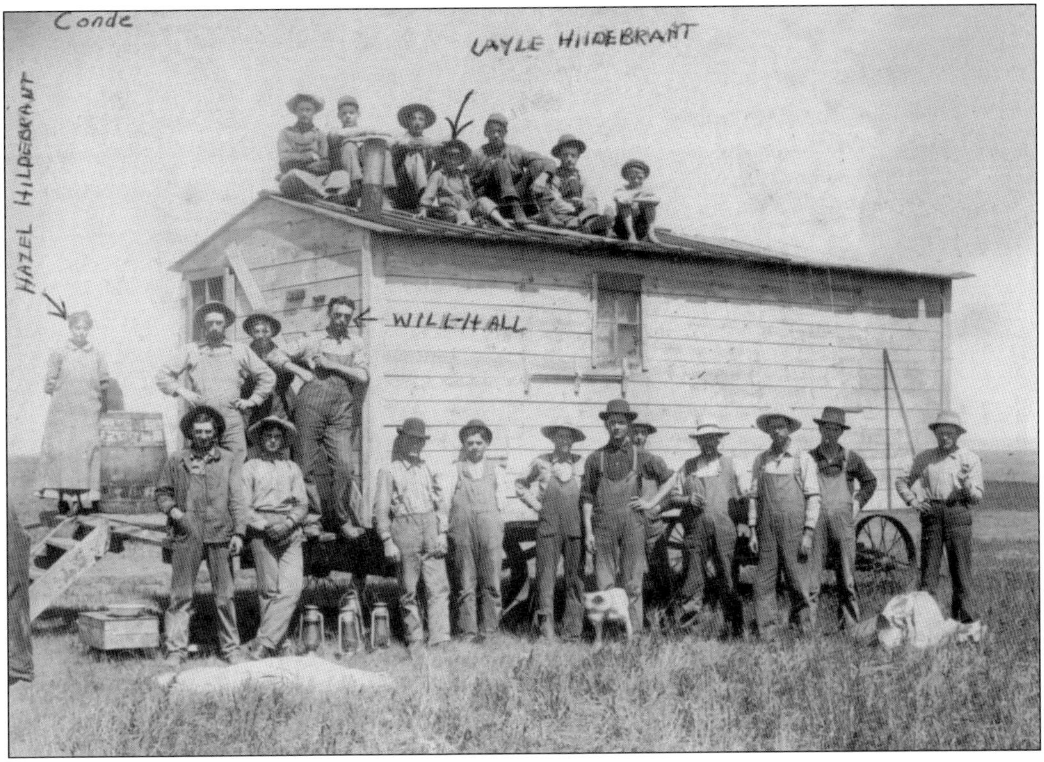

Pictured above is a cook car around 1917. Cooking for a threshing crew on a hot day inside a cook car was hard, hot work, but the crew certainly appreciated the effort. Below is a cook car on the Overby farm. (Above, courtesy of Earl Grandpre; below, courtesy of Glenn Overby.)

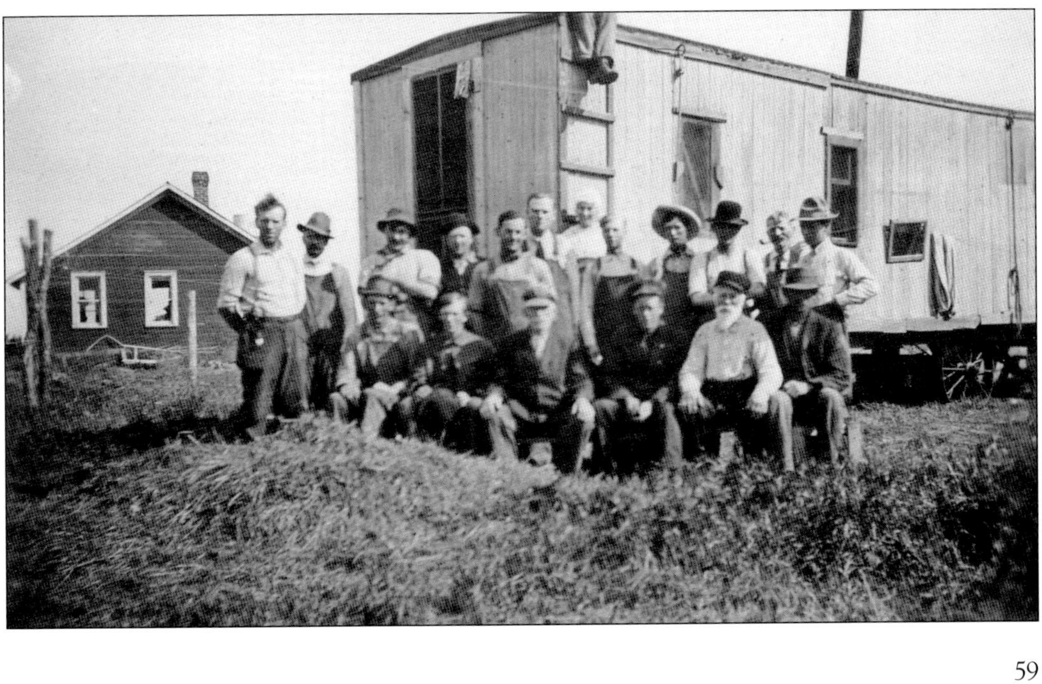

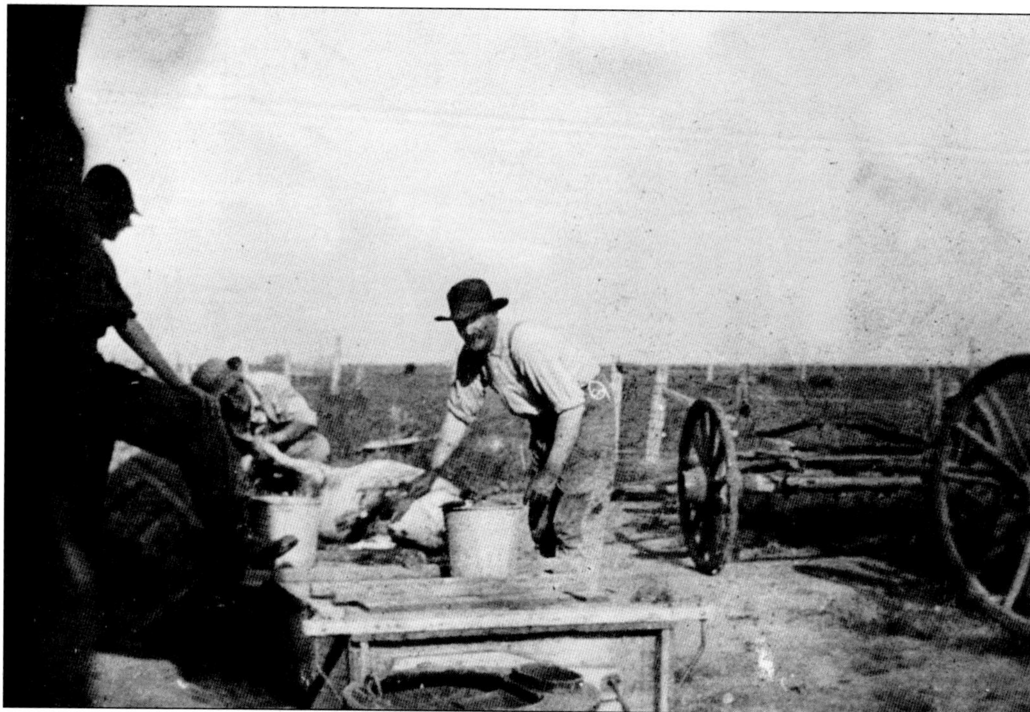

This image shows one of the Luxton men butchering a hog. Processing was either by smoking it or hanging it in the summer kitchen during the winter months, where it would stay frozen.

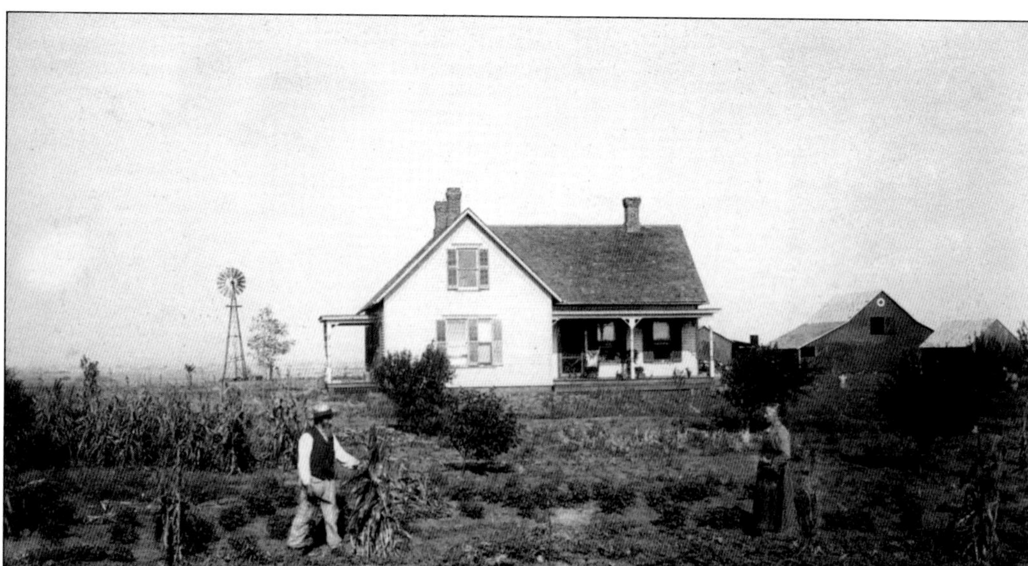

Along with butchering, early settlers relied on home gardens to provide produce for their family meals. Pictured here are Tom Luxton and his wife.

Four

Businesses, Towns, and Farmsteads

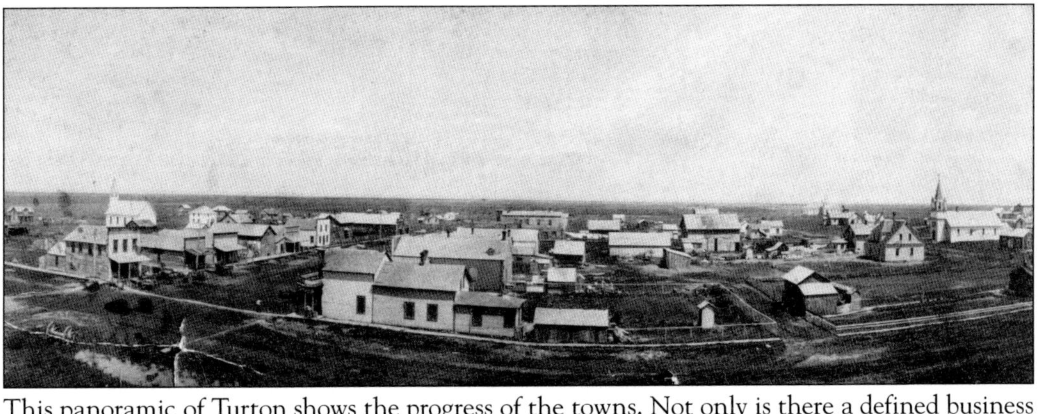

This panoramic of Turton shows the progress of the towns. Not only is there a defined business district to the left, but also two churches on the far right side and back. Paint seems to have been more available and affordable. (Courtesy of Richard Barrie.)

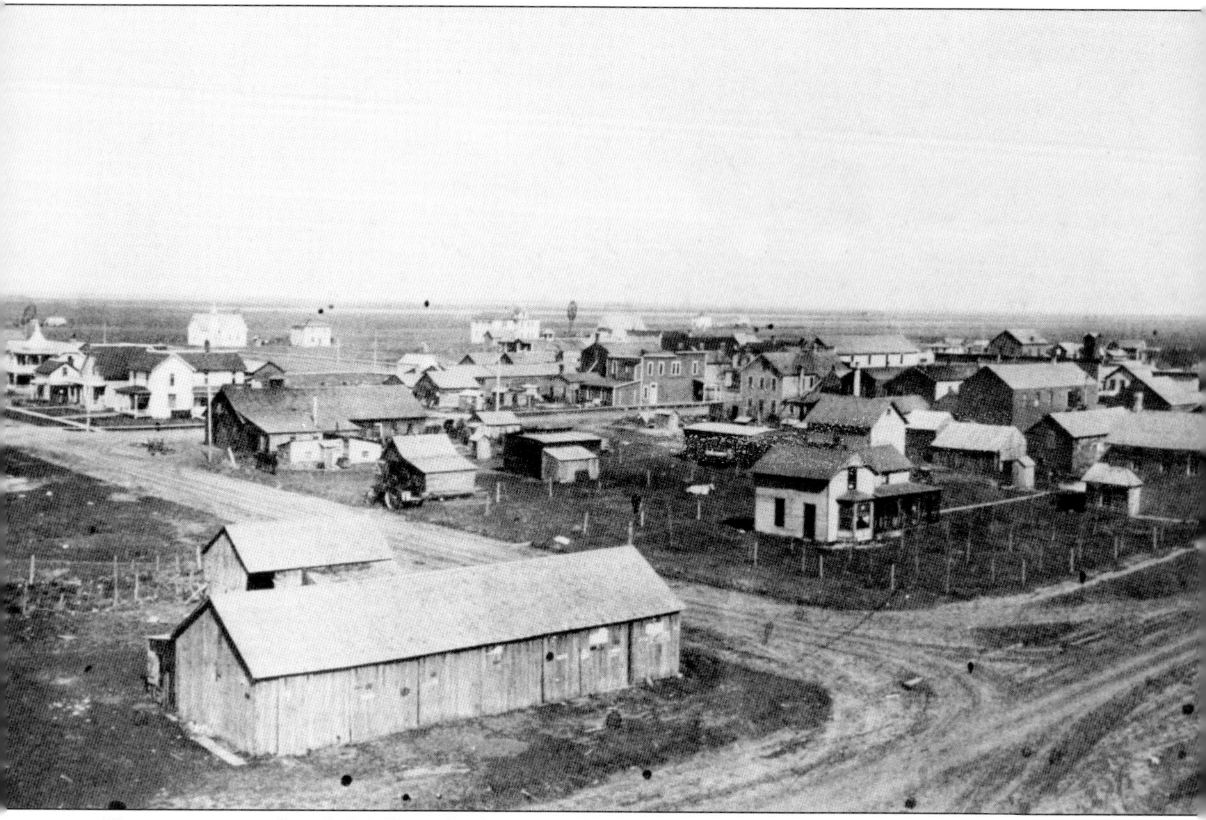

Here is a view of early Mellette looking northwest. The first settlers marked out homesteads to plant, harvest, and raise livestock and chickens. Their presence encouraged others to come and establish shops and businesses to support the growing farming economy. The early towns were often nothing more than a small collection of buildings with no trees or sidewalks, and only the rudiments of streets. Remembrances of former lives were carried here in the early settlers' minds, and they quickly began planning out towns. Those who ran the shops and businesses needed homes. As lumber became more available and more transportable via the railroad, towns began looking more like what the settlers had left behind.

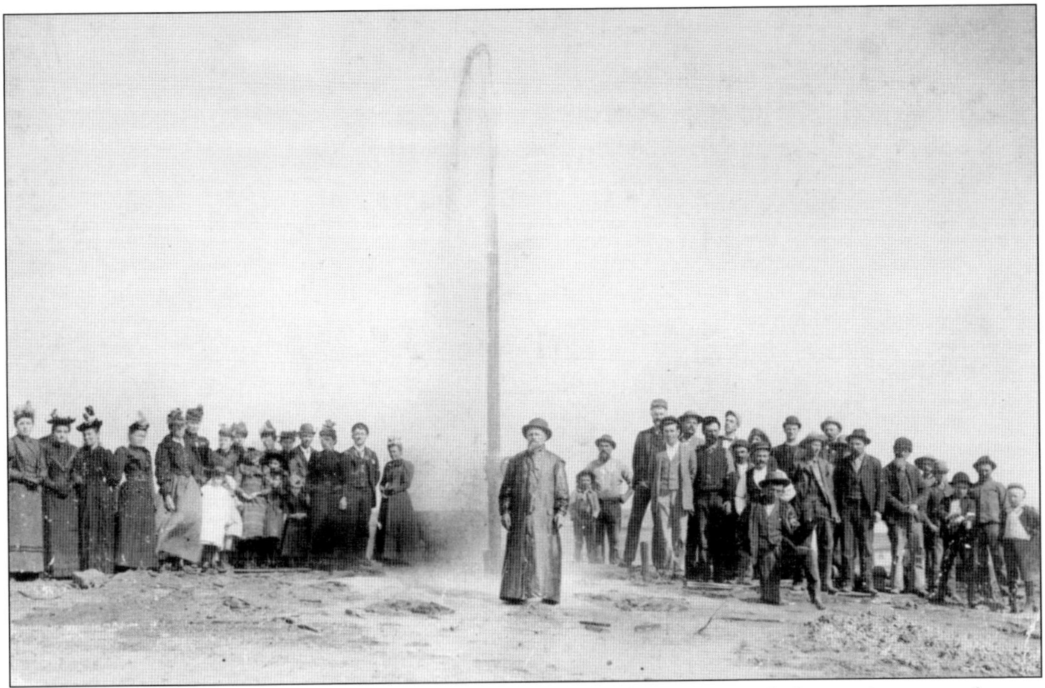

In 1893, the first artesian well drilled in the Turton/Conde area provided a vital source of water for livestock and human consumption. Everyone needed water, so when a driller came to town and was able to provide a better well at a lower price, he knew his business would thrive.

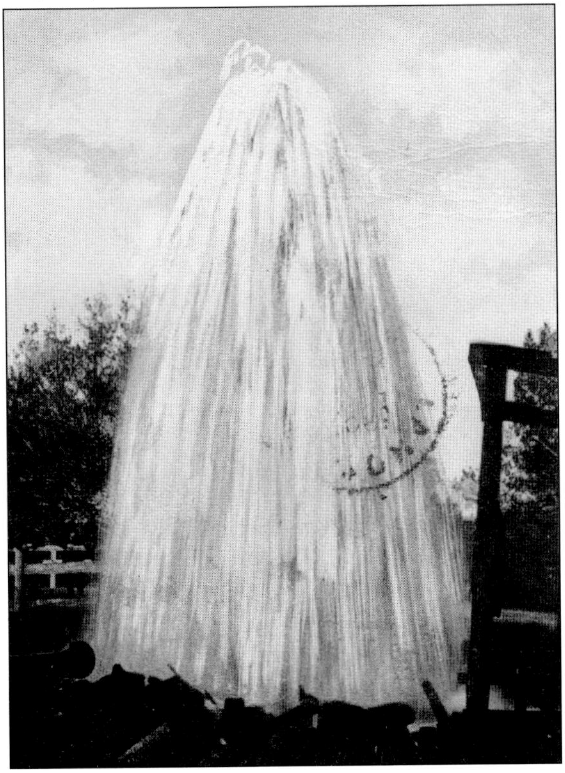

In the 1880s, finding a good source of water was an issue for the inhabitants of Redfield. A spring on Turtle Creek supplied splendid water, but too little. A well on Main Street produced water containing so much sulfur that it reminded the citizens of "one of the infernal regions." Cisterns and a well at the Chicago & North Western depot supplied the largest amount for the city until Norbeck-Nicholson dug this well. This was the biggest artesian well in the world, producing 8,500 gallons per minute. Finding this suitable source of dependable water was also paramount for the farmers. It assured a consistent supply when the farmers were at the mercy of the weather. (Courtesy of Alan Evans.)

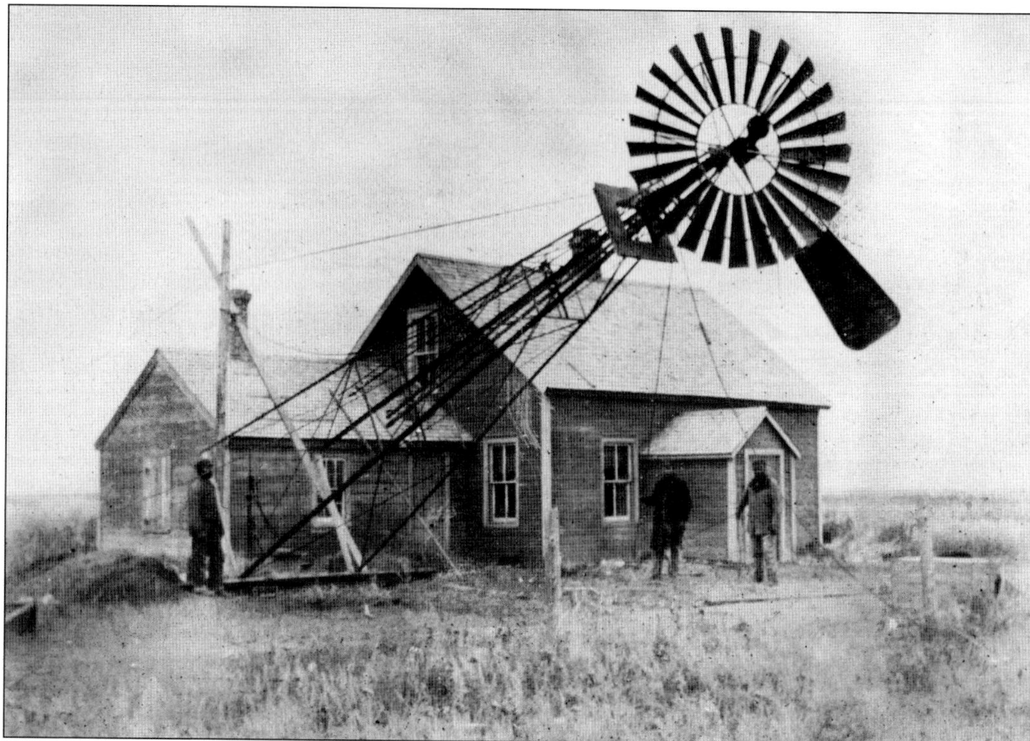

This scene captures the raising of a windmill on the Tom Luxton farmstead in 1898.

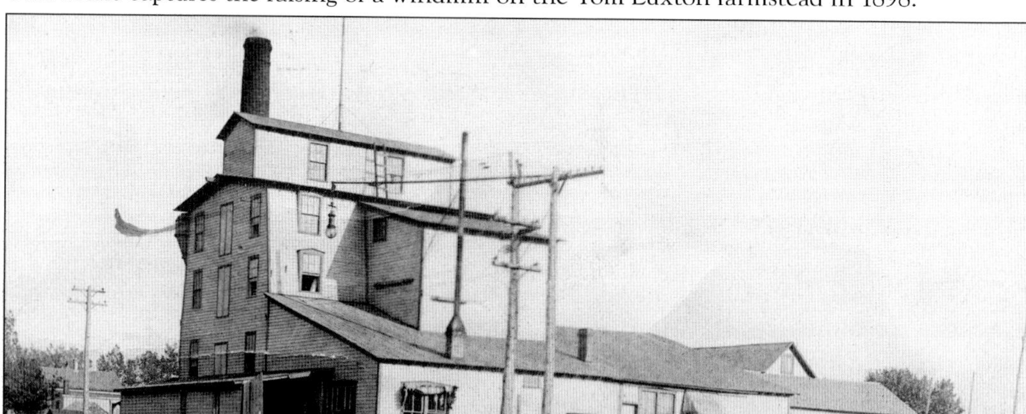

Pictured here is the Redfield Flour Mill. The Kutnewsky Brothers—Ben, Charlie, and Fred—built the mill in 1883 and later sold it to George C. Christian, a Minneapolis miller. It produced Royal Patent Flour until the 1930s, when it could no longer compete with Eastern mills. A frame building, the mill measured 30 feet by 36 feet and was five stories high. The engine house was built of brick and had a circular smokestack 65 feet high. A 50-horsepower engine driven by two large steel boilers operated the machinery, producing 150 barrels of ground flour every 24 hours. It was located southeast of the water tower.

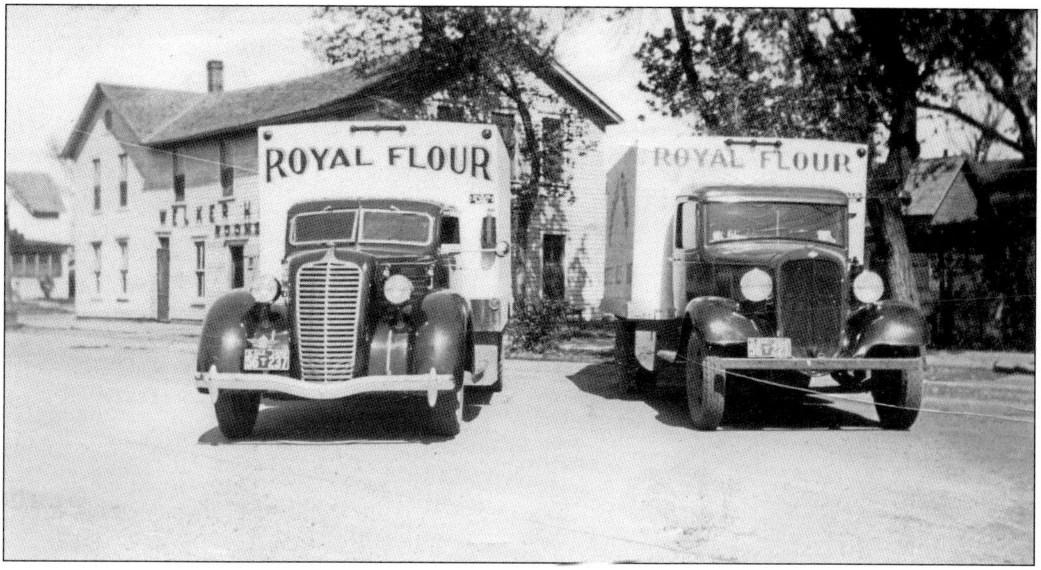

Above, flour mill trucks, parked near the Welker Rooming House, are ready to deliver Royal Flour. Below, a Royal Flour truck is on its way to an out-of-town delivery. In addition to providing flour for the area, the mill also exported to several foreign countries.

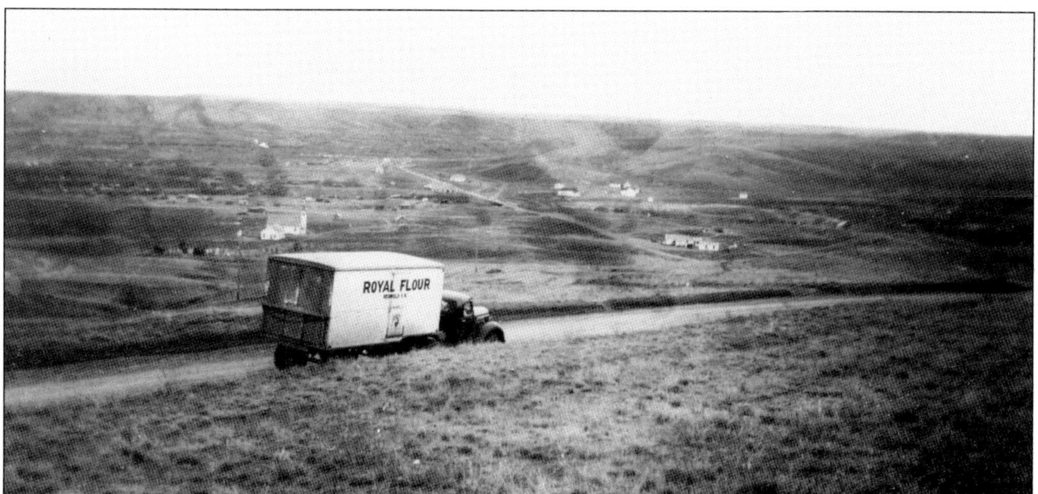

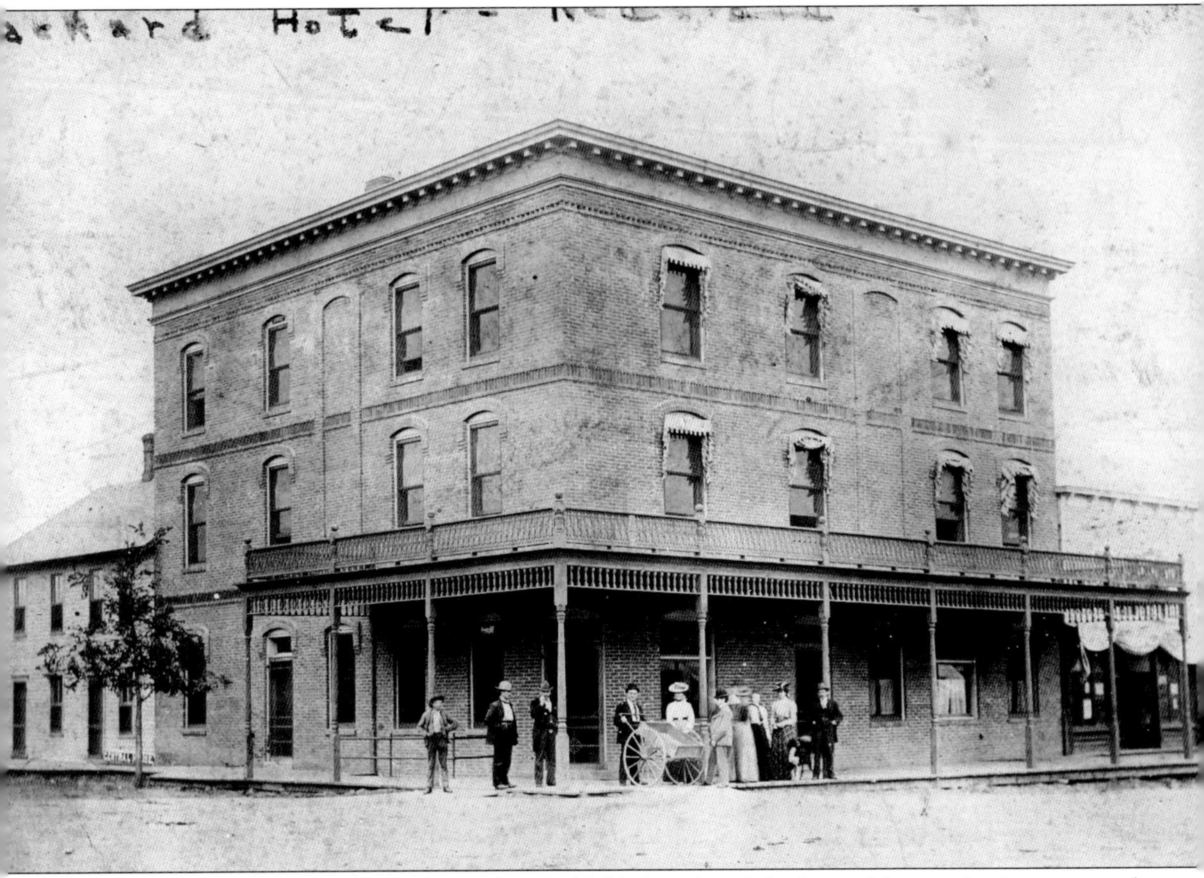

Pictured in 1897 is the Central Hotel in Redfield. It replaced the Jarvis House, which was moved to the corner of Sixth Avenue and Second Street East. Hotels and rooming houses came on the heels of the pioneers. For $2 a day, one could rent a room with a bath. In 1925, it was renamed the Packard Hotel. (Courtesy of Richard Barrie.)

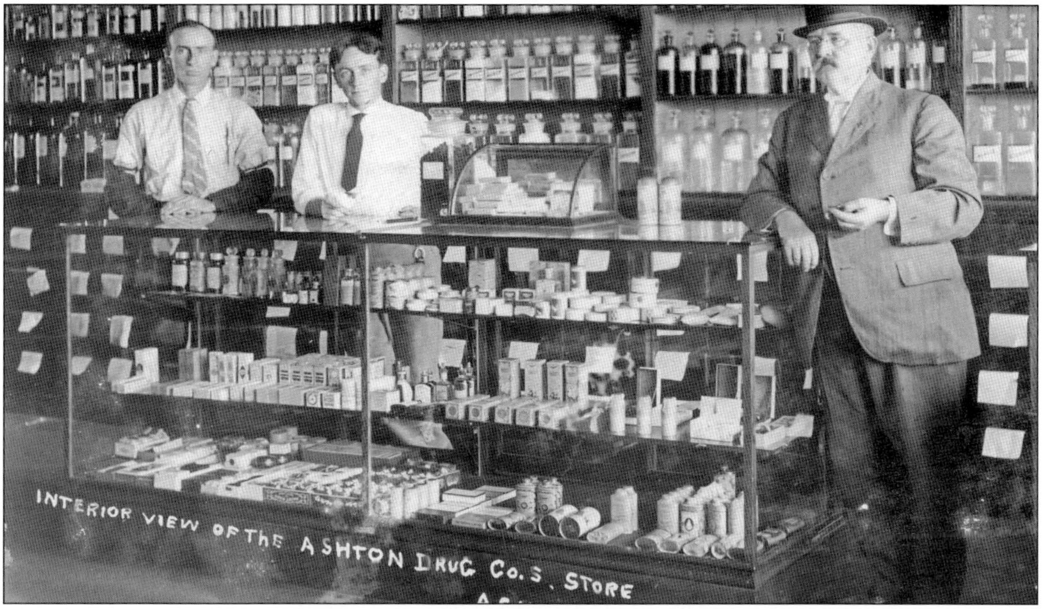

Here is an interior view of the Ashton Drug Store. Drugstores, general stores, auto and farm implement dealers, grocery stores, meat markets, and banks could all survive in these small thriving communities. The railroad provided a means of bringing goods in and taking them out. Traveling by wagon or buggy to larger business areas was limited by nonexistent or poor roads.

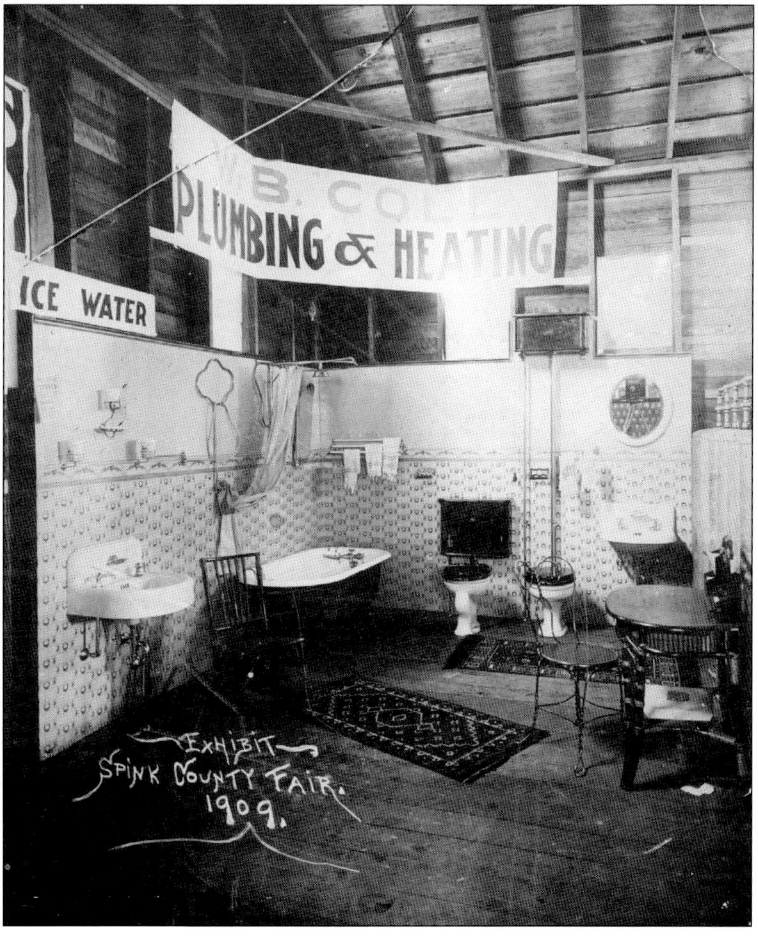

The growing towns also provided rich opportunity for the trades. Pictured here is the Cole Plumbing & Heating display at the 1909 Spink County Fair.

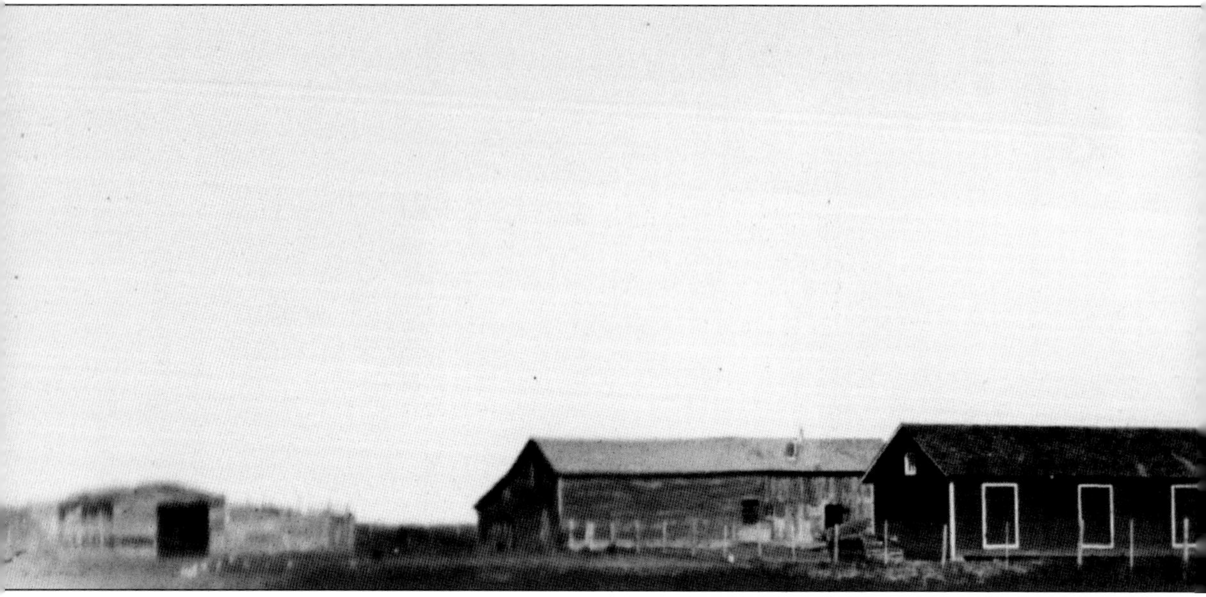

This panoramic view of the Lentz Farmstead in northeast Spink County shows a number of outbuildings including various barns as well as the house. As affluence and availability of materials became more widespread, the sod houses and simple frame houses gave way to more palatial homes and farmsteads. A good share of their entertainment was in the homes, and the people wanted to have formal dining rooms for meals and front parlors for courting and games. While many of

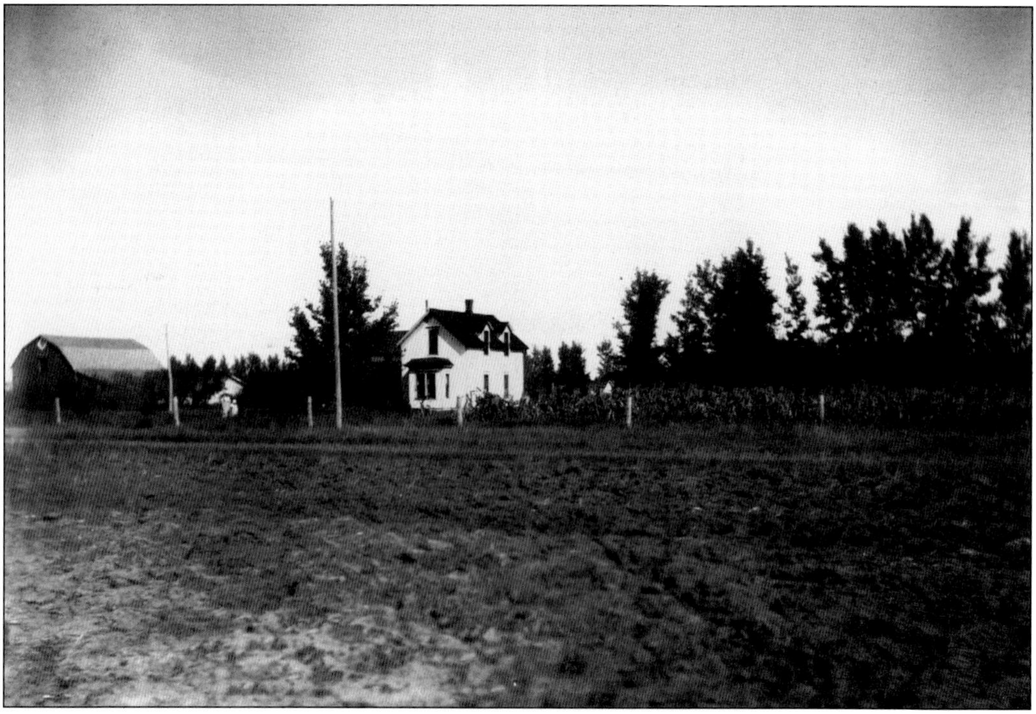

Pictured here is a farm near Conde. While many of the barns of the 1910–1920 decade had a gambrel-style roof, most of the earlier barns had a hip-style roof. (Courtesy of Rod Evans.)

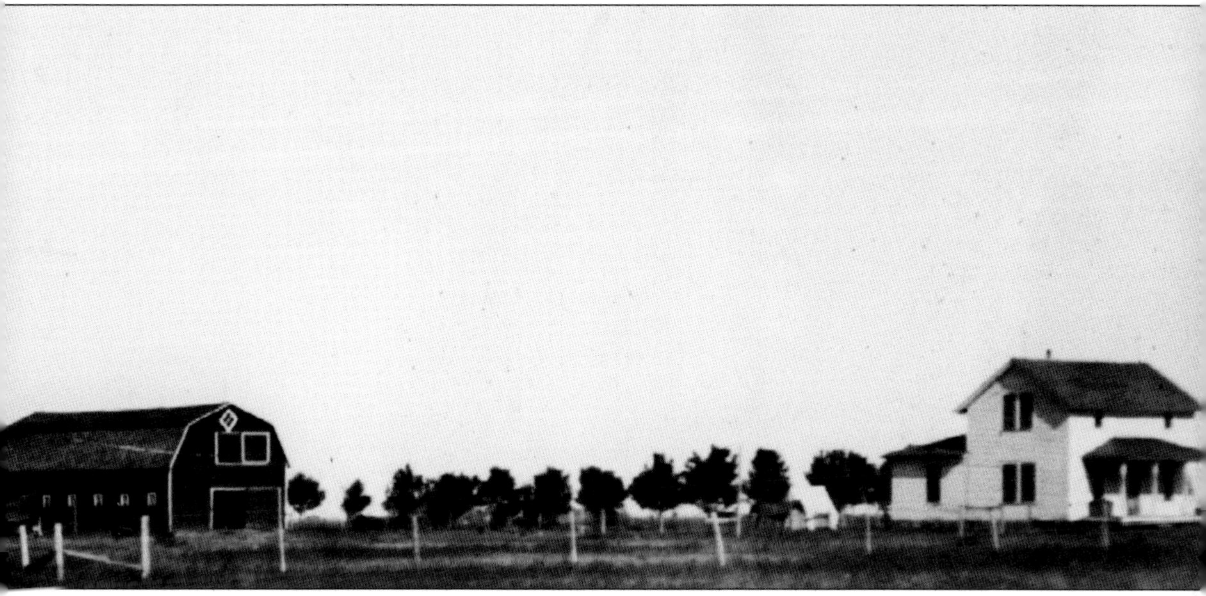

today's kitchens are spacious, most of the earlier town homes were not. The families could afford to have young farm girls serve as cooks, and the kitchens were not necessarily convenient for the help. Closets in many of the bedrooms were also quite small. Woodwork on the first floor might be the finest oak, but the bedrooms on the second floor were fir. Tree claims provided shelterbelts from inclement storms. (Courtesy of Alan Evans.)

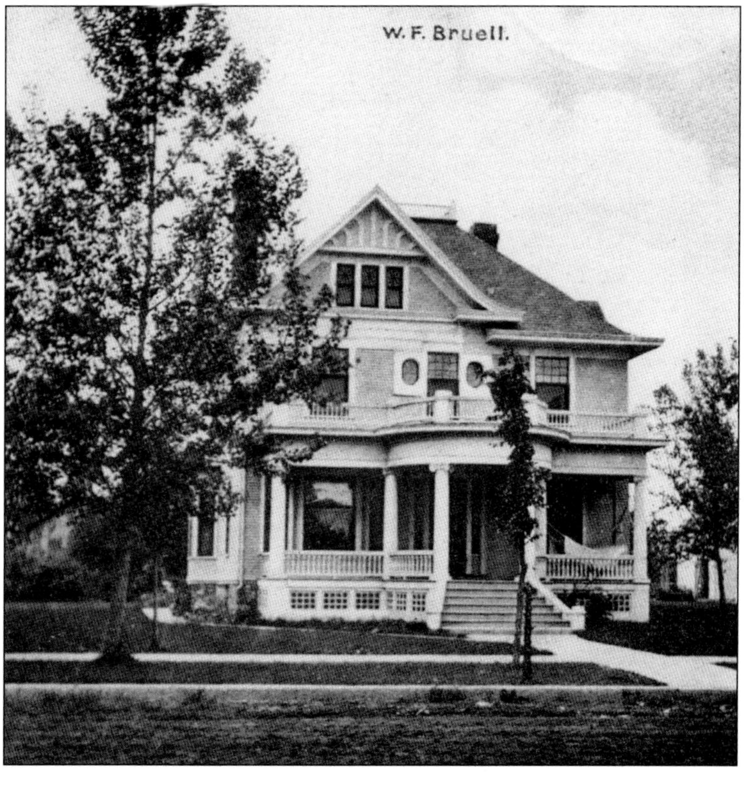

This is the home of William Bruell, who was a lawyer for the Chicago & North Western Railroad. His grandfather was a Prussian count whose estates were confiscated during the interstate wars. (Courtesy of Russell McNeely.)

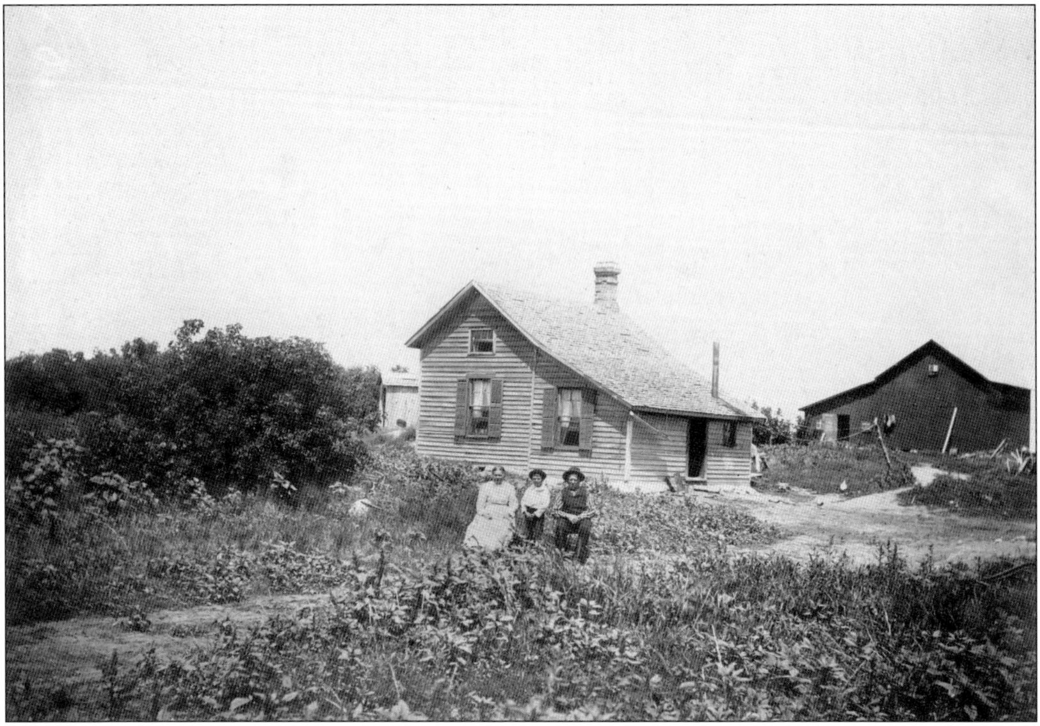

Christian and Augusta Tubandt established their home near Cottonwood Lake, the largest lake in Spink County, which is located northwest of Tulare. (Courtesy of Russell McNeely.)

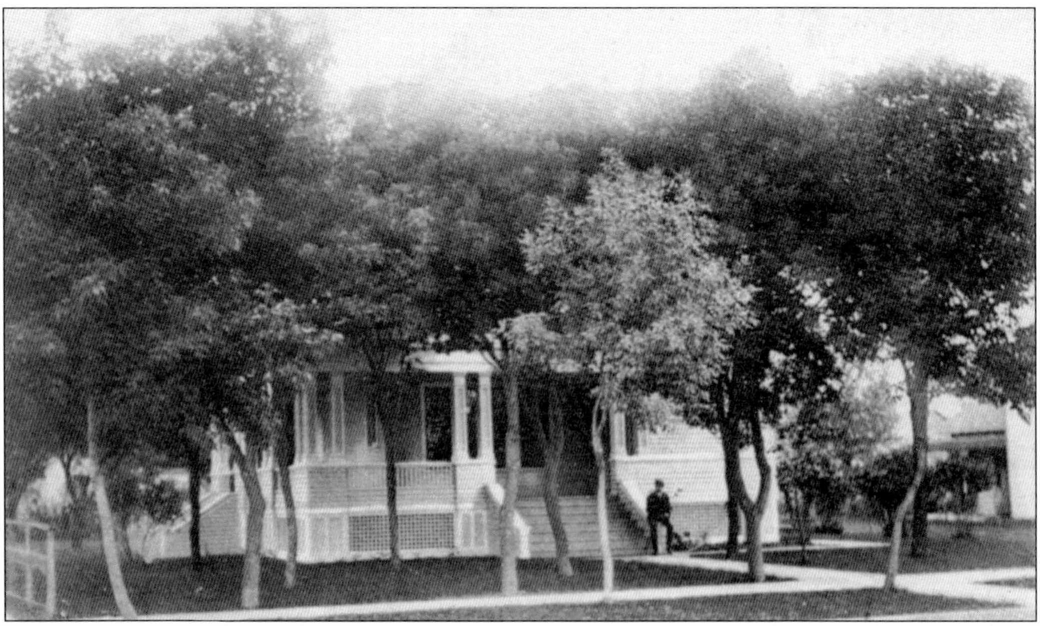

Pictured here is the Stutenroth house. Located at 326 East Second Street, Redfield, this house has not suffered from time. It continues to be a family home with a story. Former owners tell tales about a female spirit who wandered through the house. (Courtesy of Russell McNeely.)

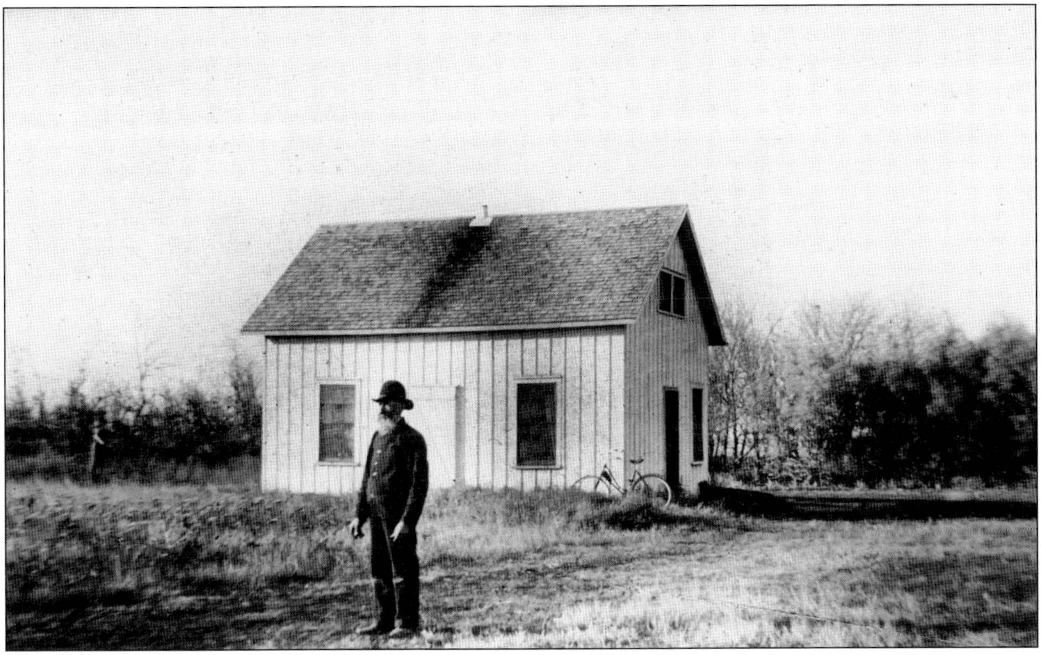

Pictured here in 1882 is the pioneer home of the Spencer family in Tetonka Township. A bicycle, a popular mode of transportation, leans against the side of the house.

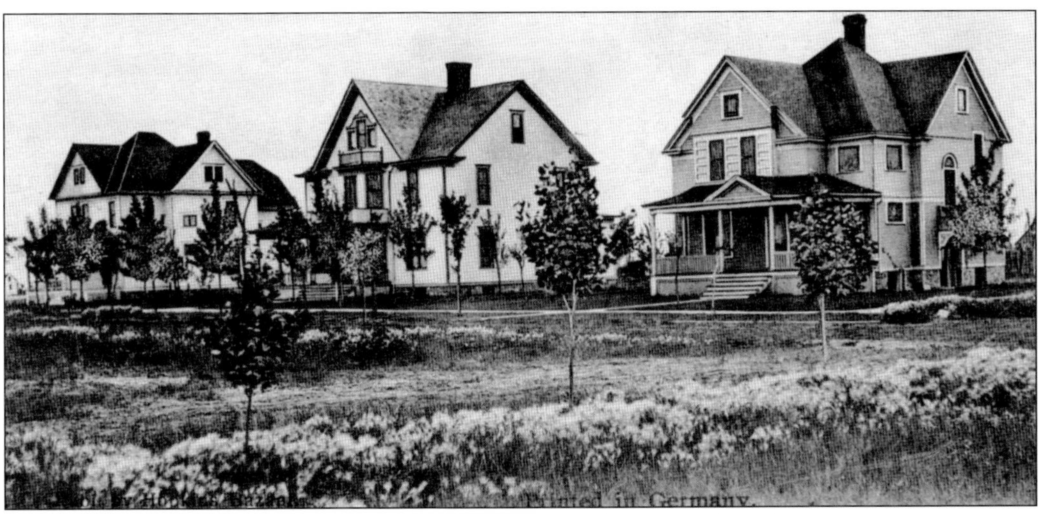

Here are three handsome homes in a row. Families still occupy these three homes. The two in the forefront were owned by Peter Norbeck (center) and his partner Nicholson (right). Behind the houses is a carriage house that supplied hot water heat to the two homes. They hired a man who lived on the second floor of that house to stoke the furnace. H.O. Fish, who ran a laundry business, bought the house later, and his son, an architectural student, drew up plans for a remodel that resulted in a Cape Cod–style house. (Courtesy of Russell McNeely.)

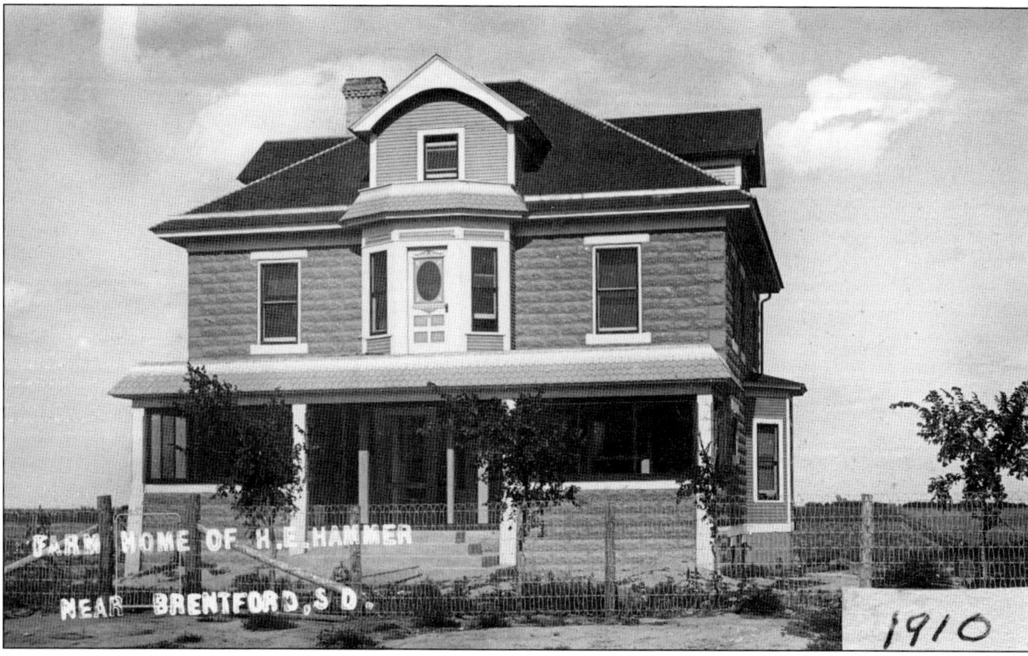

Pictured above is the Hammer Farmstead Home in 1910. It was considered a showcase farm home in its time. Below, the R.C. Styles Home is another foursquare house near Brentford.

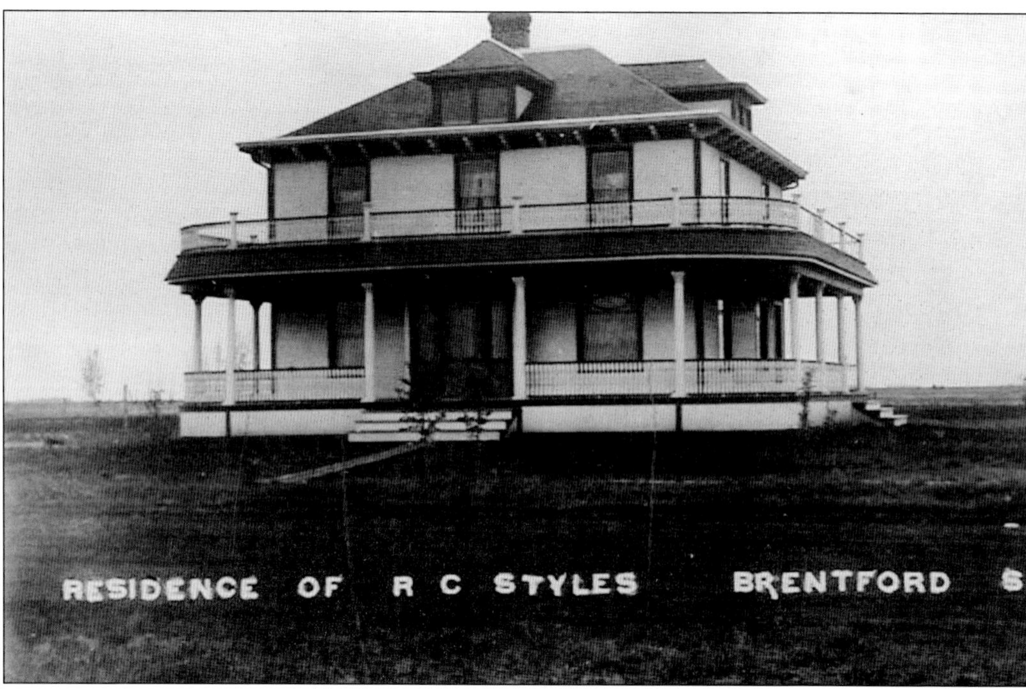

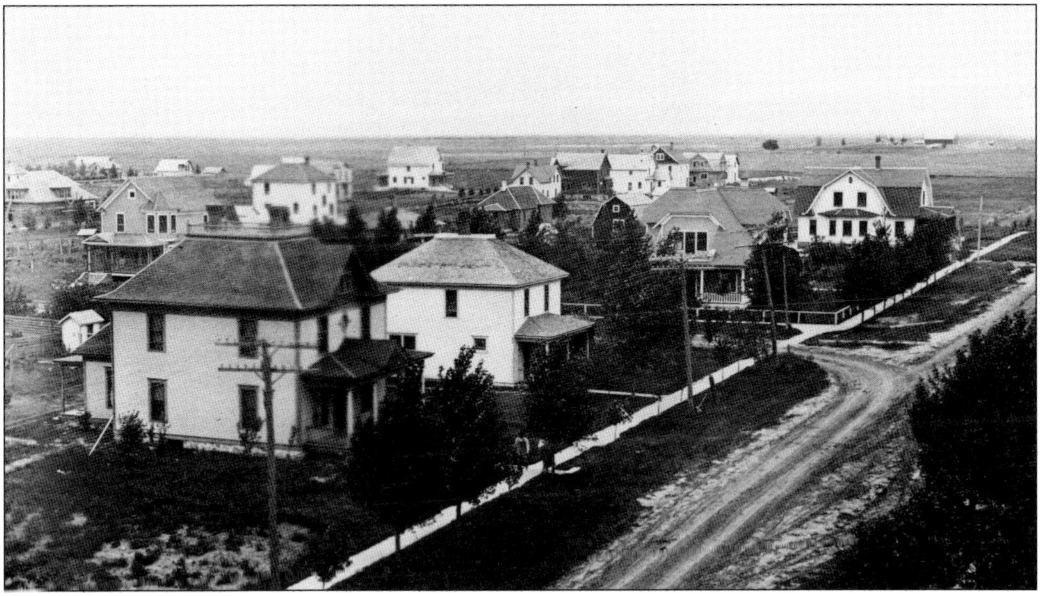

Pictured here is a residential area of Doland. The picture is dated 1913. A couple strolls along the wooden sidewalk.

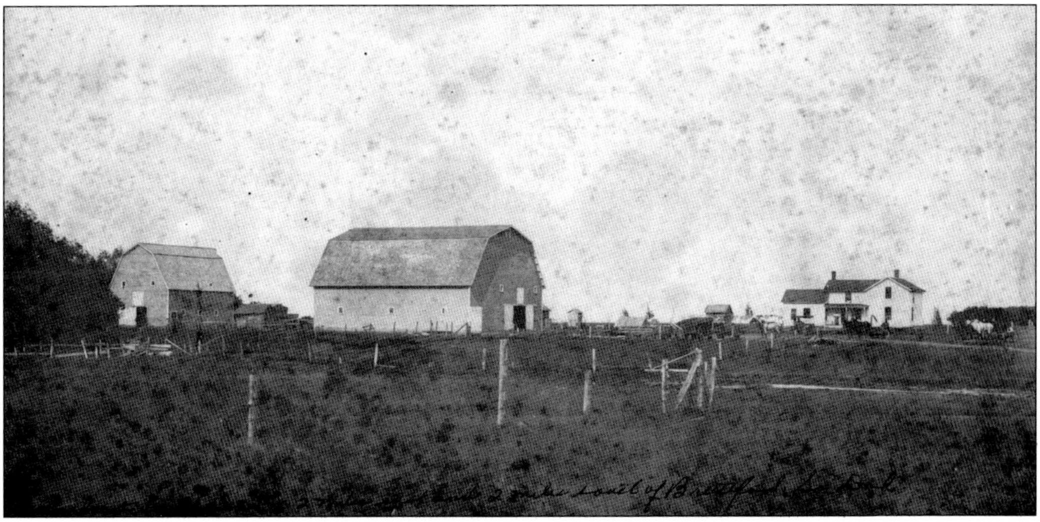

This harvest photograph shows Wil Kiser's farm in 1907. Located two miles east and two miles south of Brentford, this farm features the gambrel-style roof on the two barns. A.D. Moore had operated the farm.

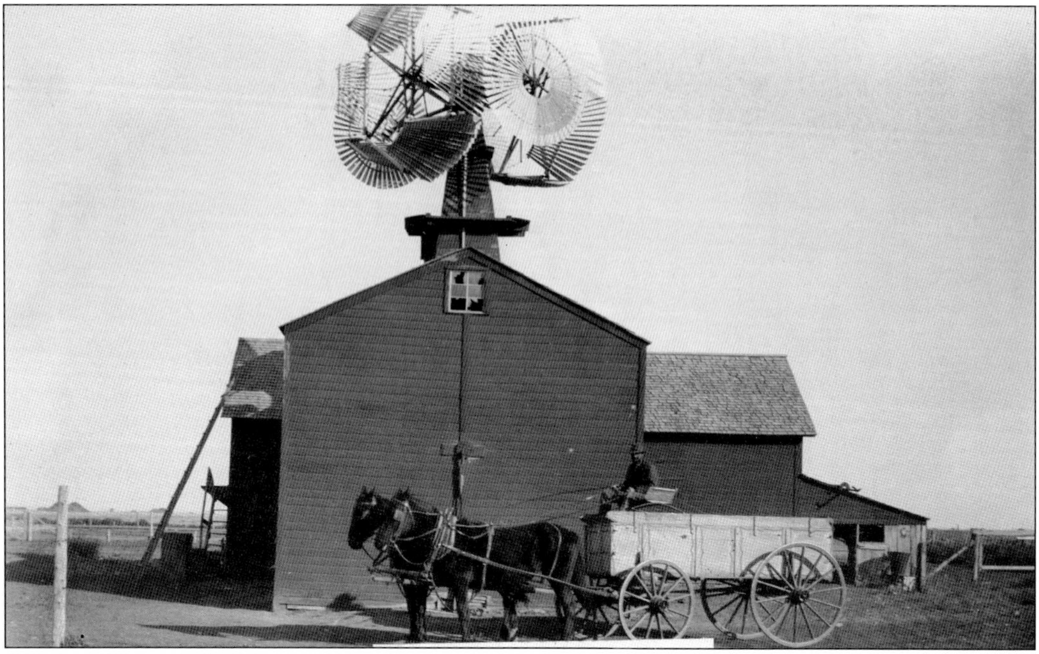

Pictured here is John Luxton with his favorite horse team. Wind power was common in 1890, when this photograph was taken.

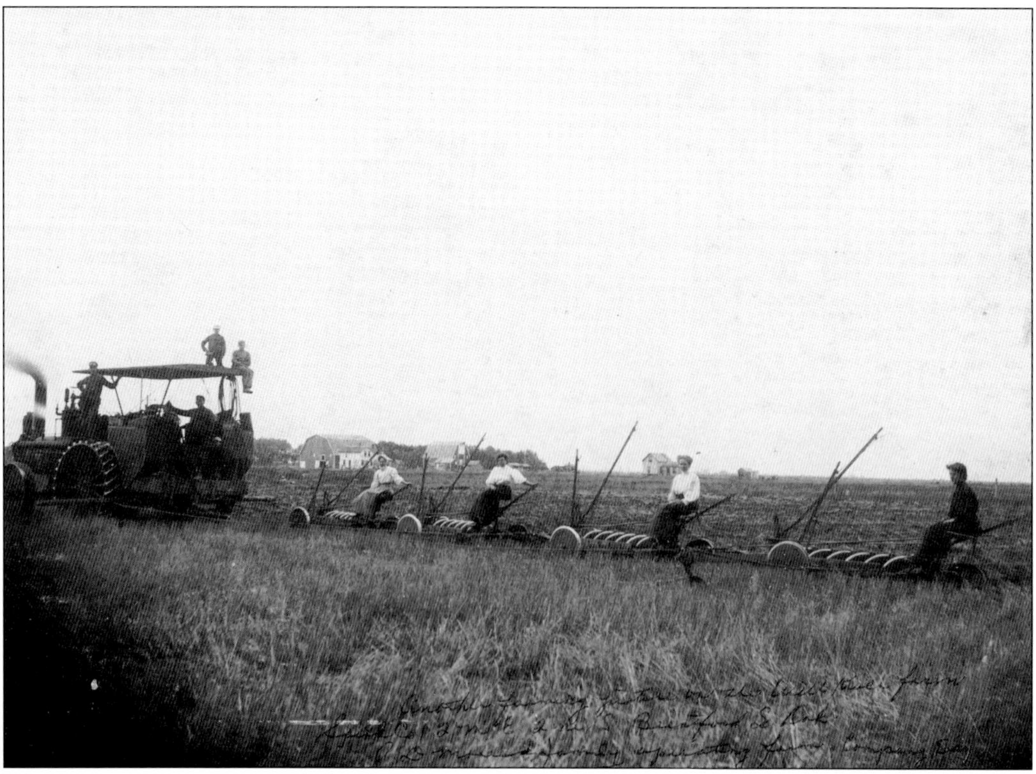

This interesting picture is of the A.D. Moore farm. A steam tractor pulls four disk plows, along with four women, each sitting posed upon a plow.

Five

CHURCHES AND CIVIC INSTITUTIONS

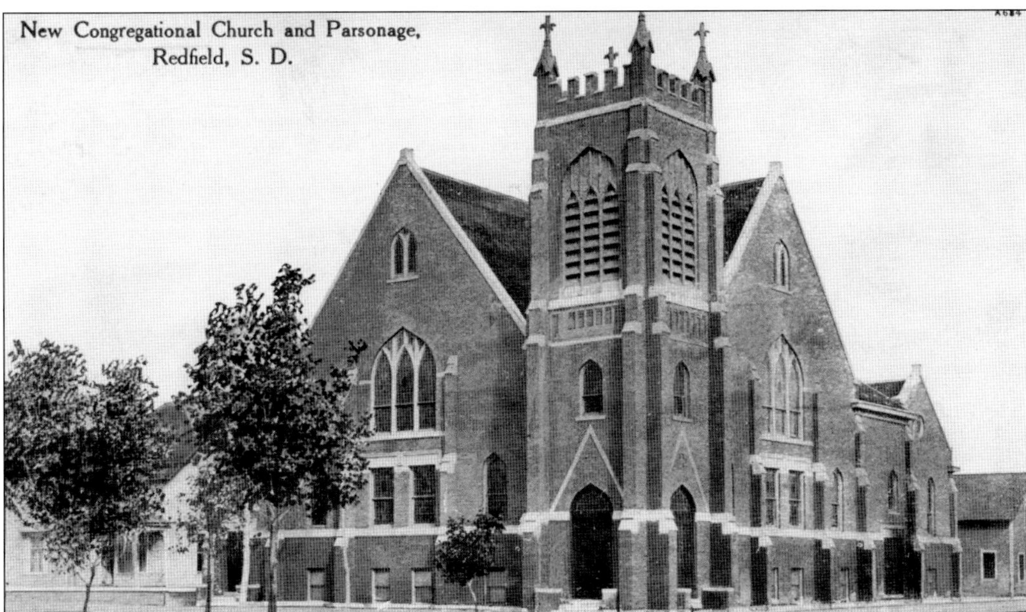

This postcard shows the Congregational Church in Redfield. Now named United Church of Christ, the Redfield congregation still worships in this same edifice. Their first church was a boxcar. (Courtesy of Russell McNeely.)

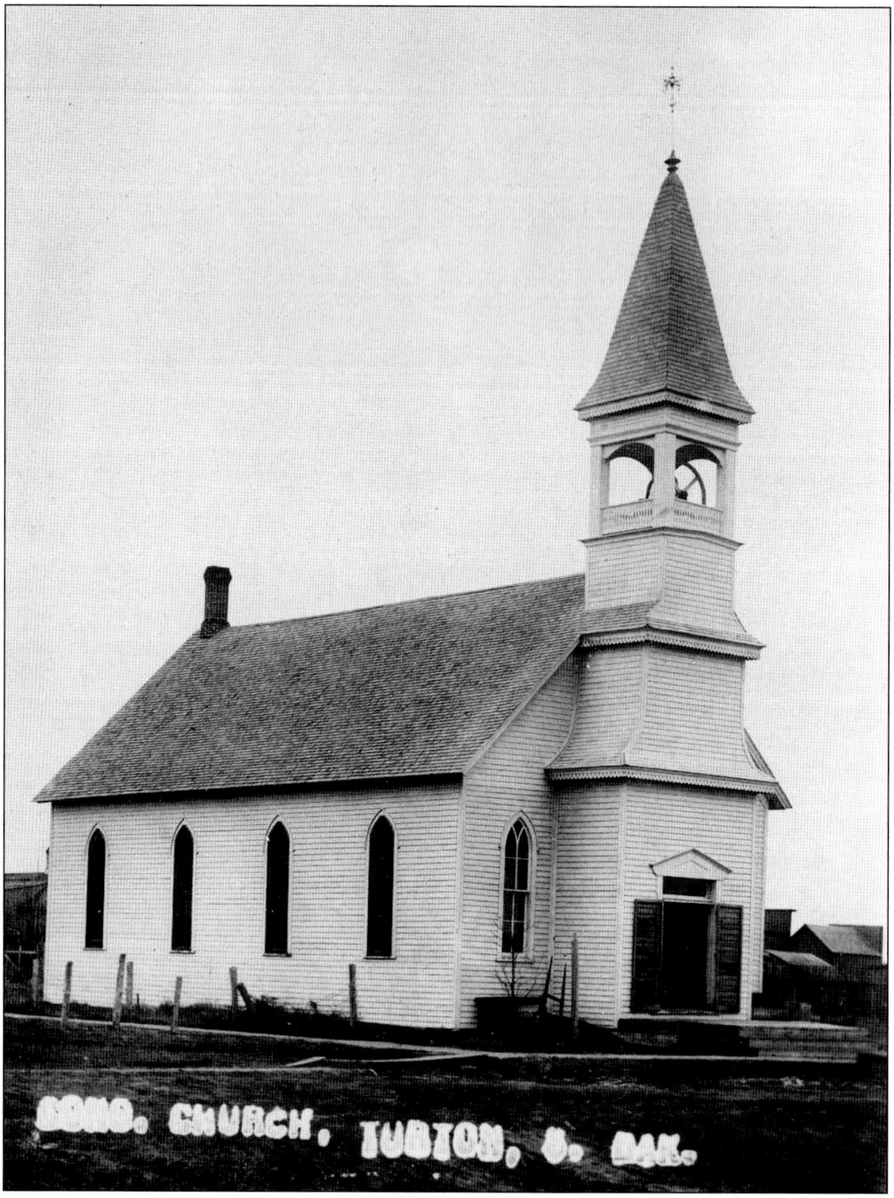

This Turton Congregational Church has been preserved and services are presently held there once a year. As the county grew, more religious leaders began migrating to the area to serve the spiritual needs. Preaching, baptisms, weddings, and Sunday services would be held in the various homes until they could muster the money to build churches in the local towns or in centrally located areas of the county. These prairie churches often included sod houses and schools. Many of the parishioners did not mind the weekly hour's drive over the prairie to spend an hour in God's house thanking Him. The elements certainly had tested many of these early people, and many considered God a foundation in their life. Along with their spiritual life were the organizations that provided fellowship and recreation and governmental agencies that provided security and order. Many of these organizations were familiar echoes of the pioneers' past: the Masons, Eastern Star, and a library. When trouble arose, the jailhouse was a means of handling it. (Courtesy of Doug Jensen.)

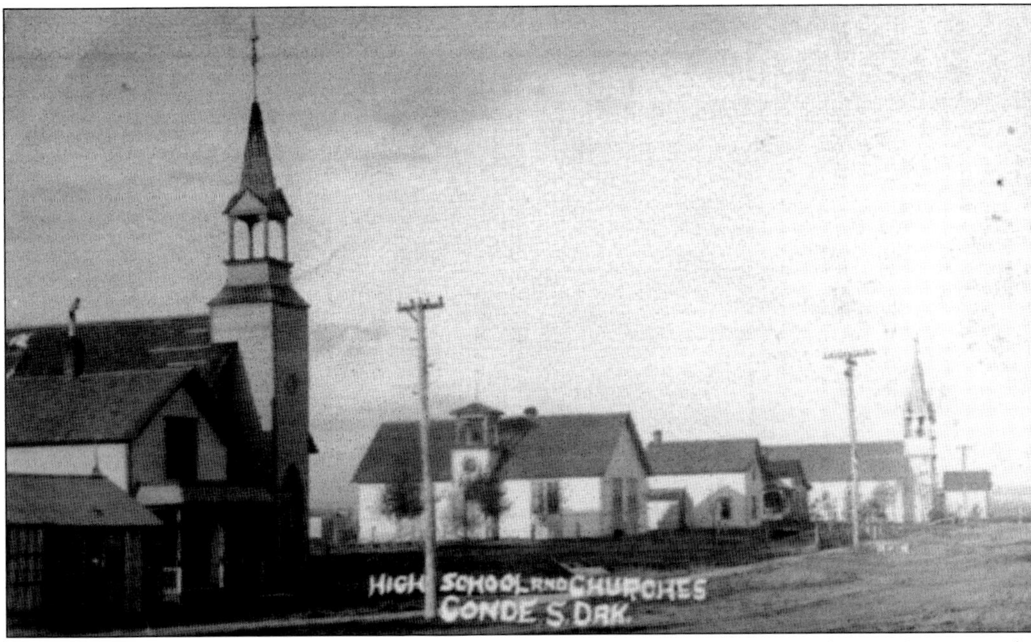

Conde's Baptist Church stood between its parsonage and the school. Typical of early towns, the churches were built in the same areas. The Catholic Church is at the end of the street. (Courtesy of Doug Jensen.)

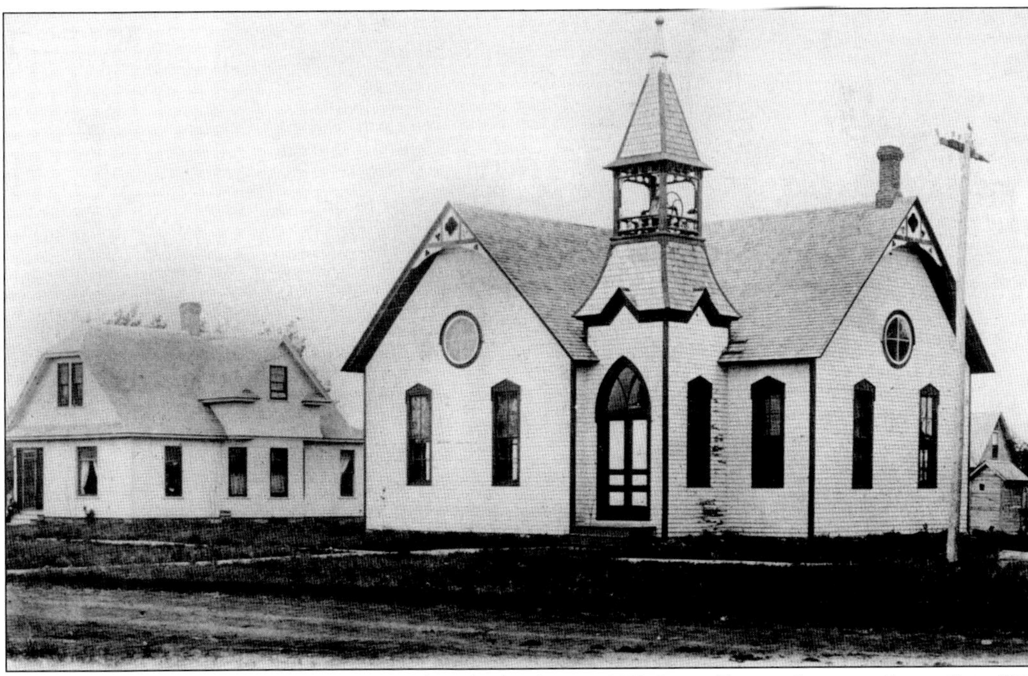

Pictured here is Conde's Methodist Church, built in 1887. Initially, settlers worshipped in J.E. Barnes's sod house, and later the Beotia School, before taking their services to town where they used the railway depot and again another school. Shown here in 1910, the Conde church featured leaded glass windows.

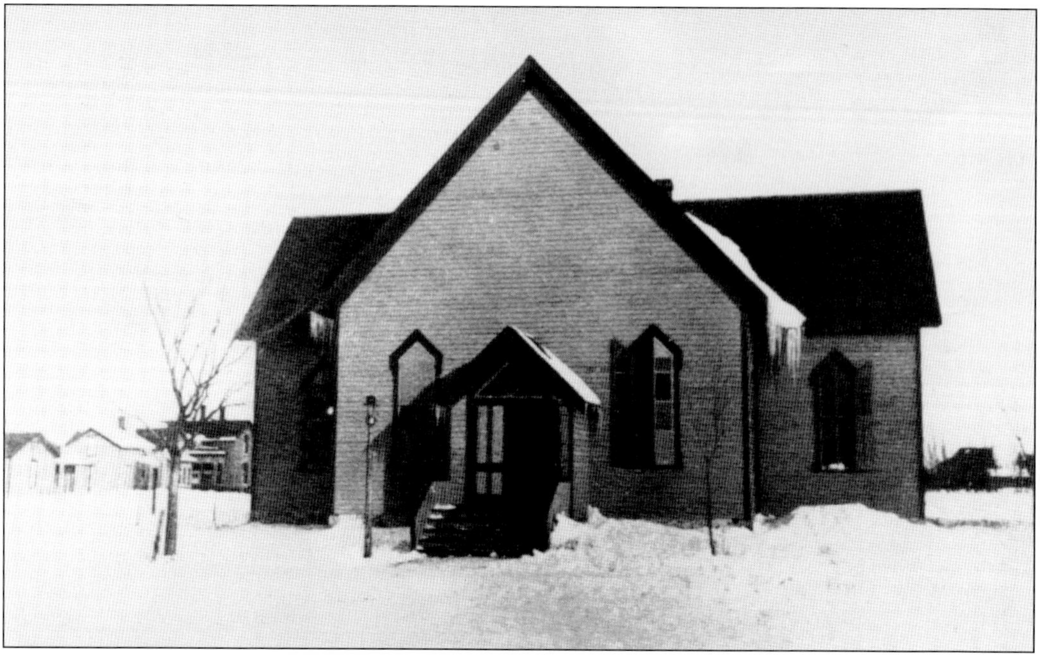

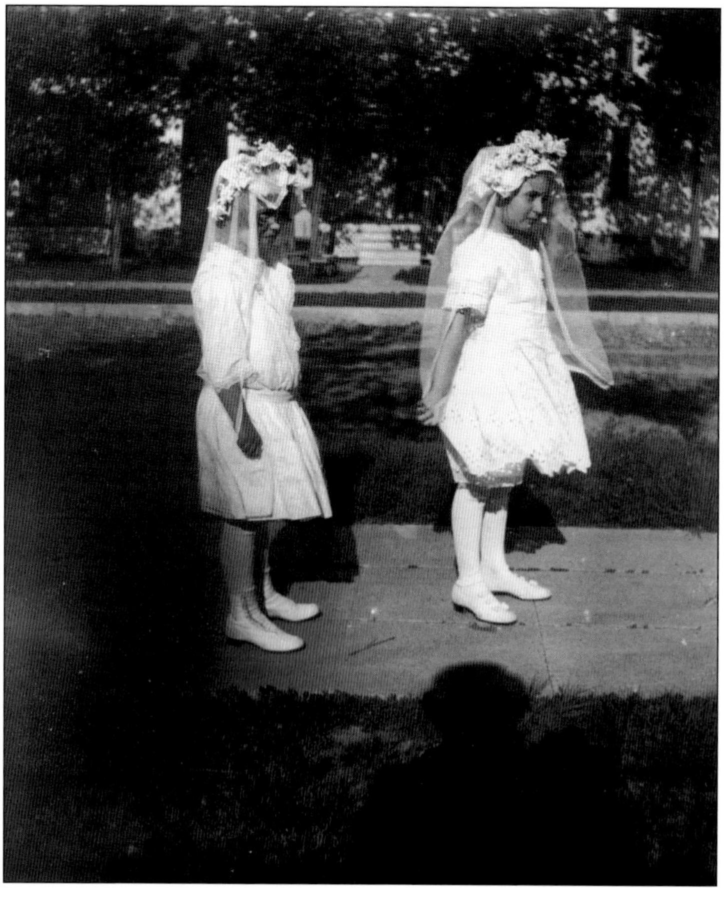

This is the first St. Bernard Roman Catholic Church, built in 1884. When the parish constructed a new church in 1910, the Swedish Lutherans purchased the old church, moved it, renamed it St. Paul Lutheran Church, and used it until 1919 when that church merged with Our Savior's Lutheran. It was moved once more and took on a new life as the church's parsonage. Diane and Henry Dunkel have made it their home since 1969. (Courtesy of St. Bernard Catholic Church.)

Two unidentified girls pose in their First Communion attire at Conde's St. John Catholic Church. (Courtesy of Alan Evans.)

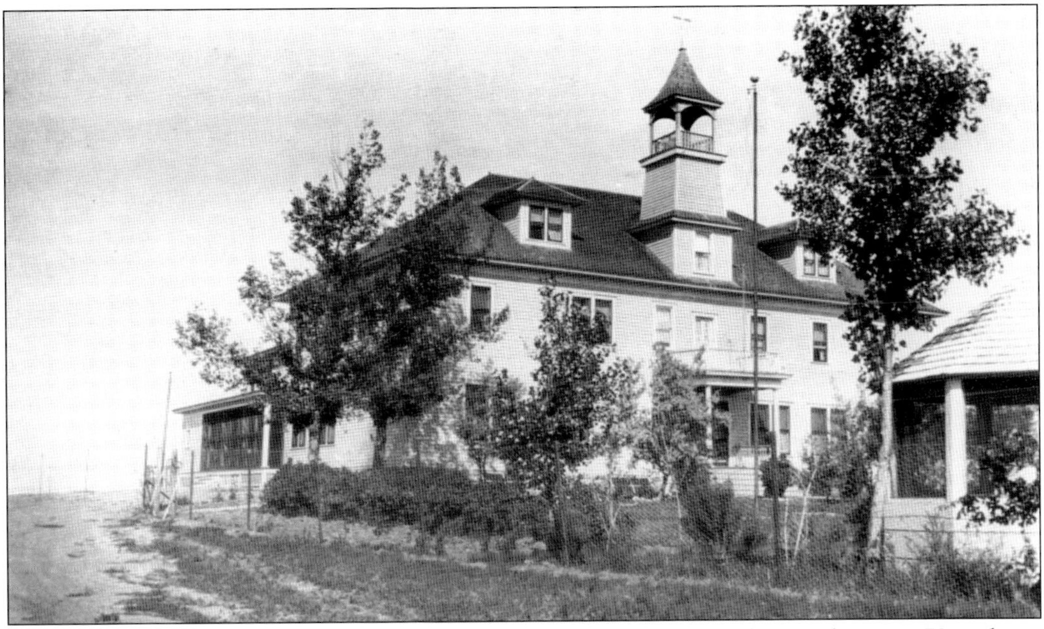

Seen here is the Little Flower Home. Located on hill west of Turton, this was home to 73 orphans and a day school for 33 children from the surrounding area at the time when an attic fire on March 21, 1932, destroyed it. The Sisters of Charity of St. Louis under the auspicious of the Diocese of Sioux Falls operated the school and orphanage. (Courtesy of Richard Barrie.)

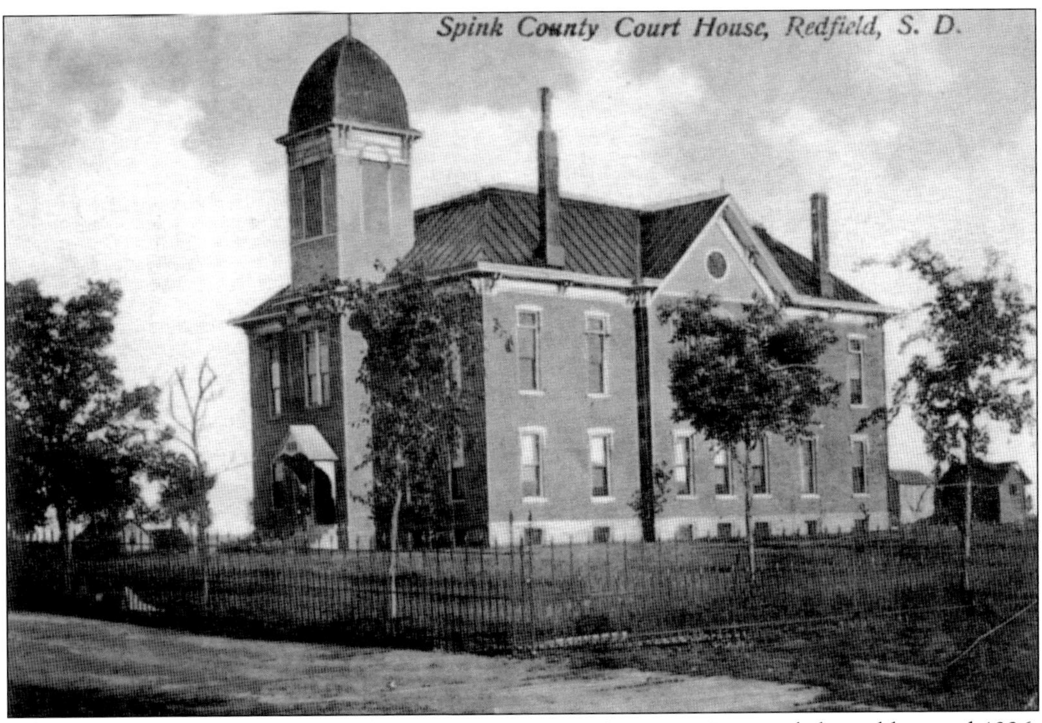

This is the third courthouse in Spink County, pictured in 1911. It served the public until 1926, when a new structure was built.

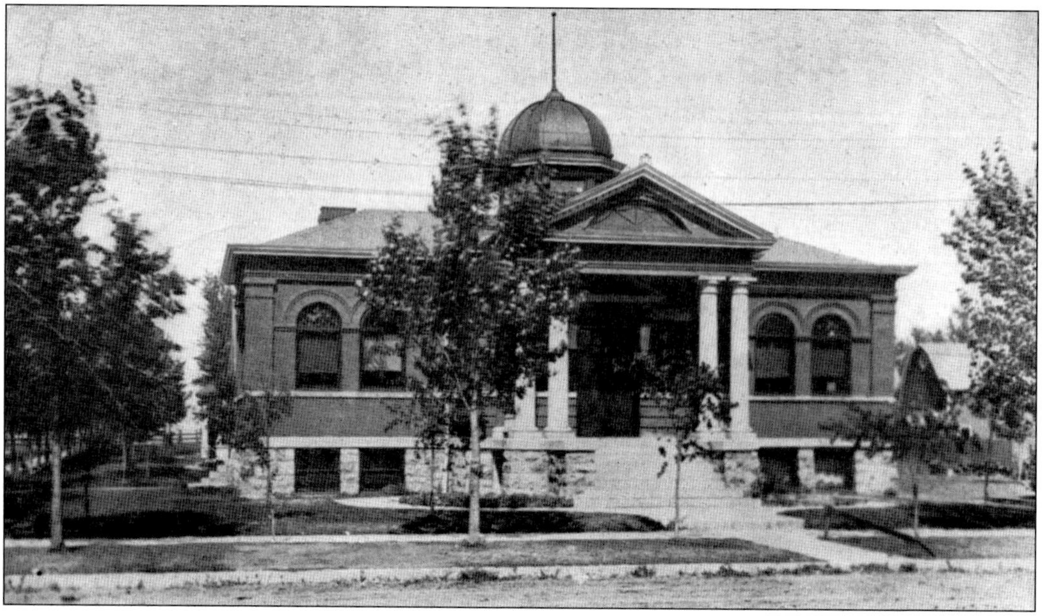

Pictured above, Redfield's Library is the oldest operational Carnegie Library in South Dakota. This postcard is dated to 1910. Below is the Ashton City Hall. From the spring of 1885 to November 1886, it served as the Spink County Courthouse. (Courtesy of Russell McNeely.)

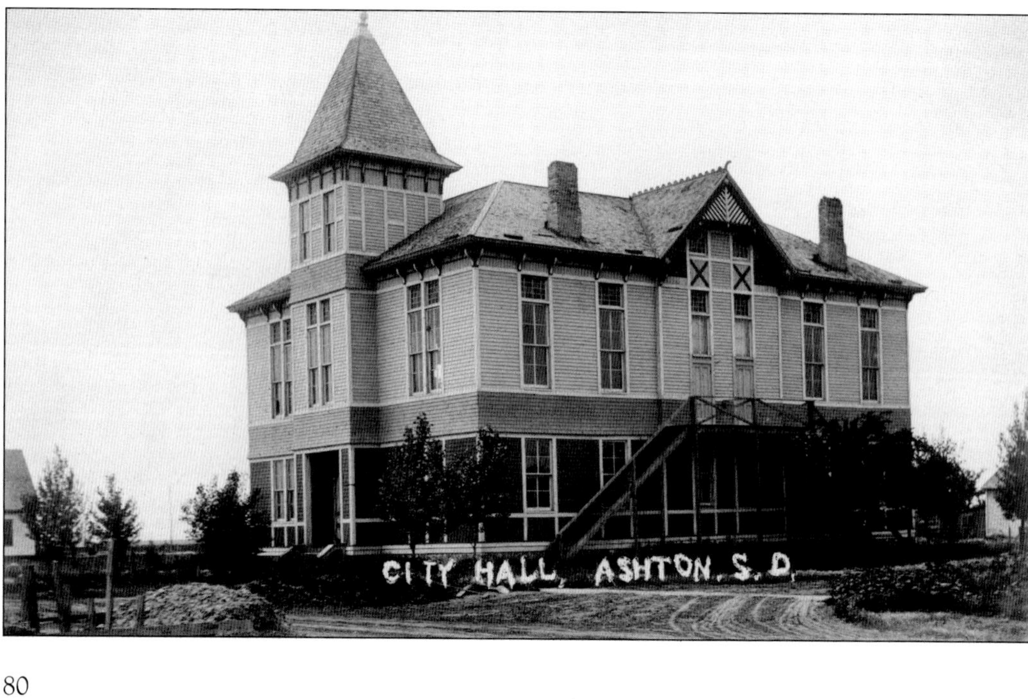

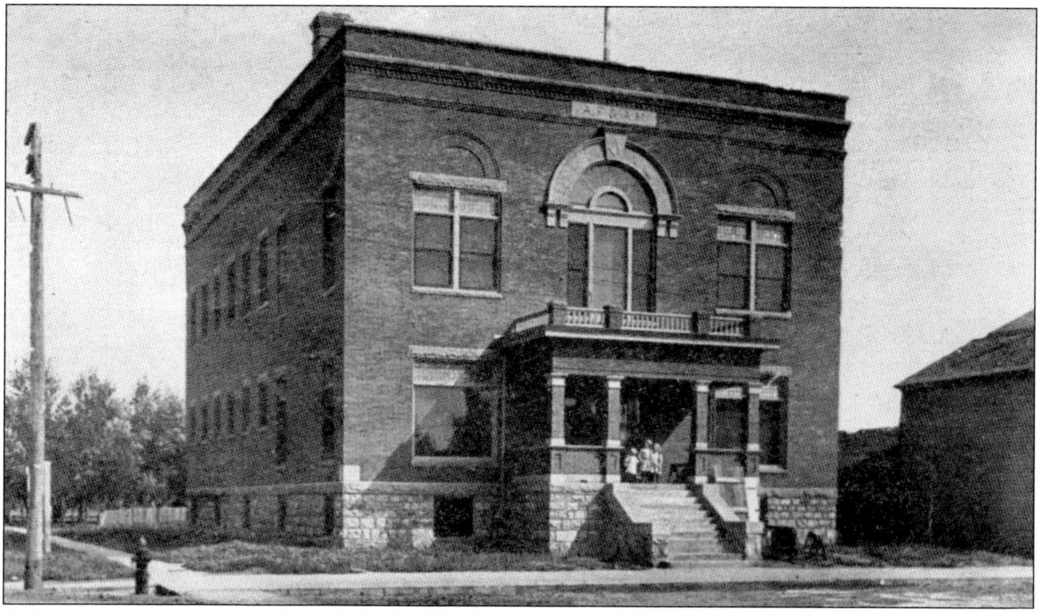

While no longer used by the Masons, the Masonic Temple remains on Main Street in Redfield. Through the efforts of Ken Siegling and his son Rod, the structure still holds historical significance. (Courtesy of Russell McNeely.)

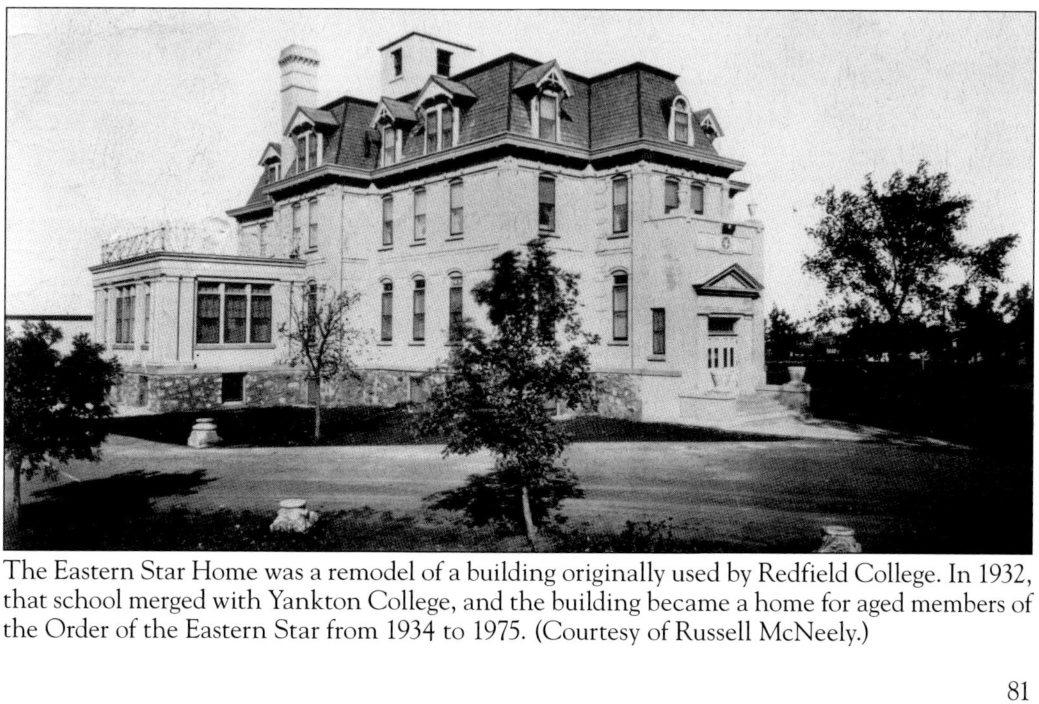

The Eastern Star Home was a remodel of a building originally used by Redfield College. In 1932, that school merged with Yankton College, and the building became a home for aged members of the Order of the Eastern Star from 1934 to 1975. (Courtesy of Russell McNeely.)

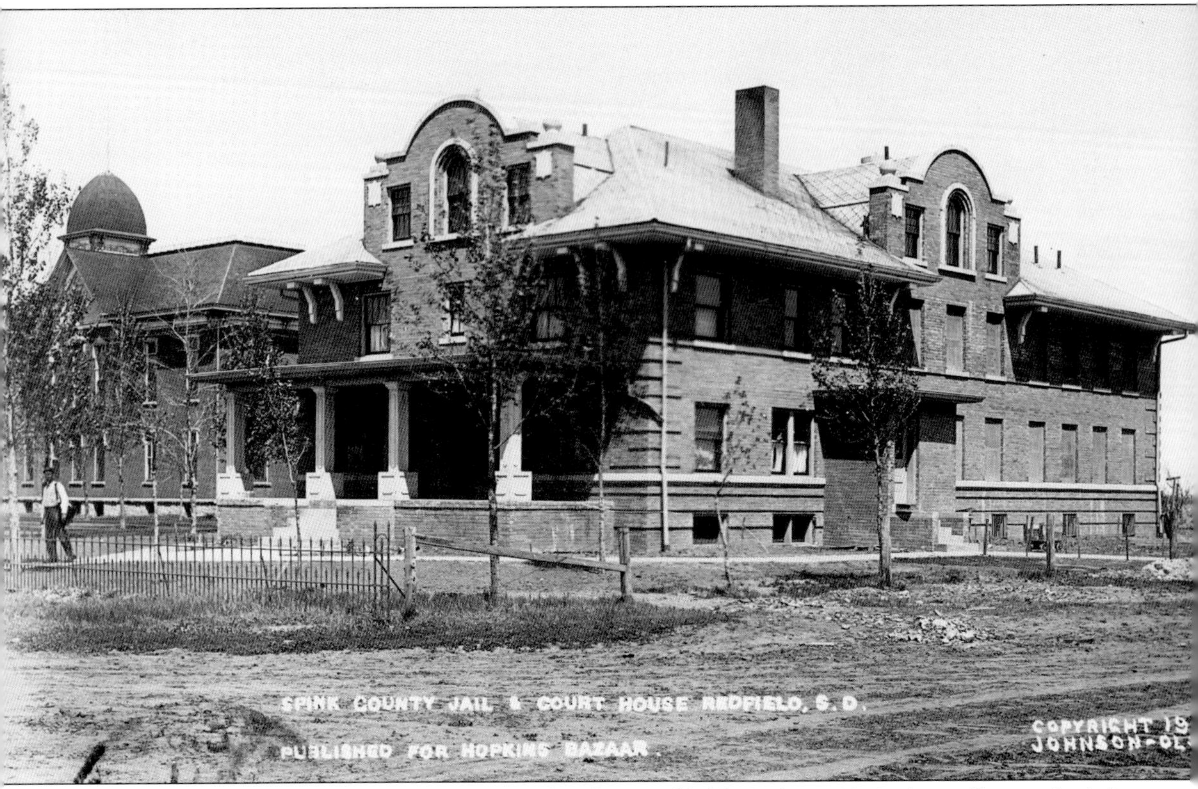

Here is the Spink County Courthouse and Jail in Redfield. Built in 1910, the jailhouse (right) had prisoners in the basement, processing offices on the first floor, and family housing for the sheriff on the third floor. The Spink Courthouse, a replacement of an earlier wooden structure, stands to the left. (Courtesy of Russell McNeely.)

Six

EDUCATION

Pictured here is an early Spink County school in Beotia Township. This school, located in the northeast part of Spink County, opened in the late 1880s and closed in 1942. Education was very important to early settlers, and Spink County offered a broad range of educational experiences. It had its public rural schools and districts and private schools in the form of a high school academy, a grade orphanage and school, a college, and a state school for the "feeble-minded." The Homestead Act of 1862 set up townships consisting of 36 square miles or sections. Of the 36 sections, two quarter sections were set aside to rent out to fund rural and town schools. This school opened in the late 1880s and closed in 1942. It sits in dilapidated condition on an abandoned farmstead near its original location.

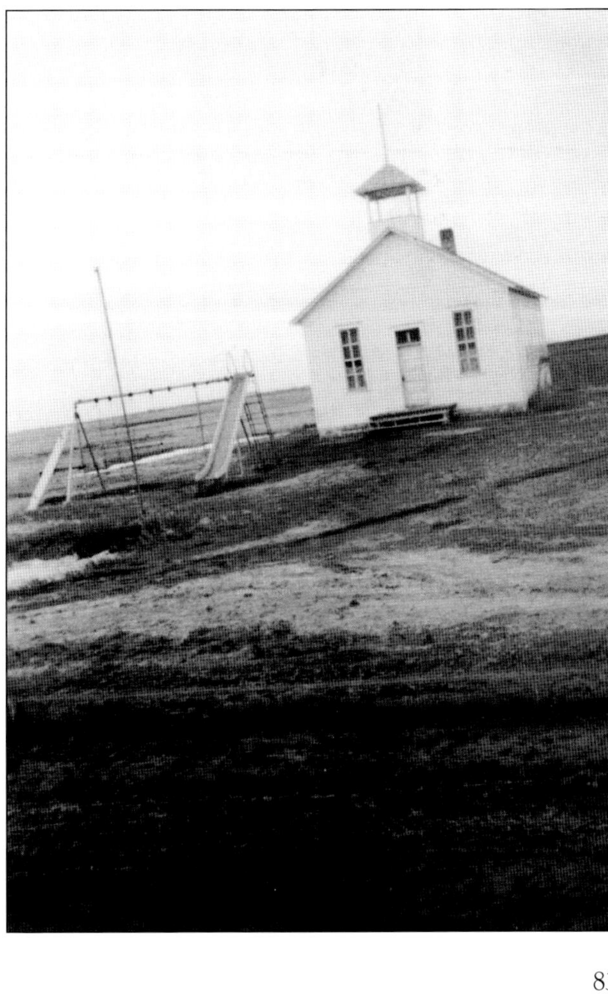

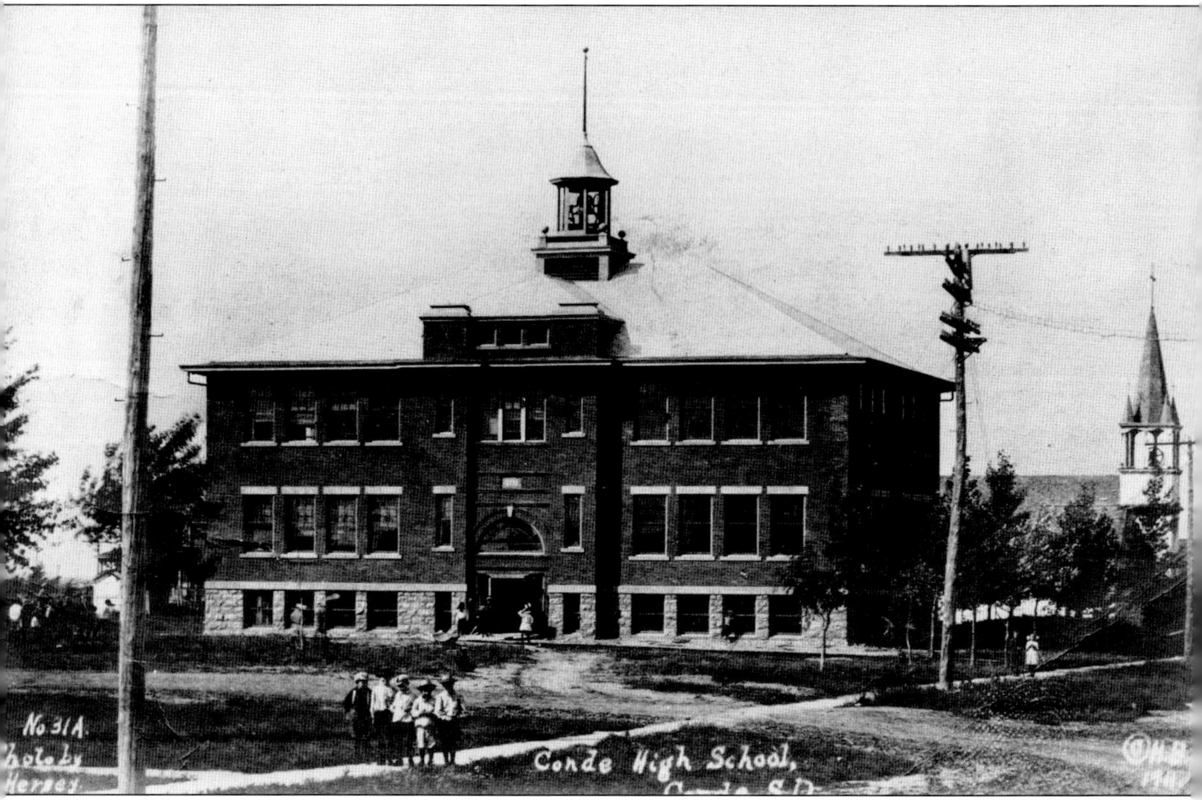

This 1912 postcard shows the Conde High School, complete with bell tower to call the Conde students to class, with unidentified children posing in their school finery. To the right is the Catholic church. (Courtesy Doug Jensen.)

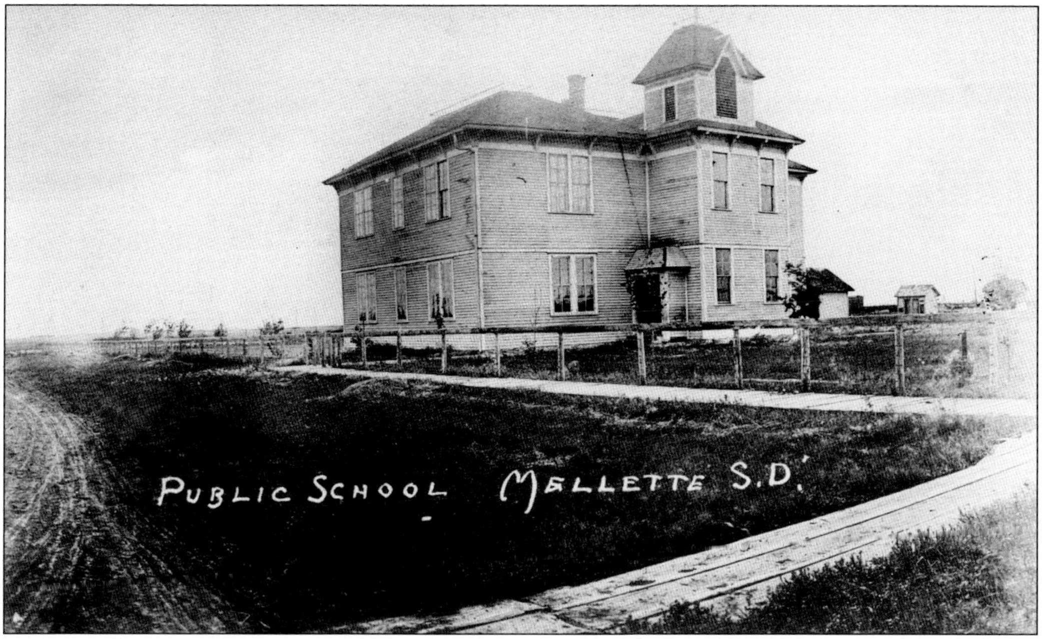

This public school in Mellette, a two-story building, was constructed in about 1883 or 1884. Most of the towns started to establish schools early in their history. The Homestead Act of 1862 set aside two quarters of land in each township to provide income for education. Some, like the shanty, were created out of existing buildings. Others had a dual purpose by combining with a church. And others were new structures. Some are still in existence today serving students. Others only lasted a short time. (Courtesy Rod Evans.)

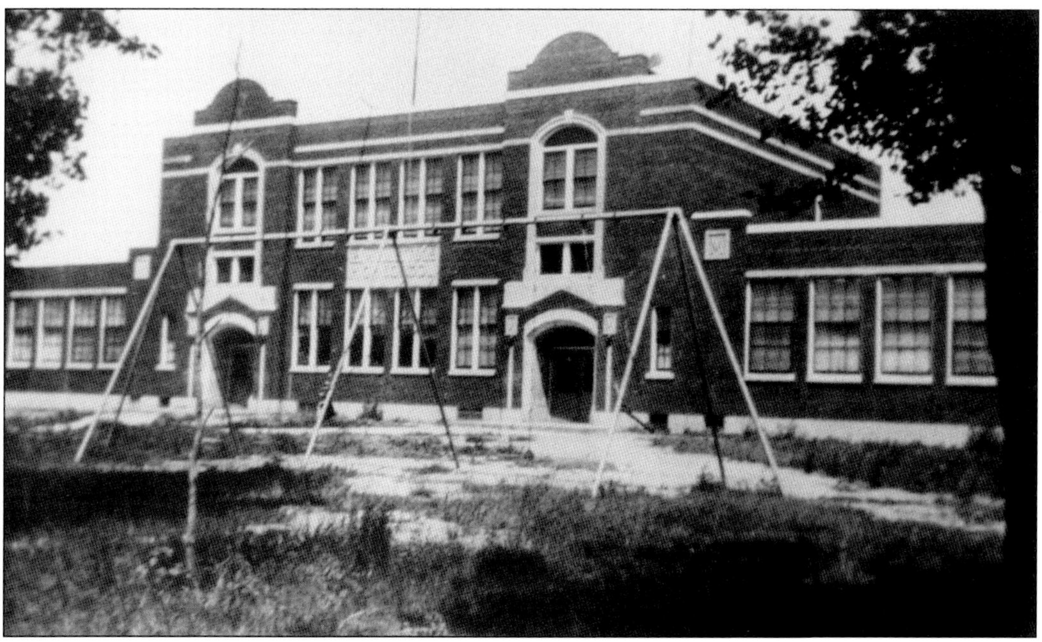

In 1916, this school was built on the same site as the original Mellette school. It housed all 12 grades. Most Spink County schools had graduating classes by the early 20th century. (Courtesy Rod Evans.)

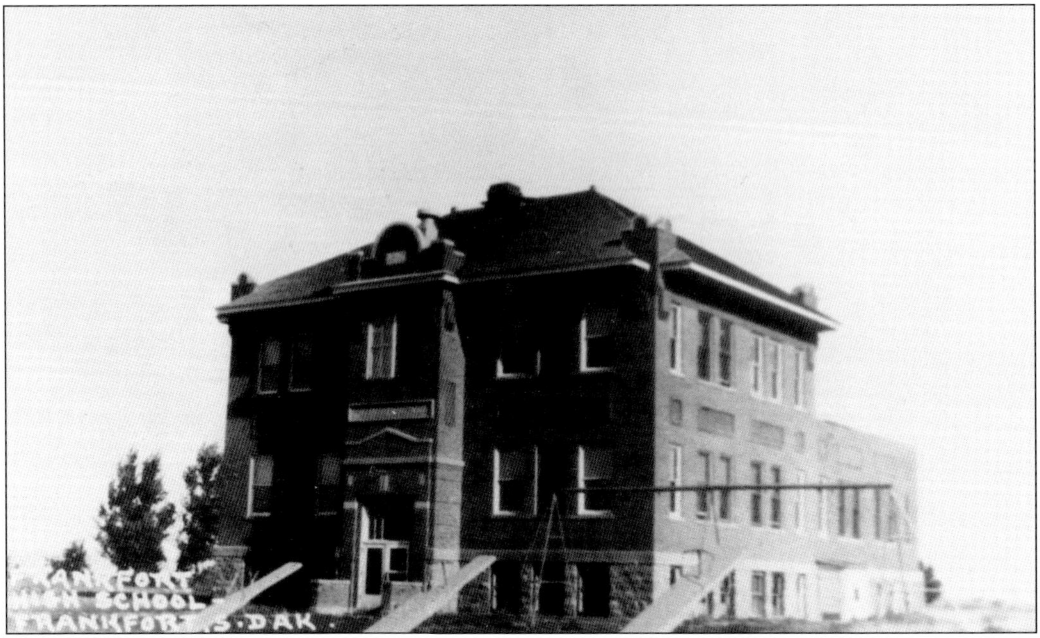

The Frankfort school is pictured here. Erected in 1912, this school served elementary and high school students until 1960, when the high school students came to Redfield.

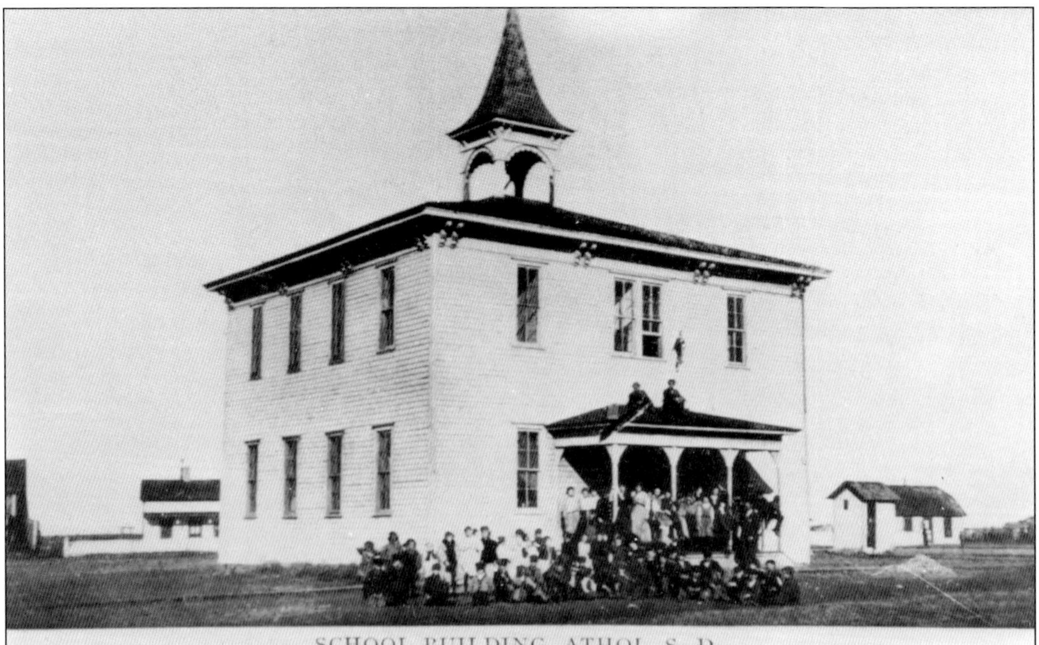

This is the old Athol school building, with students posing outside. Built in 1883 or 1884, it served both grade school and high school with its first graduating class in 1910. On the right is the necessary outhouse. (Courtesy Russell McNeely.)

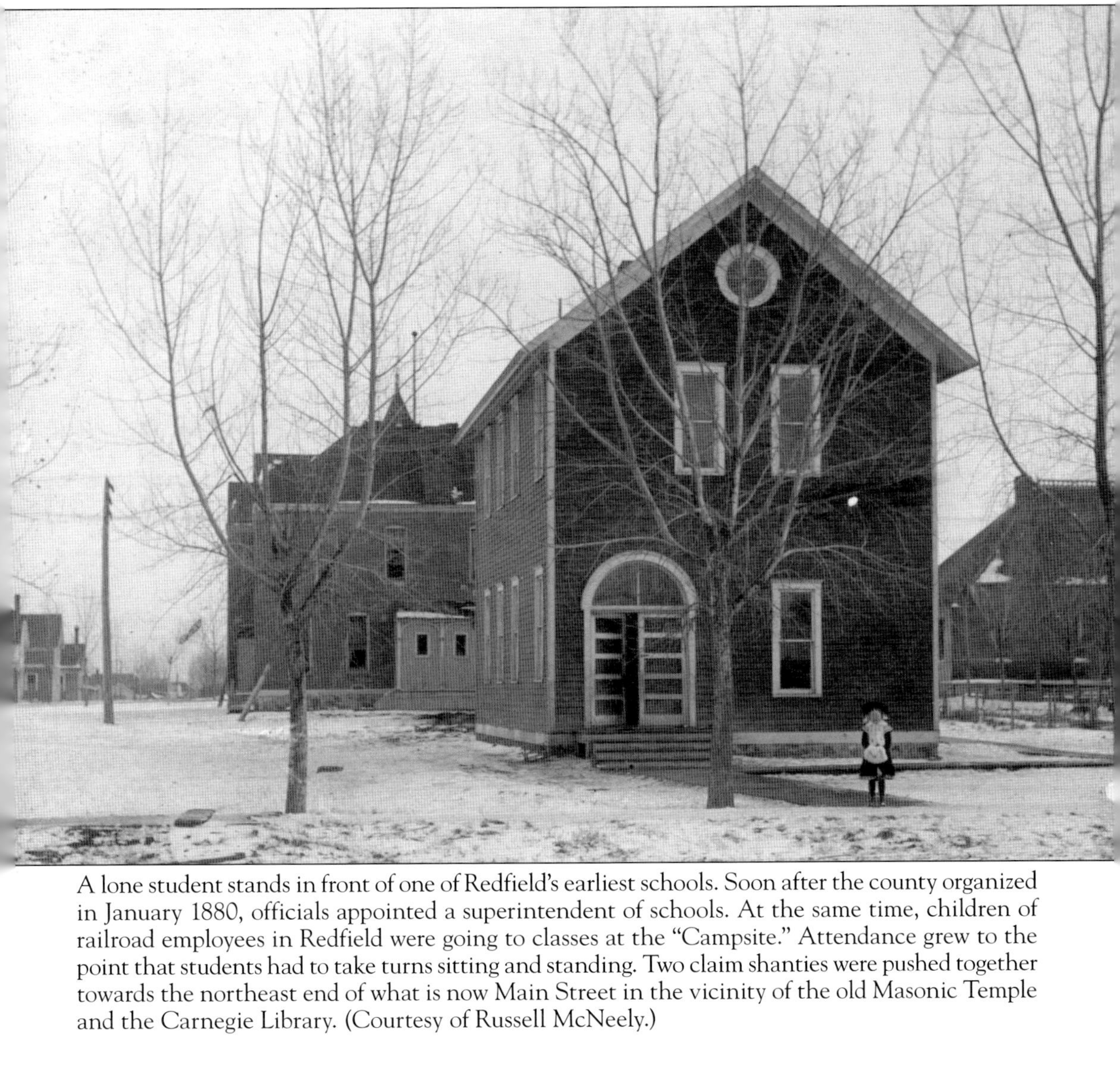

A lone student stands in front of one of Redfield's earliest schools. Soon after the county organized in January 1880, officials appointed a superintendent of schools. At the same time, children of railroad employees in Redfield were going to classes at the "Campsite." Attendance grew to the point that students had to take turns sitting and standing. Two claim shanties were pushed together towards the northeast end of what is now Main Street in the vicinity of the old Masonic Temple and the Carnegie Library. (Courtesy of Russell McNeely.)

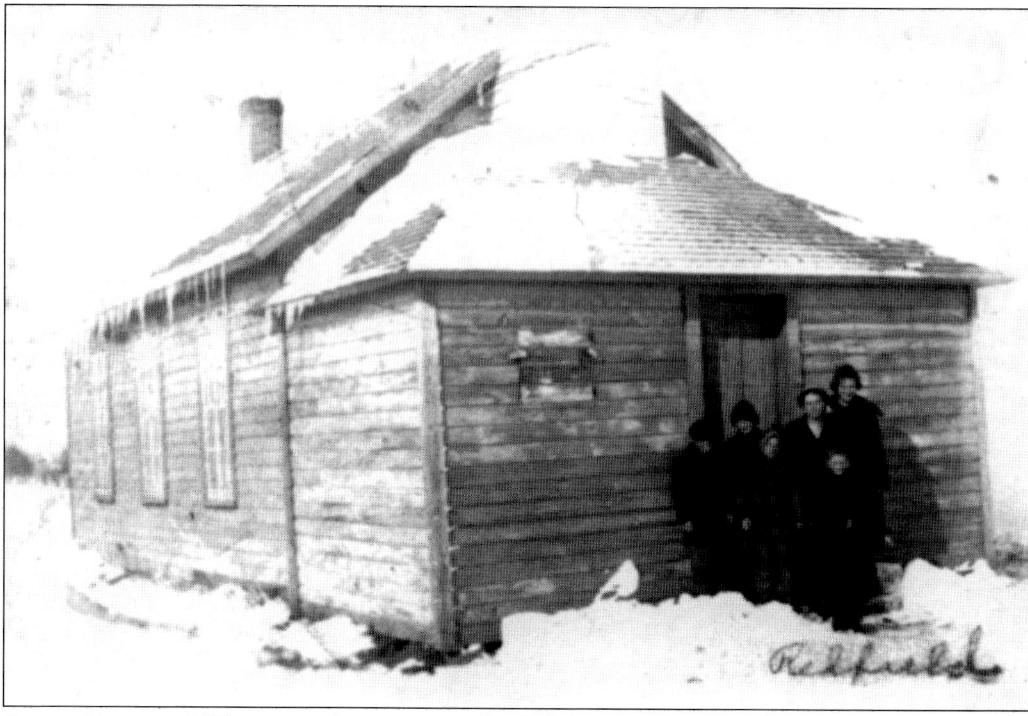

Pictured here in 1919 is a rural one-room school. Selma Madson taught at this country school near Redfield.

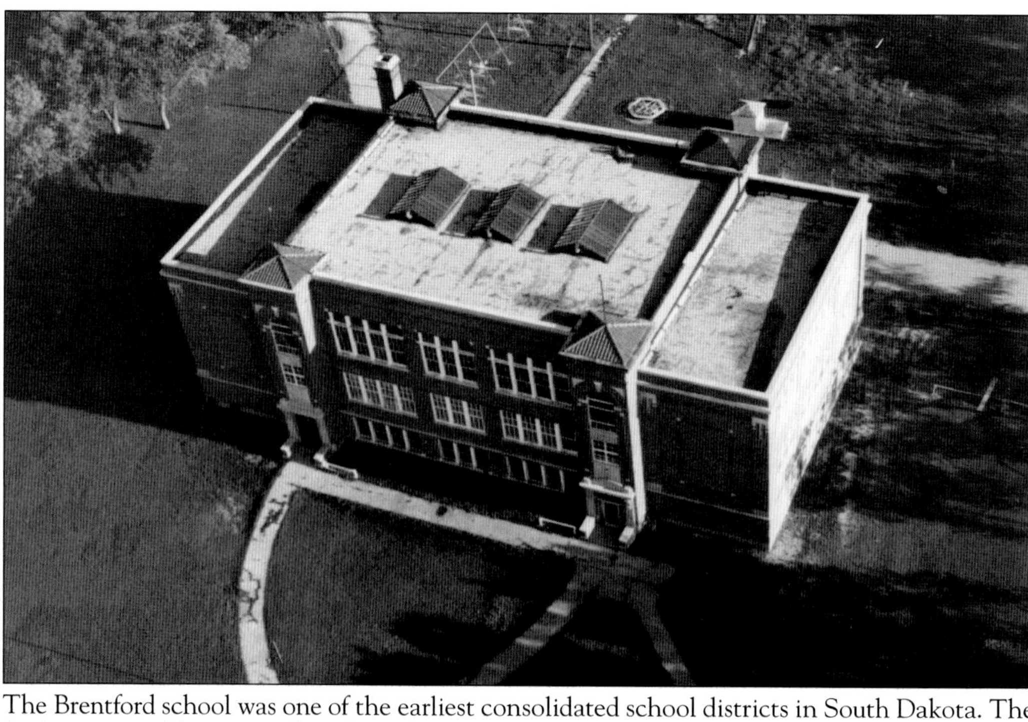

The Brentford school was one of the earliest consolidated school districts in South Dakota. The facility pictured here served students from 1921 until its closing in 1980.

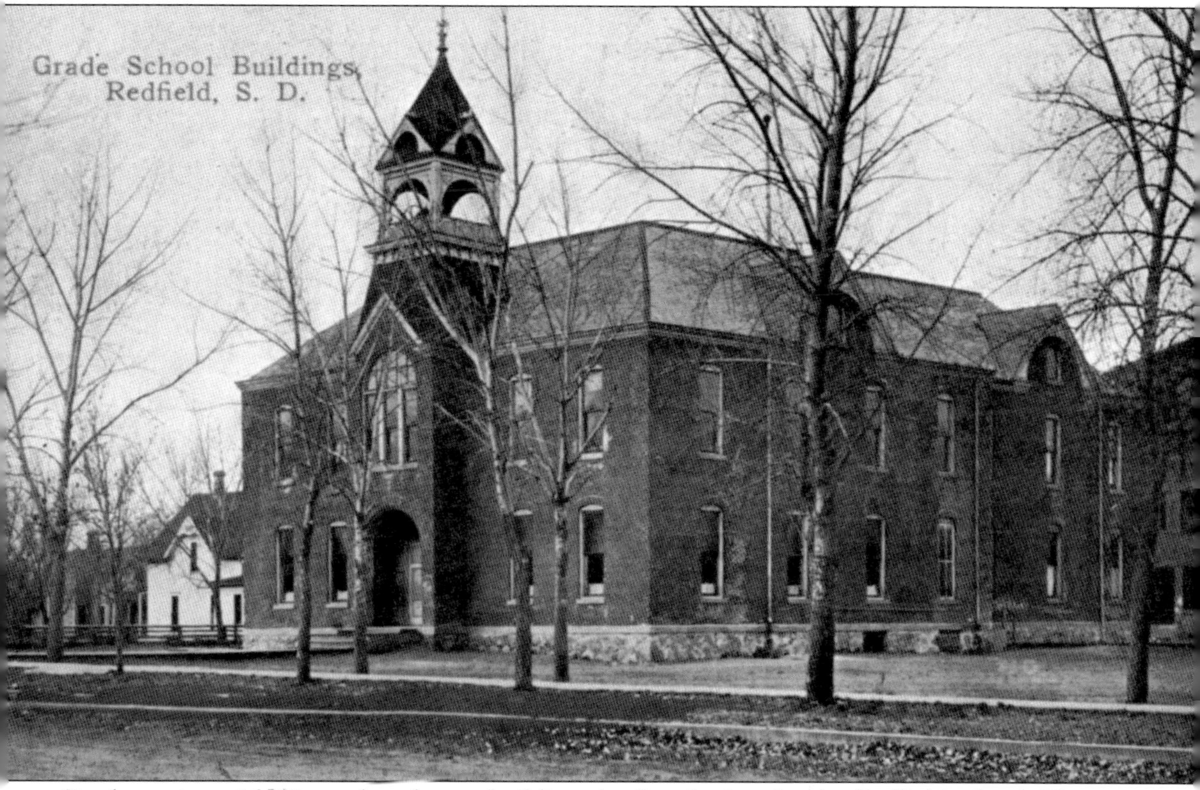

By the spring of 1882, workers began building the first facility for the Redfield school. They erected a two-story building running north and south where the present school sits. This first endeavor featured a gabled roof and tower but was only a single room wide and three times that in length. Its first floor provided education for grade school, but in 1885, the second floor for the high school was finished. The first class graduated May 31, 1894. When the school census grew, school planners expanded the building to the west (making the school six rooms wide), added a roof with dormers, and installed a tower and belfry to the east facing Second Street. In 1908, the growing population necessitated another addition built to the west side of the grounds and used for upper grades and high school. In 1909, this school was built with a gymnasium and domestic science department in the basement, elementary school on the first floor, and high school on the second. Eventually it became the grade school. (Courtesy Spink County Museum.)

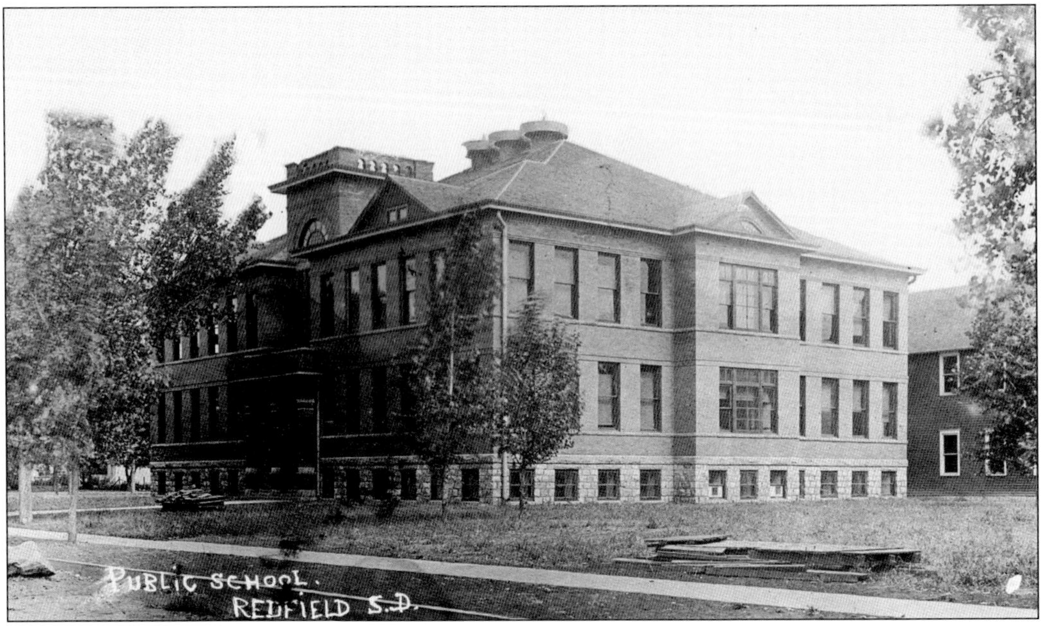

Pictured above is another Redfield school built in 1909. This plant featured a gymnasium in the basement, elementary school on the first floor, high school on the second, and domestic science in the attic. Eventually it became the grade school. It possibly had structural problems. Local historian John Solheim remembers that his dad salvaged the cupolas and tin from some of the ceiling, and John and his brother Art built a shower house out of the tin. In 1917, the structure below became the mainstay of the school.

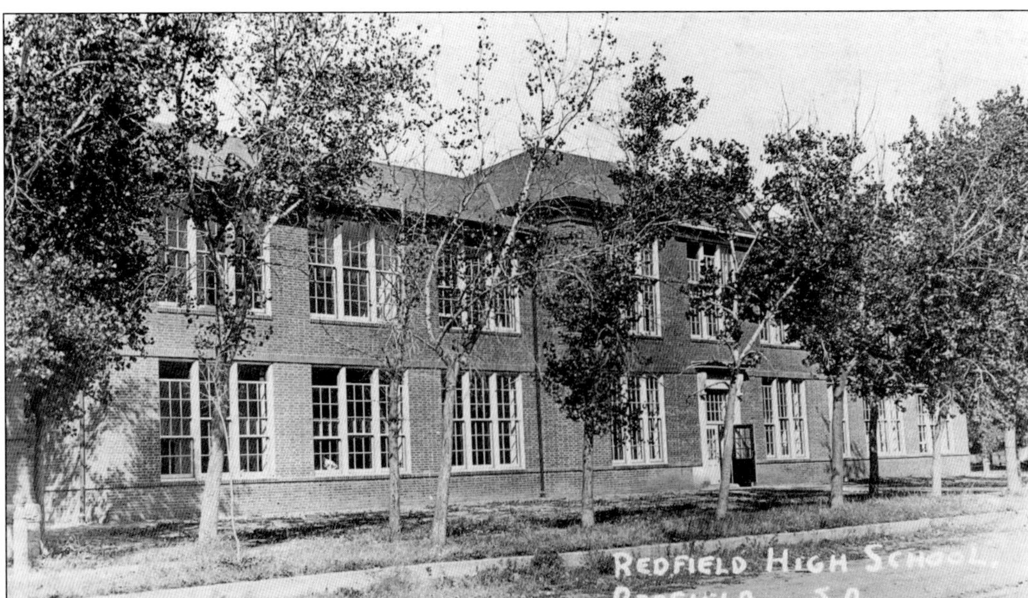

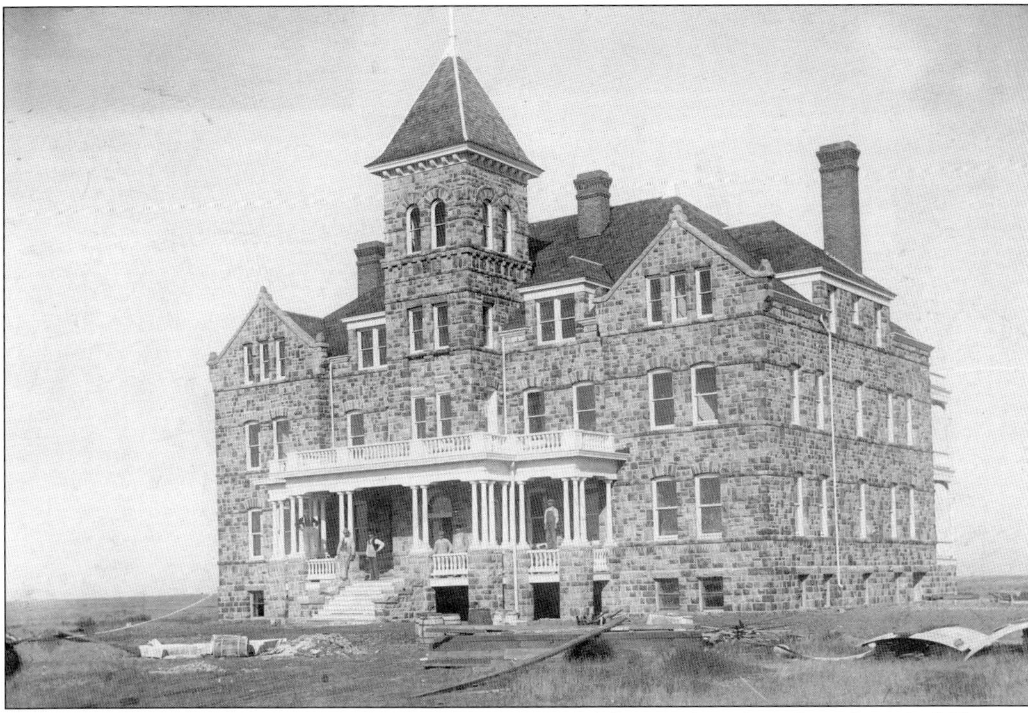

Pictured here is Granite Hall. Legislation in 1899 required the South Dakota State Board of Charities and Corrections to provide a facility for the feeble-minded of the state. Redfield citizens donated 160 acres of prairie north of Redfield. Constructed of Sioux Falls granite, this is the first building. The institution began admitting residents on February 2, 1902. (Courtesy Russell McNeely.)

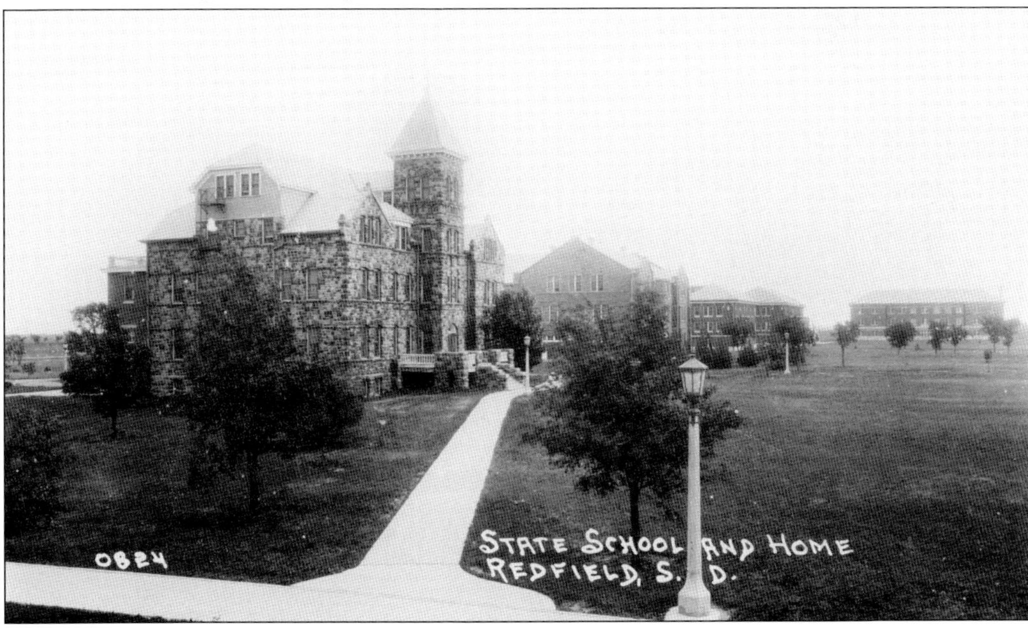

Granite Building (left), as it was later called, originally housed all residents and employees including administrators. Later an administration building and dormitories (right) were added. (Courtesy Russell McNeely.)

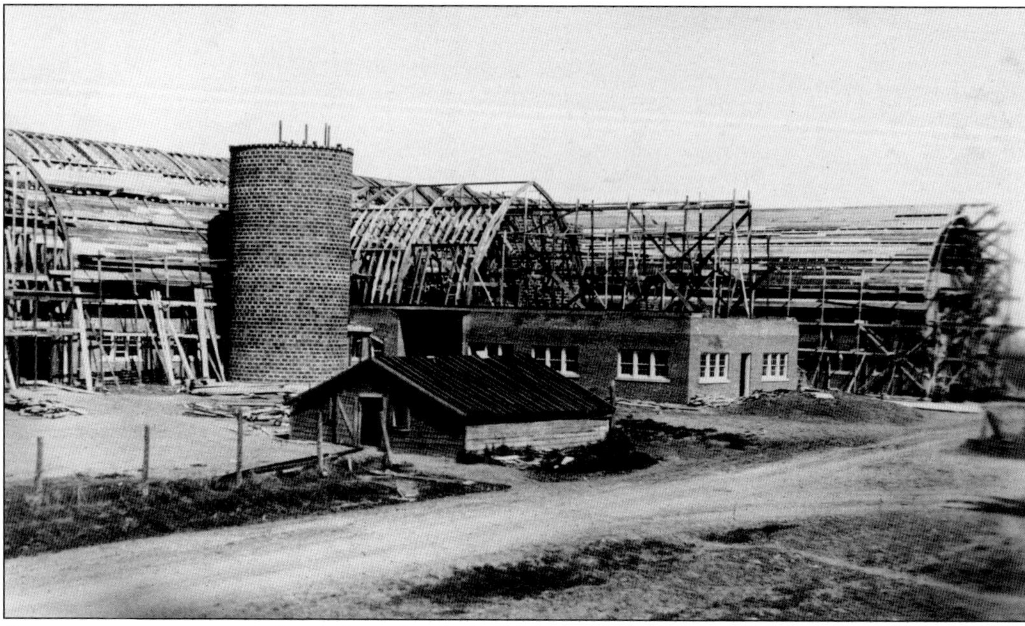

Barns were a common sight at the school. At one time, the State School and Hospital was self-sufficient. The employees and residents had a prize-winning dairy herd that provided milk and related products for the school's consumption. (Courtesy Russell McNeely.)

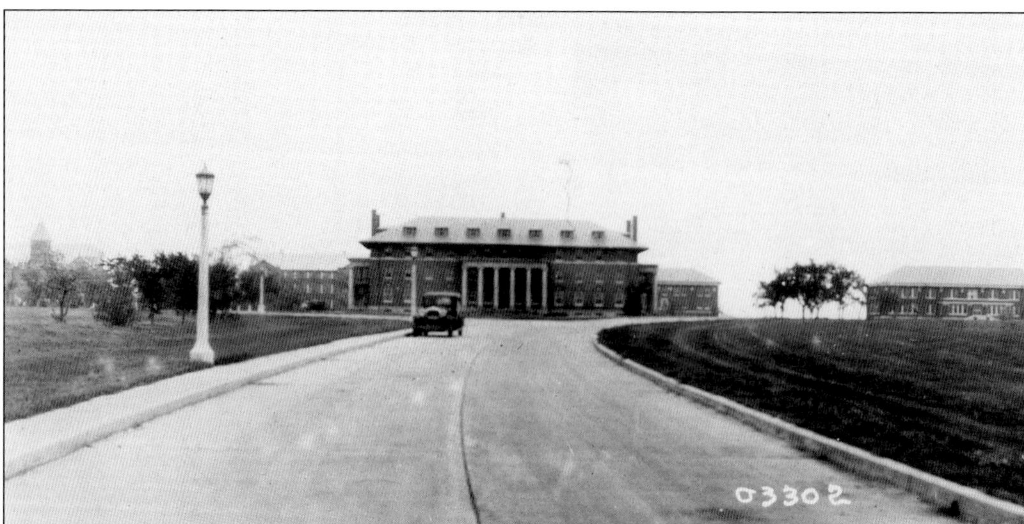

Here is the new Administration Building. This photograph, dated 1944, shows the view coming onto the grounds. (Courtesy Russell McNeely.)

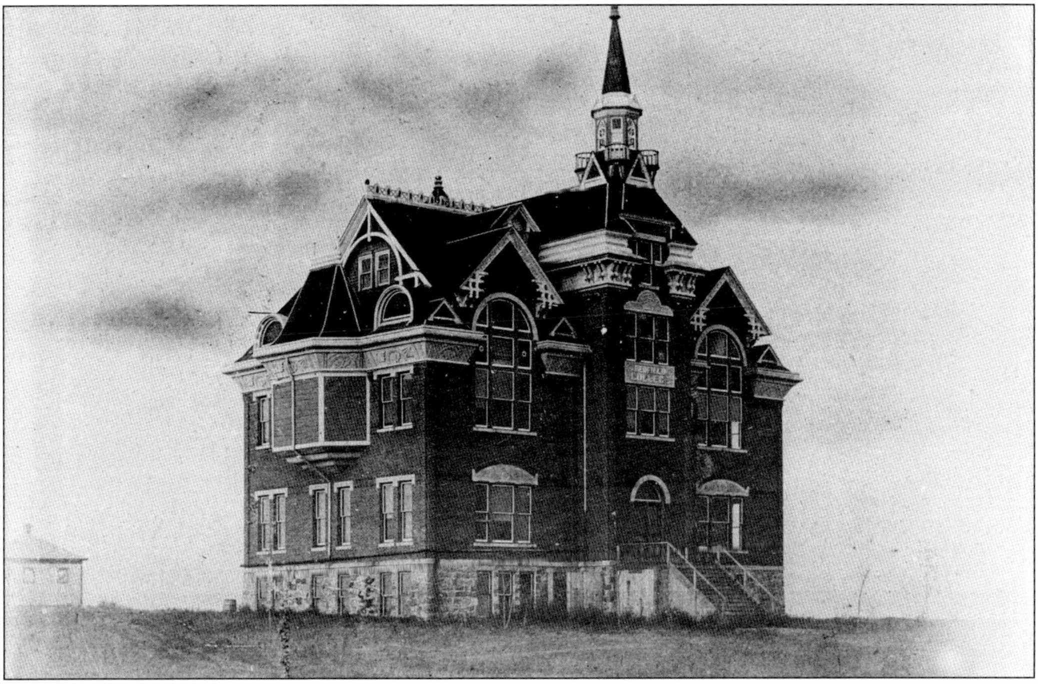

Surrounding towns joined efforts to establish a college in Redfield. Sponsored by the Northern Association of Congregational Churches, 11 students began classes at Redfield College in 1887 with classes held in the auditorium room at the Congregational Church. On January 26, 1888, students and faculty moved into this building.

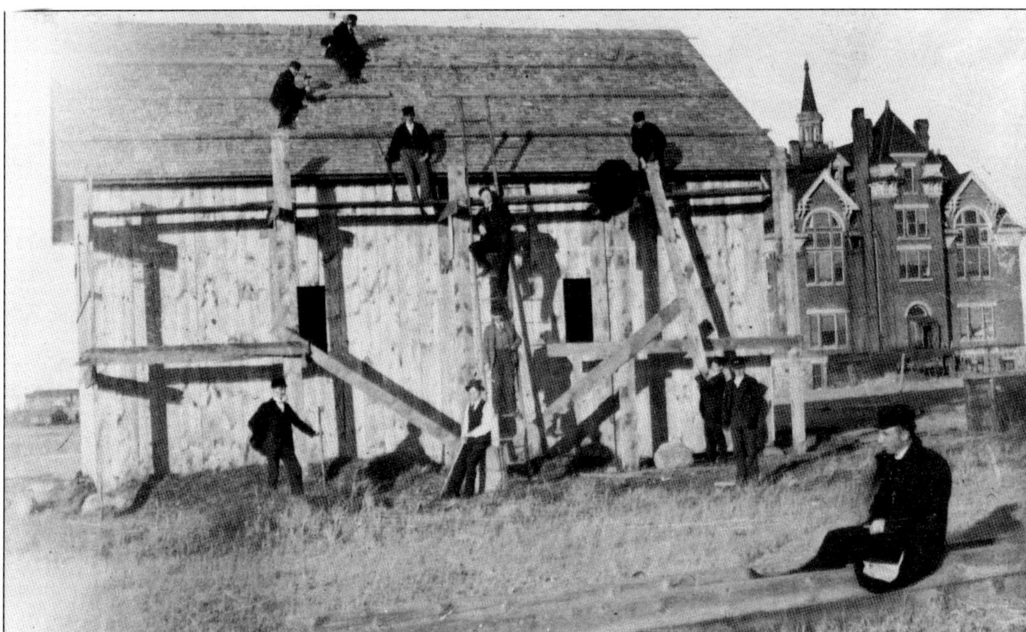

Pictured here are workers constructing an outbuilding at Redfield College. The school consisted of four departments: college academy, normal, commercial, and music, and offered a bachelor's degree until 1916. It became a seminary in 1912.

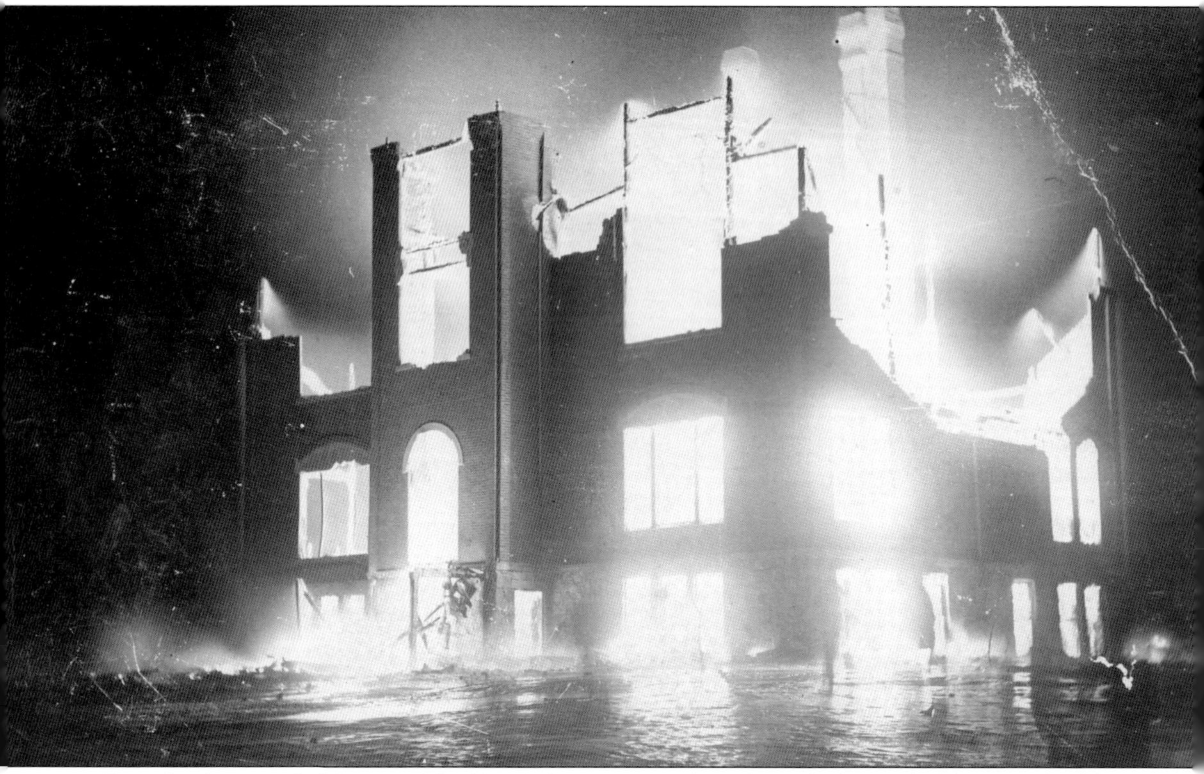

Fire whistles sounded January 26, 1896. A fire was spreading through the roof of the main building at the college. The fire company arrived promptly, but the pipe connected to the city well lacked a coupling to fit the fire hose.

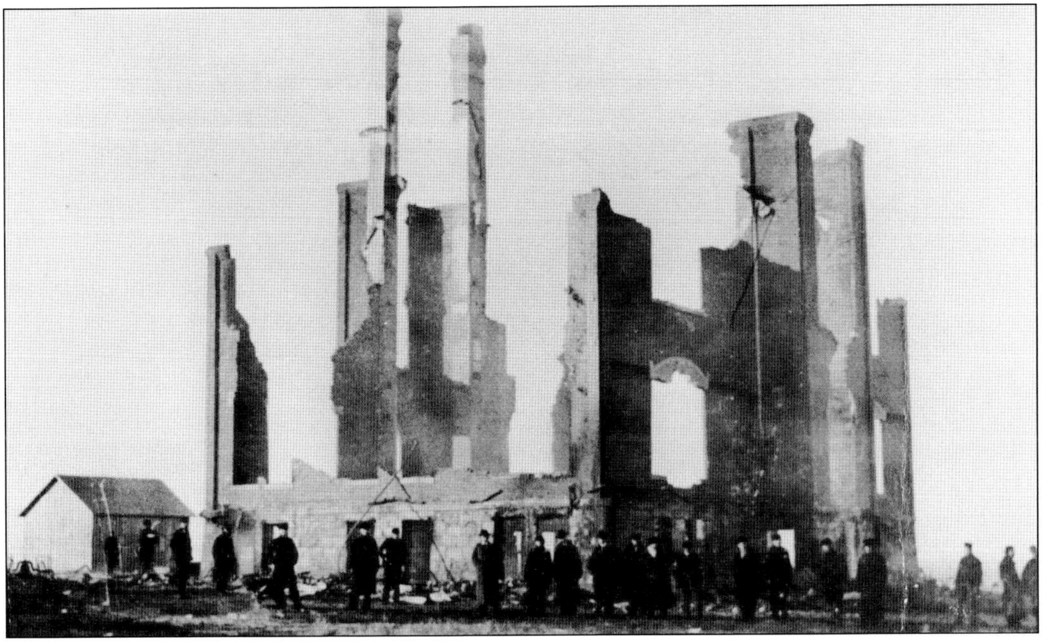

The day after the fire, faculty and townspeople gathered around the shell of the building. The loss was great; the building had cost $20,000 but was only insured for $8,000.

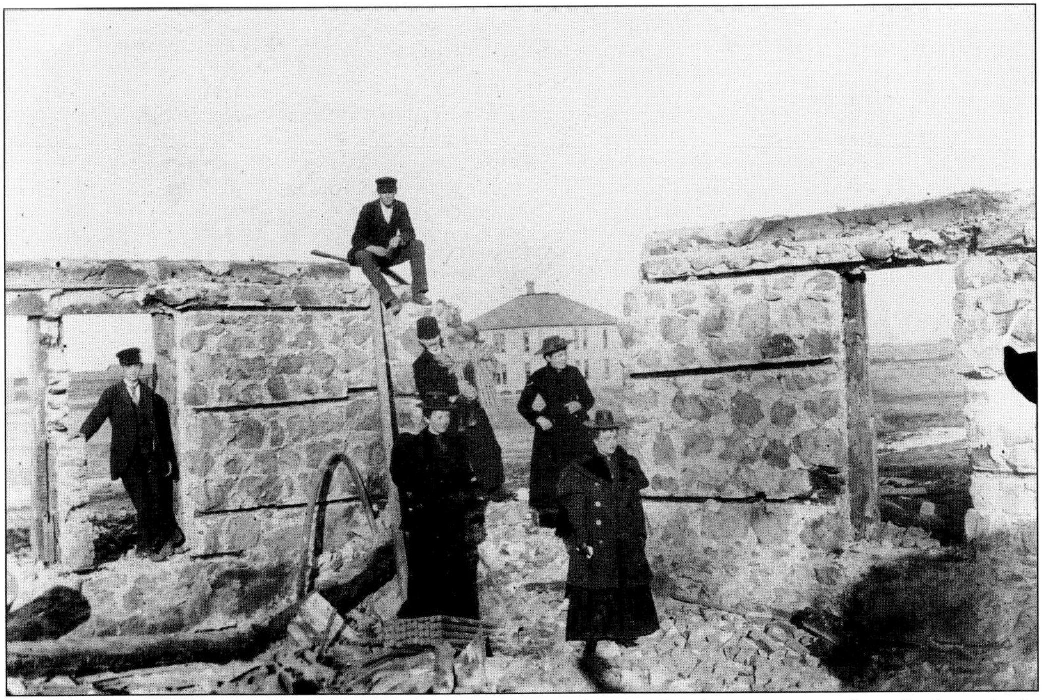

Students take a closer look at what was once their school. The fire company found a large hole in the floor in front of a heating stove, suggesting that the fire was caused by either an open door on the stove or a defective flue.

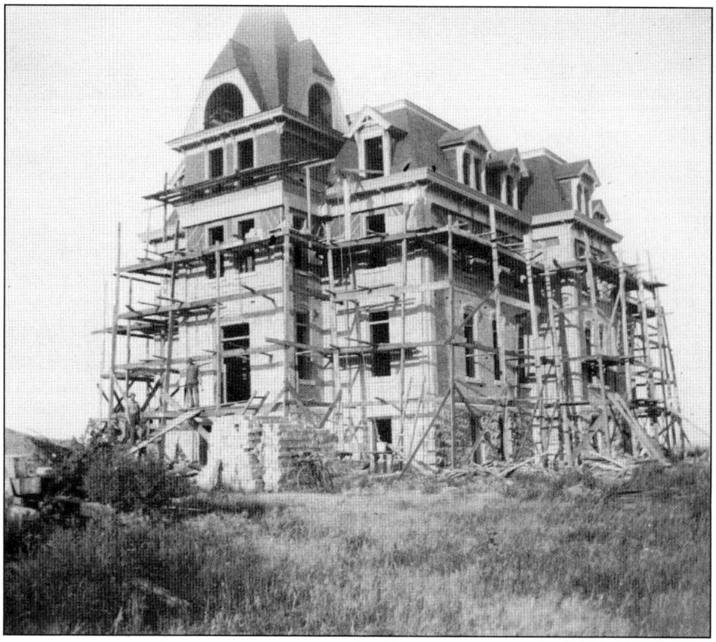

Built in 1883, the Grand Hotel at Columbia lived up to its name with hot and cold running water, electric bells, and mahogany woodwork. It was the site of many political and social events until Aberdeen won the Brown County seat election in 1890. Redfield College purchased it in the summer of 1896, dismantled it, and moved it. Three floors were floated down the James River on barges and the rest was shipped by train. It took $25,000 to rebuild the facility on the original site.

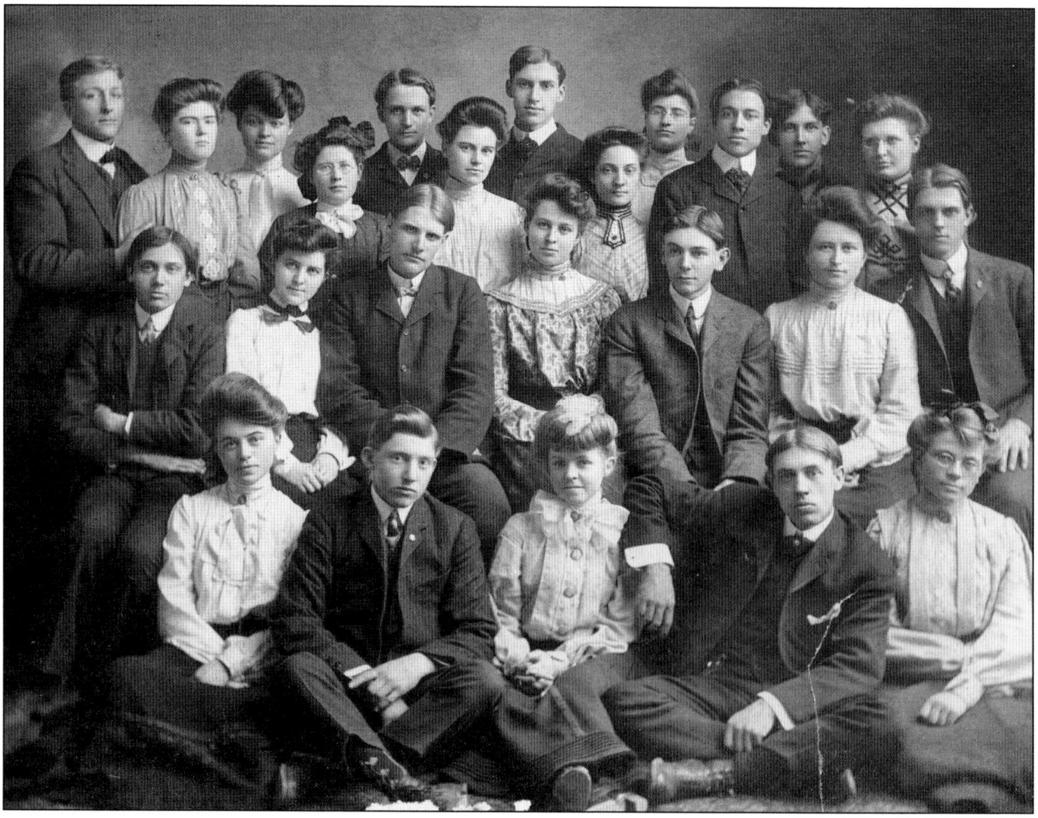

These students at Redfield College look ready for courses to begin at the new main building. The fire had actually been a blessing. The eastern investors who had held the title forgave the mortgage.

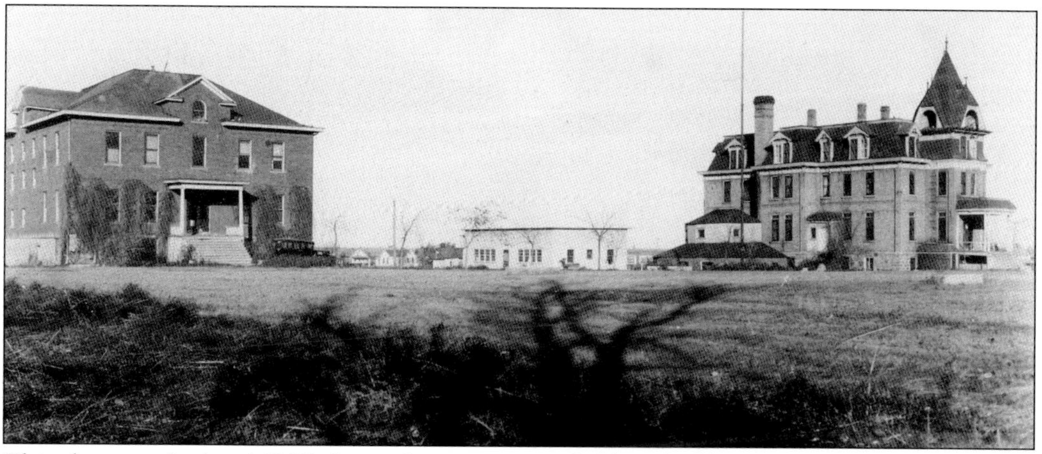

This photograph, dated 1905, shows the gymnasium (left) and Old Main (right) ready for classes. The lower floor housed the kitchen and dining room, while the first floor held the chapel, reading room, and library. Male students lived on the second and third floors. Female students lived in a boarding house called the Ladies Cottage. It was across the street to the east. Gym, music, and meeting rooms were on the first floor of the gymnasium, and laboratories were on the lower level.

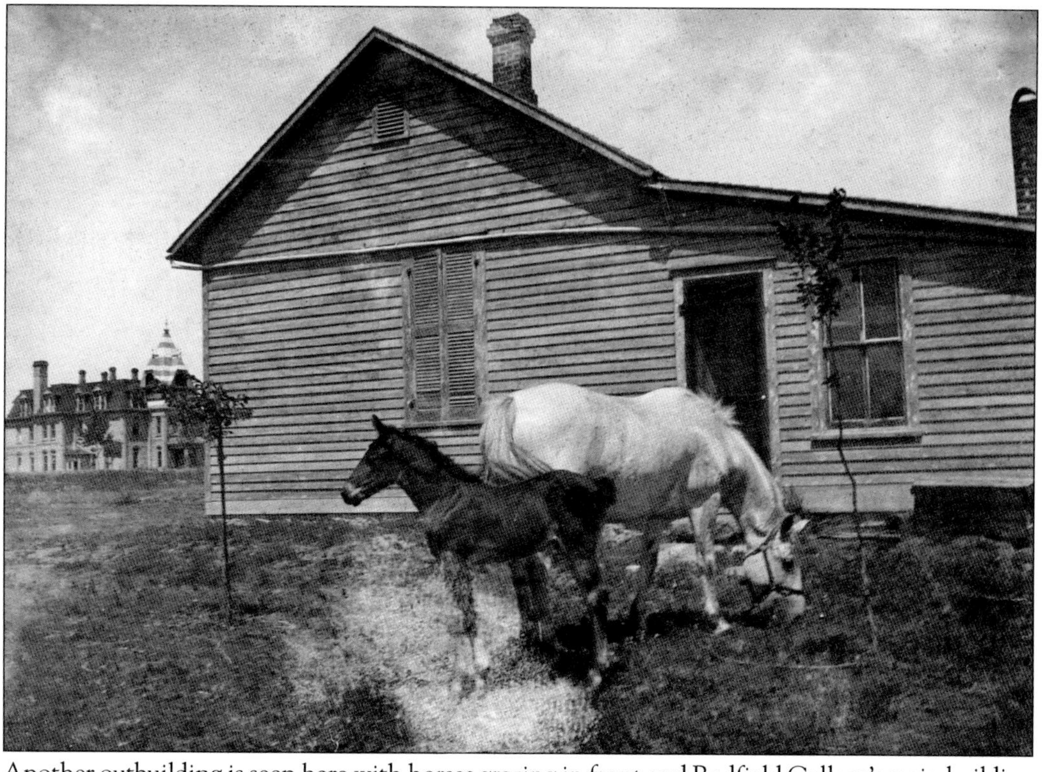

Another outbuilding is seen here with horses grazing in front and Redfield College's main building in the background.

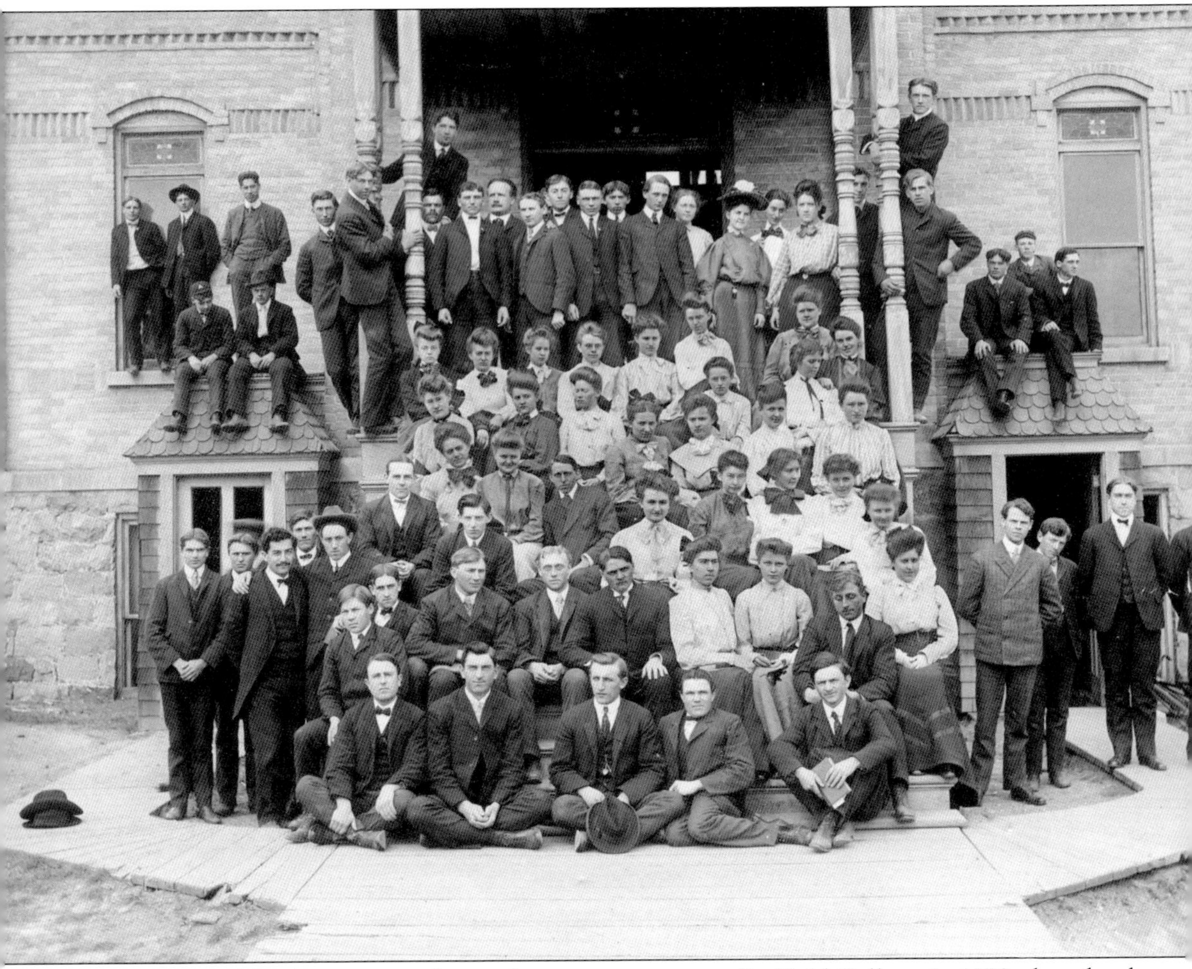

Students and faculty pose together at the main entrance to Redfield College. In 1932, the school merged with Yankton College, and the building became a home for aged members of the Order of the Eastern Star from 1934 to 1975.

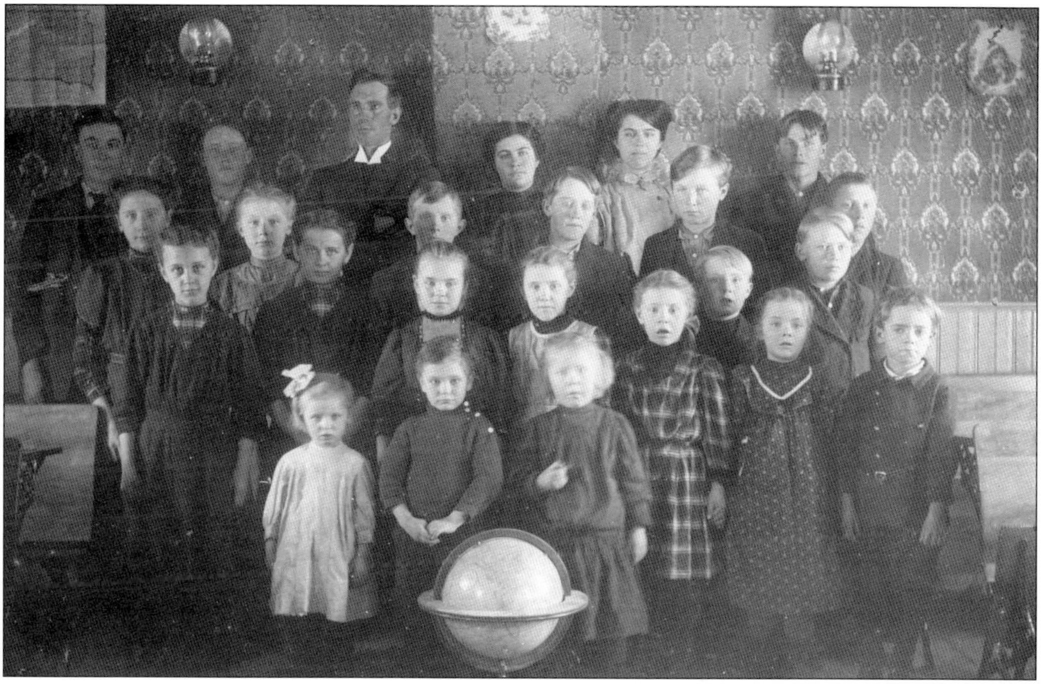

Teacher and students pose in their classroom with their globe at Redfield School in 1919. Pictured are, from left to right, (first row) Clifford Gardener, Alma Schultz, Ella Schultz, and Frank Schroeder; (second row) Ella Hague, Elsie Hague, Verda Gardner, Lelia Binger, Edna Binger, Edwin Schultz, and Walter Schultz; (third row) Myrtle Hague, Bertha Schultz, Will Binger, Herman Schultz, Dick Schroeder, and Walter Binger; (fourth row) Frank Hague, Fred Schultz, teacher Robert J. Lunday, May Pierce, Adda Pierce, Leo Schultz.

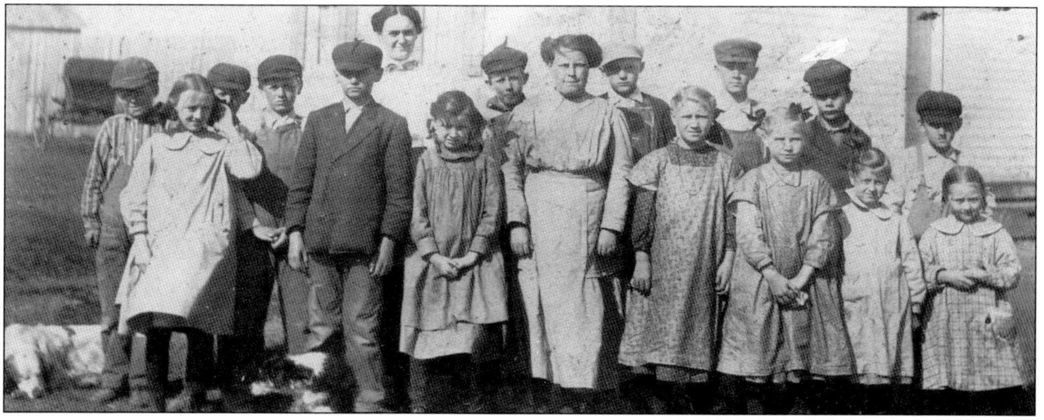

Students at Clifton School District No. 8, school No. 5 pose with their teacher. Pictured are, from left to right, (first row) Dana Harlow, Wayne Milford, Harriet Ellyson, Kate Baseler, Ann White, Mabel Luxton, Oscar Luxton, and Marion Harlow; (second row) Harry White, Donald Milford, Maurice Harlow, Gilbert Luxton, Harry Milford, James Harlow, Clark White, and Clarence Luxton; (third row) teacher Beulah Taylor. The school was built in 1884.

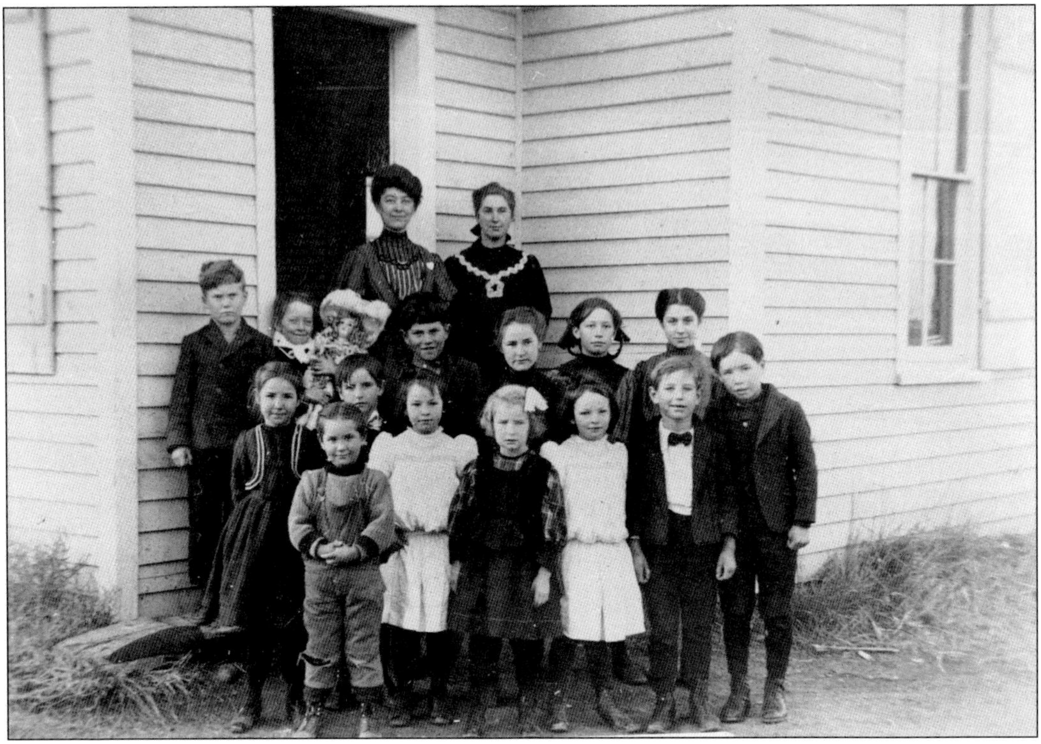

This teacher posed with her students at Deiter School in Spink County in 1907. The little girl second from left in the third row is holding her doll. This school has been restored and is part of Fisher Grove State Park.

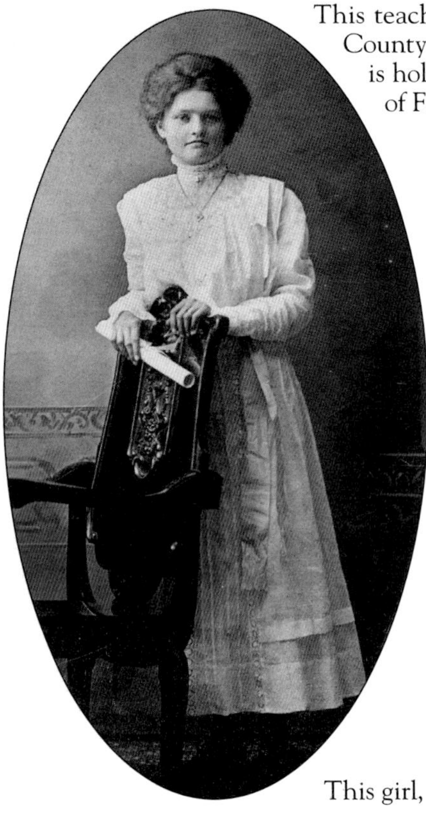

This girl, having graduated, poses with her diploma in hand.

Seven

Fun and Games

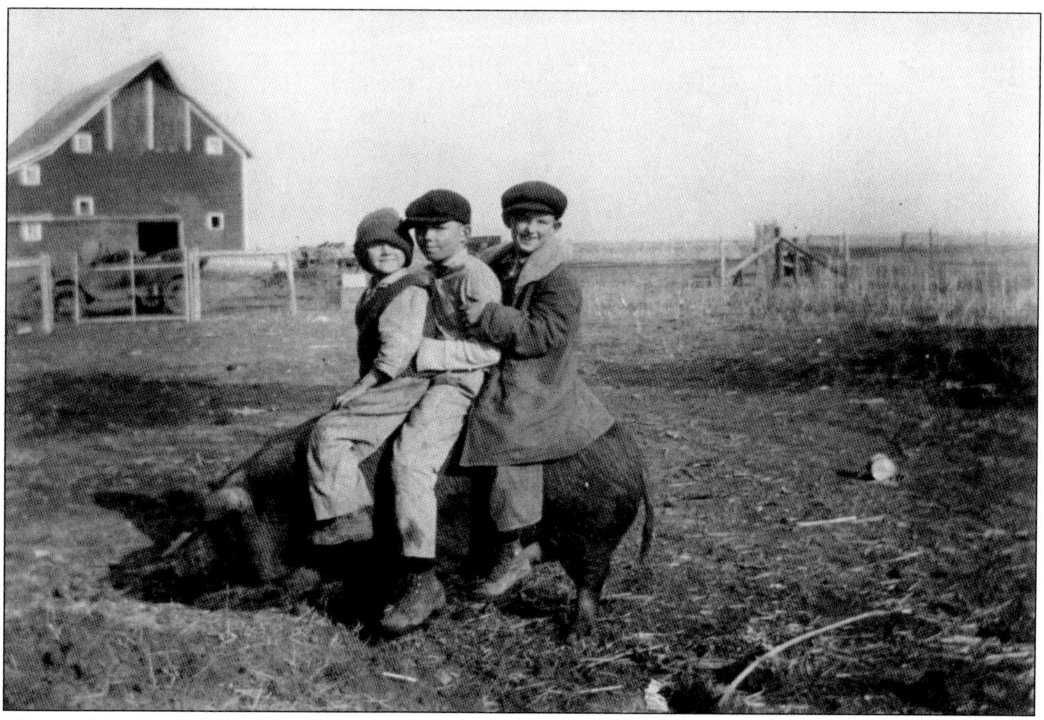

These three boys have fun riding a hog. Many of the early South Dakota stories passed down to us are of danger, hard labor, and medical backwardness, and we tend to think that there was little fun or color in the lives of the town citizens and country residents. Yet there are numerous photographs of play, parades, bands, theater, and sports. There was much fun and enjoyment to be had during the early years of Spink County. (Courtesy of Rod Evans.)

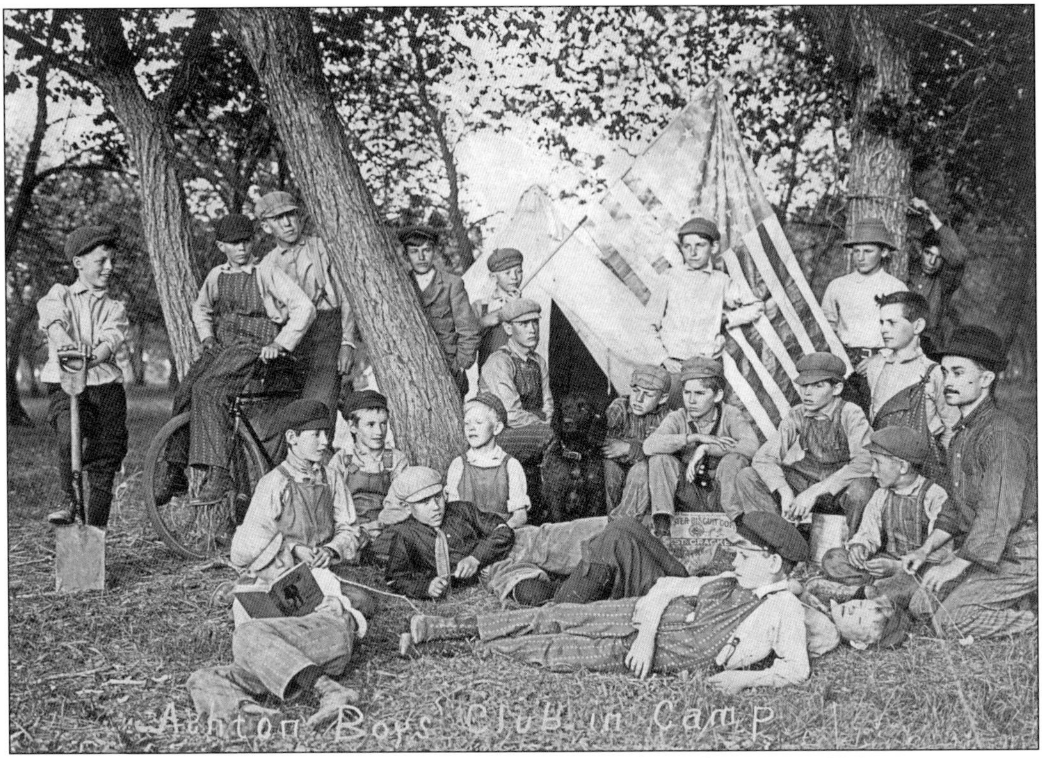

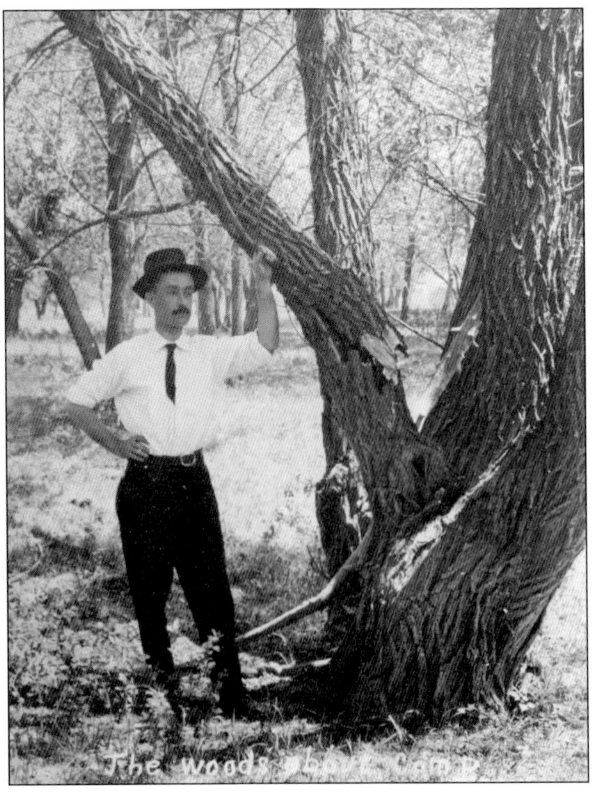

The Ashton Boys Club poses in front of their tent. All the accouterments of a good campout are visible: a flag for patriotism, a bike to be shared, a dog, makeshift seats, binoculars, a good book, and a spade to take care of business.

The camp leader poses in the woods above Camp Ashton. The semi-formal dress seems out of place.

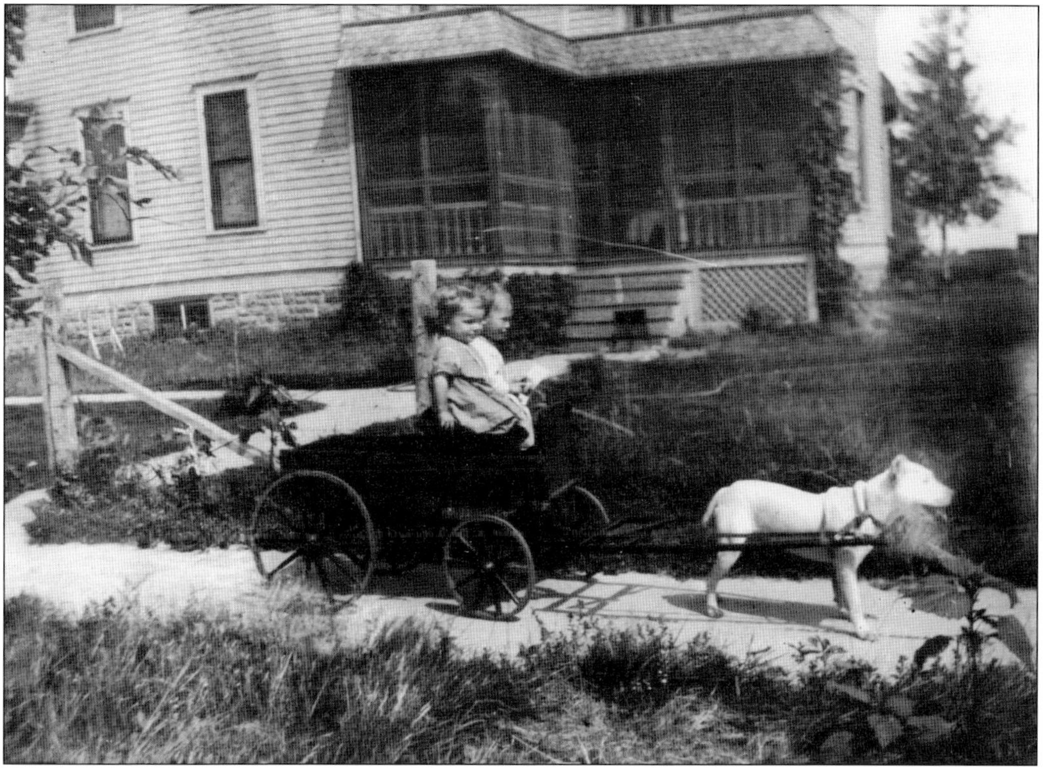

These children ride in a cart pulled by a dog. (Courtesy of Alan Evans.)

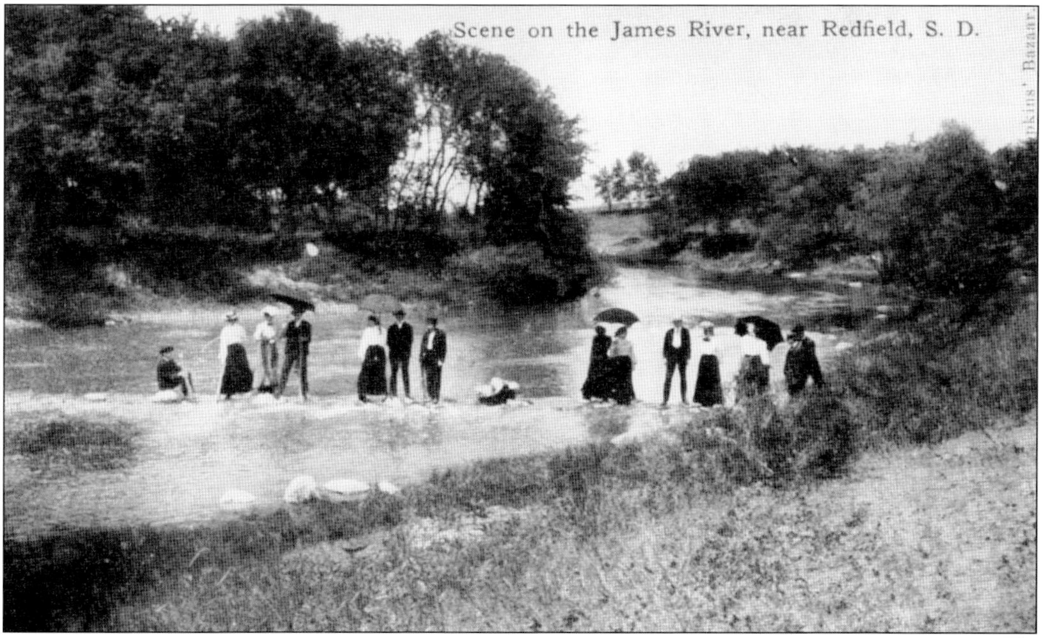

The areas surrounding banks and rivers often served as recreation spots. This postcard shows a summer outing at the James River.

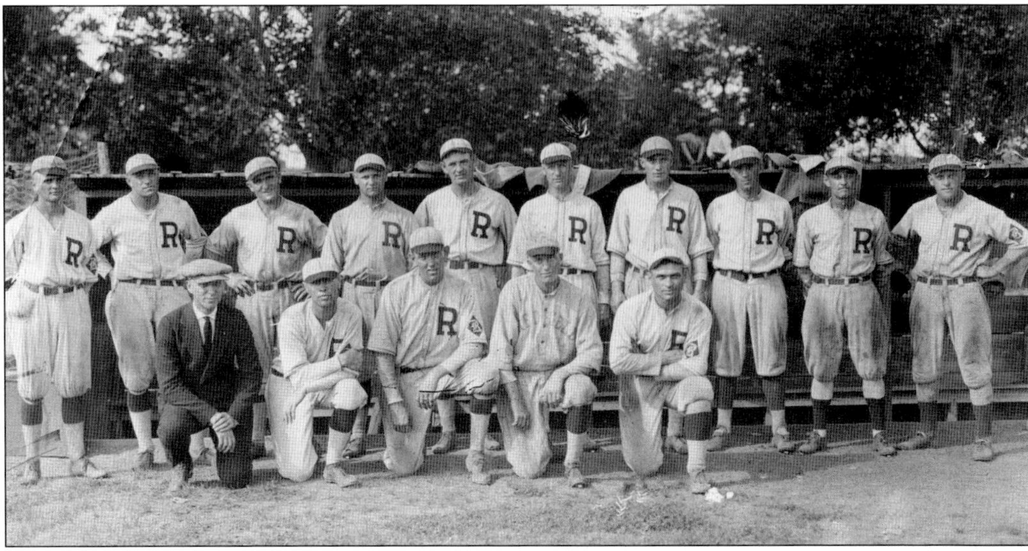

Pictured above is an early Redfield baseball team. Sports were very shortly made a community activity as town populations in the county stabilized and civic services were established. Leagues of town baseball teams developed particularly early. This is not surprising since a baseball diamond is relatively easy to lay out on the expansive land of the prairie. Similarly, football fields were amenable to the terrain. Basketball was more of a challenge in Spink County. An early Conde basketball team from 1935 is pictured below.

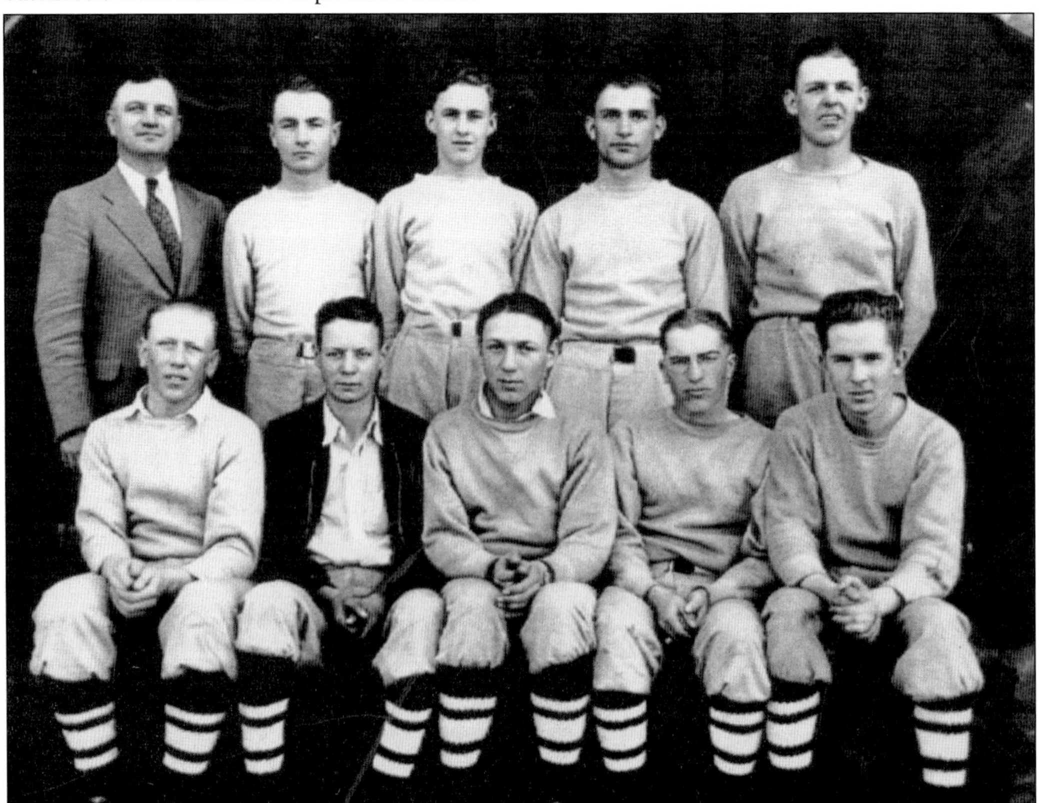

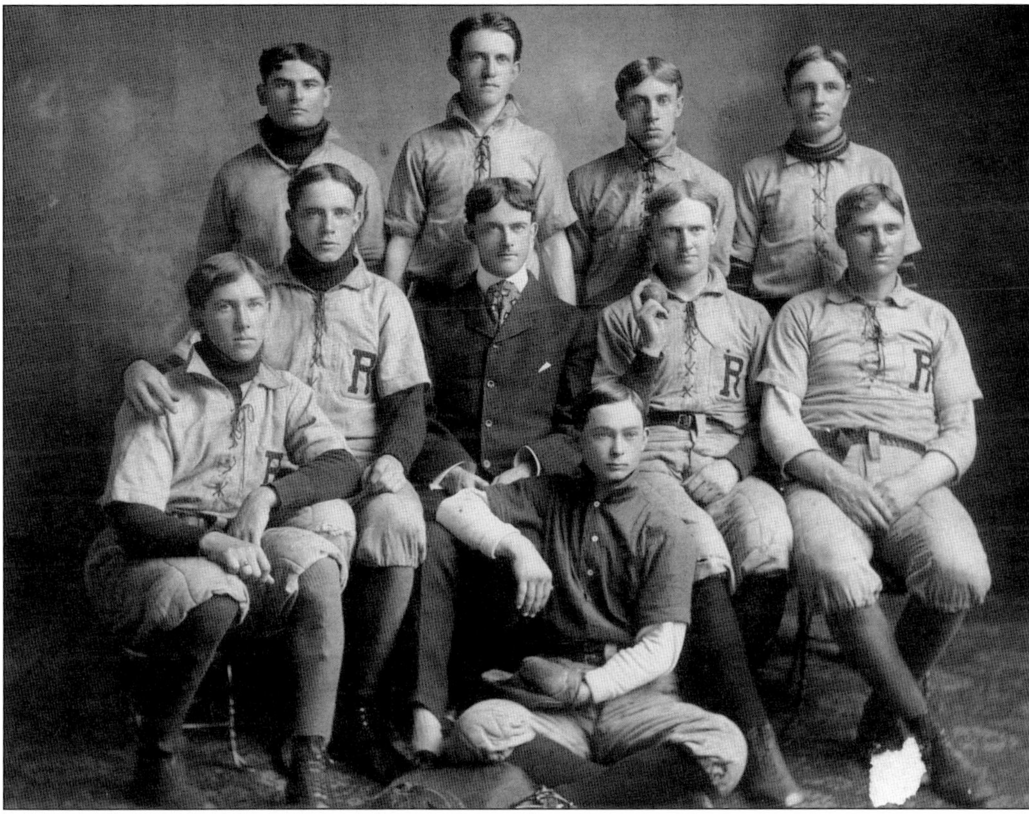

Redfield College fielded its own sports team. Above, an early 1900s baseball team poses for a team picture. Pictured below is the college football squad in 1902. Solely a school activity, basketball was played in facilities with low ceilings and rafters, building columns scattered around the court, and playing areas smaller than today's regulation. While short of photographic documentation, coeds played basketball in the 1920s.

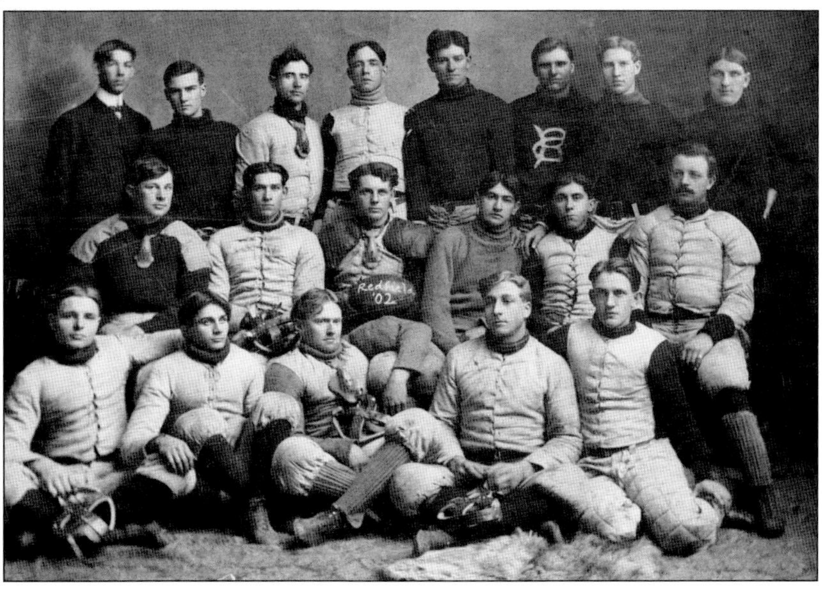

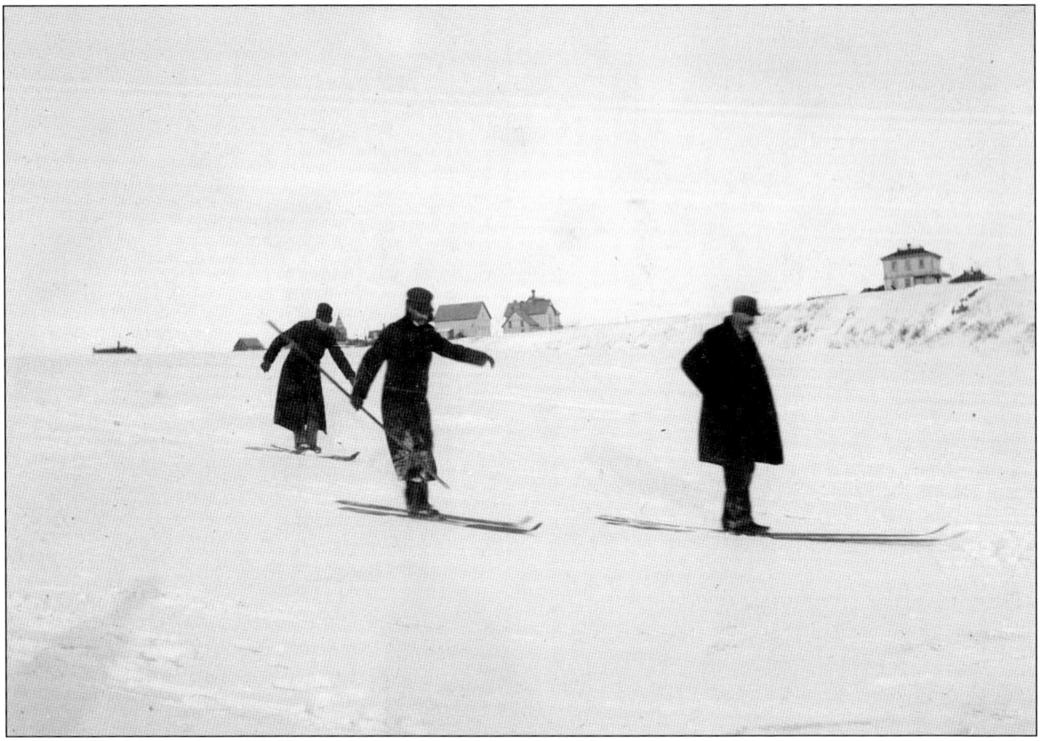

Cross-country skiing was popular, as seen in the late 1890s photograph above. As pictured below, mishaps were all too common.

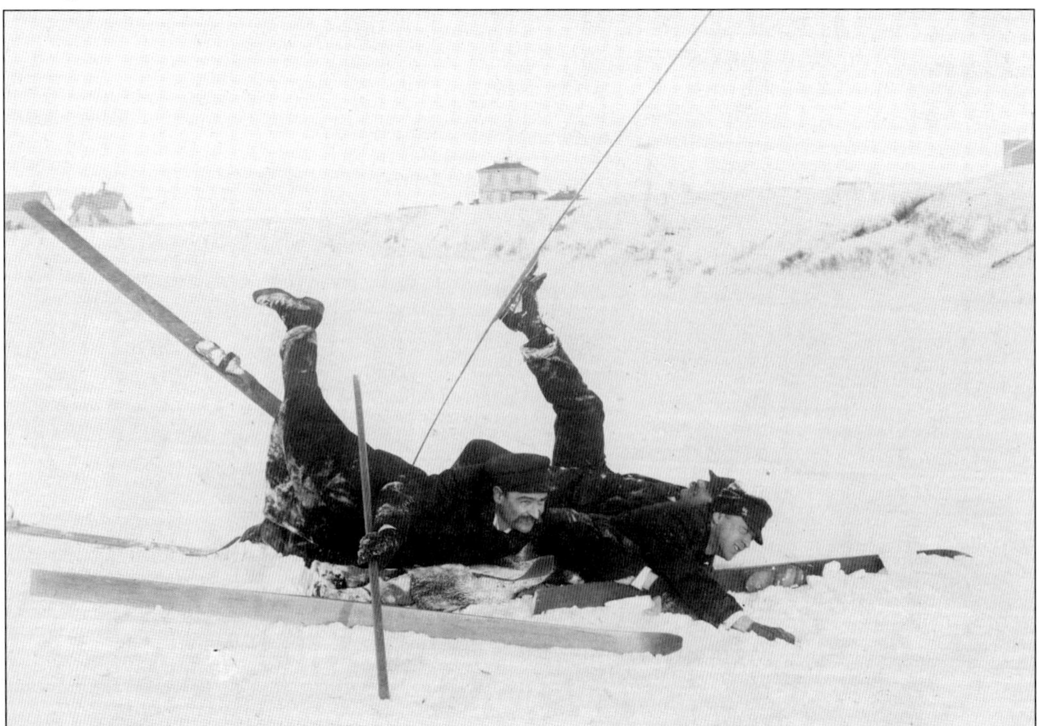

The fun was questionable for those who had to dig the trails from the snow. This image is from the winter of 1896–1897.

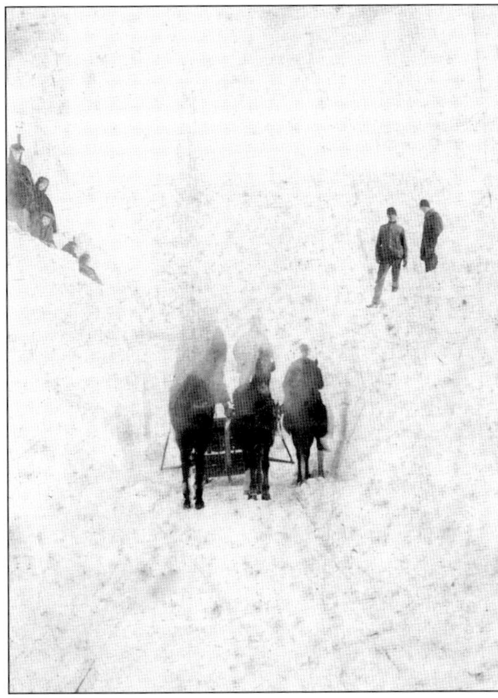

Redfield prides itself as the Pheasant Capital of the World and Spink County still hosts a large pheasant population, but this photograph shows the popularity of duck hunting prior to the successful introduction of the Chinese pheasant.

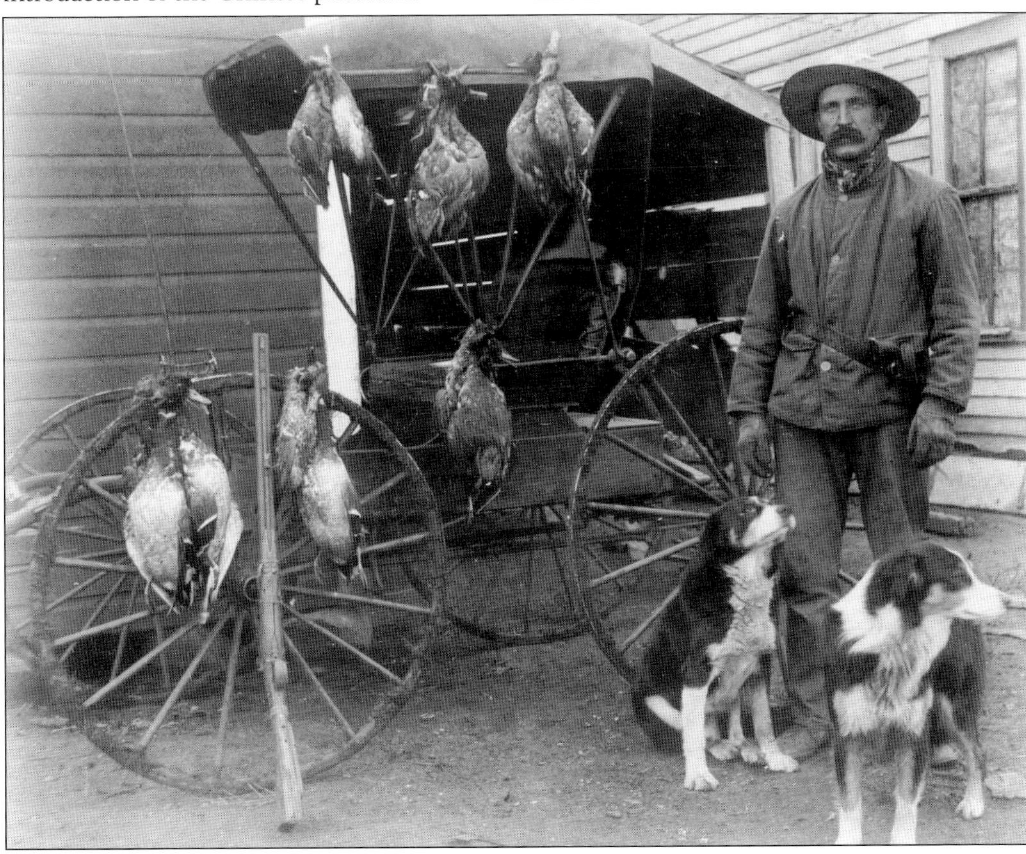

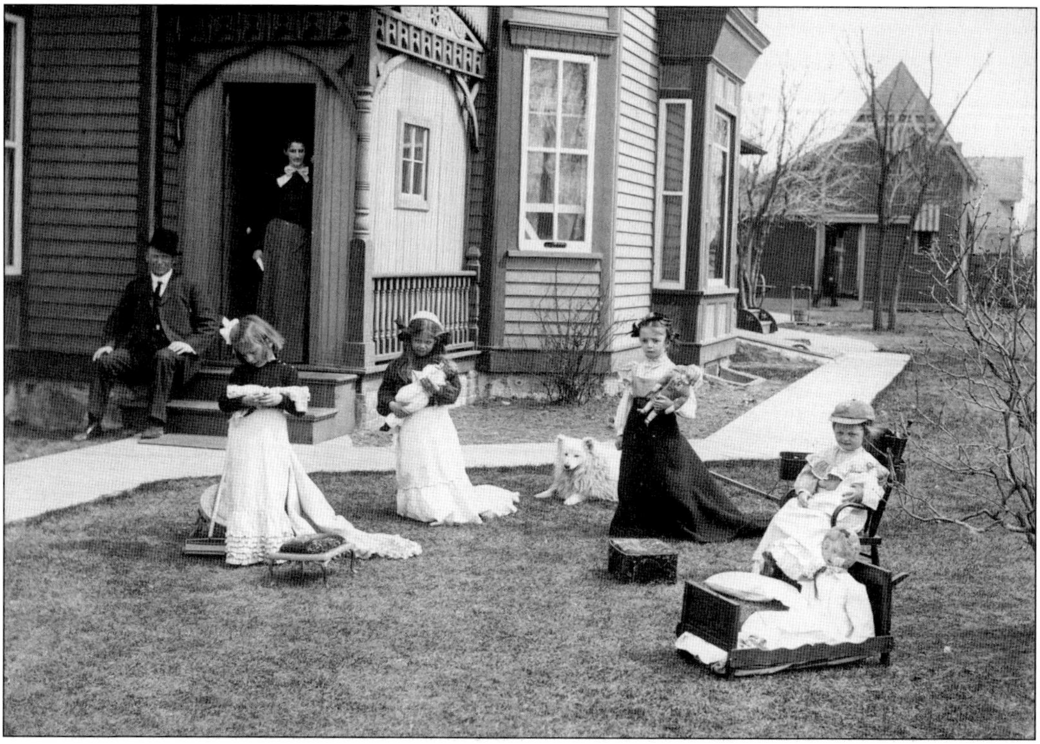

These youngsters are playing dress-up. Lucille Issenhuth on the right plays dolls with Pauline Pool. Edward C. Issenhuth is seated on the front step of his home, and an unidentified woman stands in the doorway.

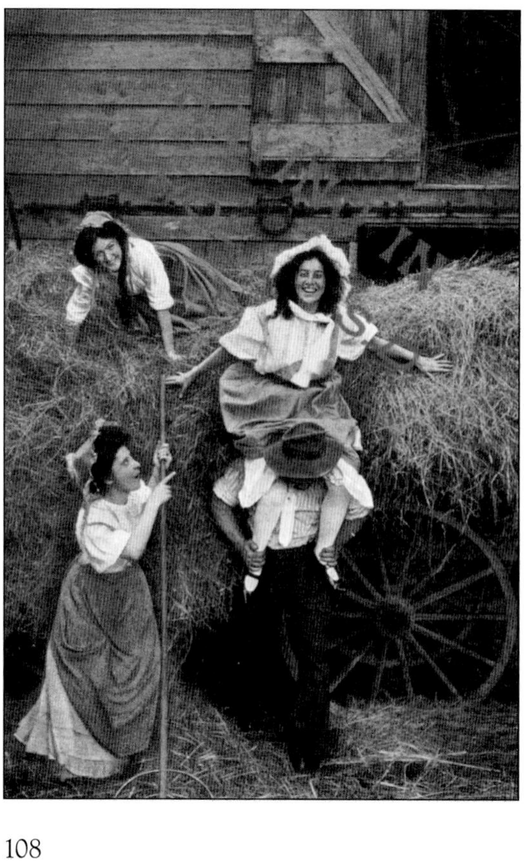

Everyone has great fun around a wagon of hay, as seen in this Athol postcard dated 1910. (Courtesy of Russell McNeely.)

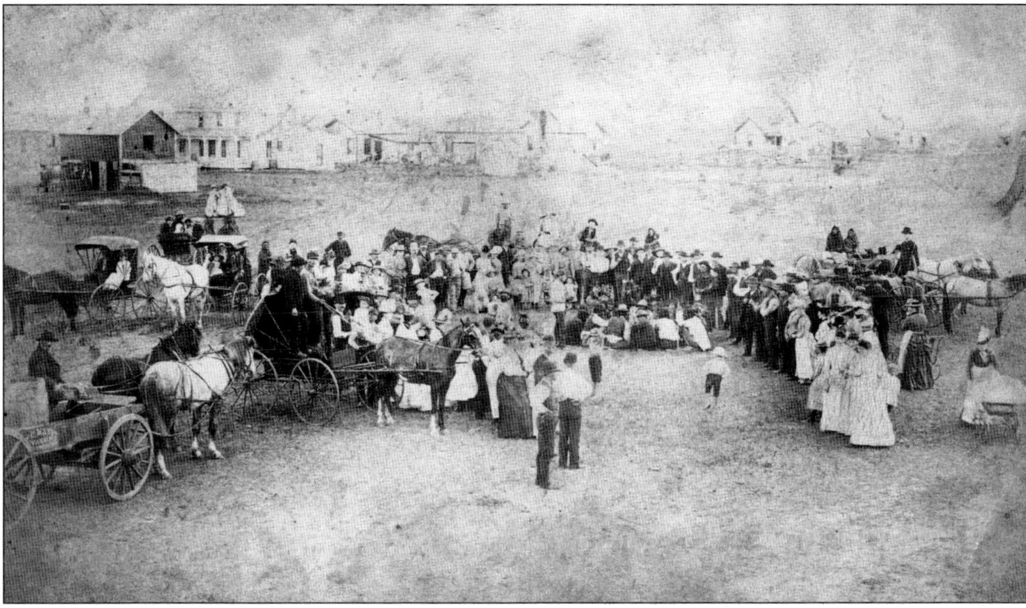

This is the Gellaterbury donation. Residents gather for a celebration in Mellette on July 4, 1886. (Courtesy of Rod Evans.)

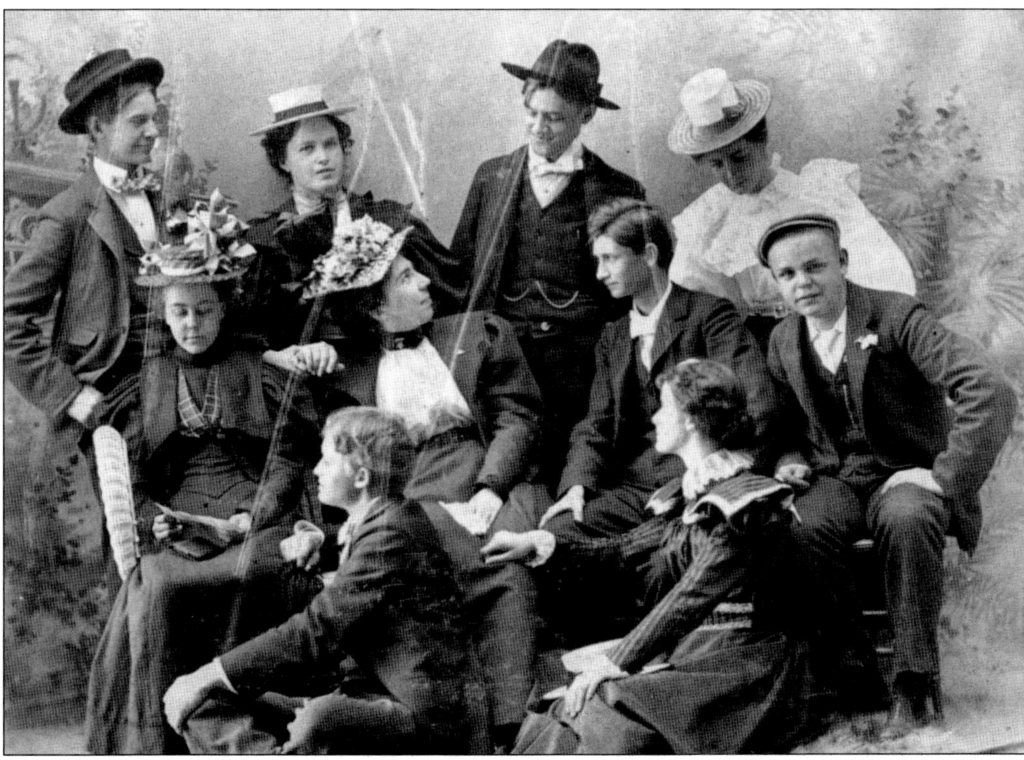

This portrait of Redfield citizens by Anderson includes (first row) Frank Packard and Lillian Riggs; (second row) Elaine Blaine, unidentified, Harlan Packard, and unidentified; (third row) two unidentified, C. Damuth, and B. Stutenroth.

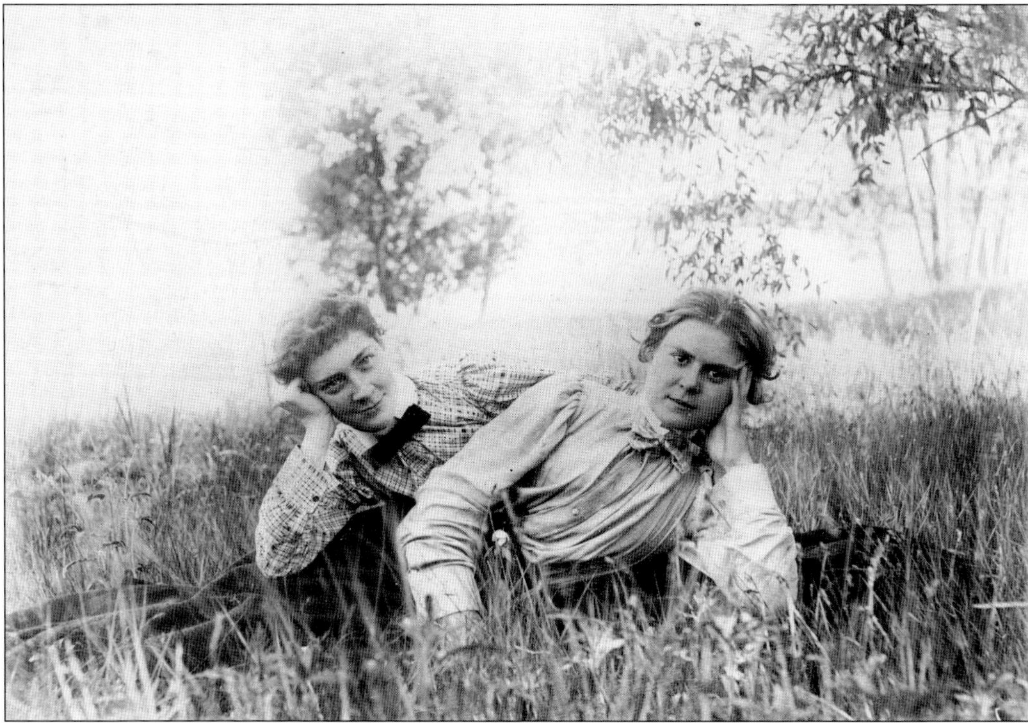

These two young ladies were photographed while enjoying a picnic. (Photograph by Lindrooth; courtesy of Spink County Museum.)

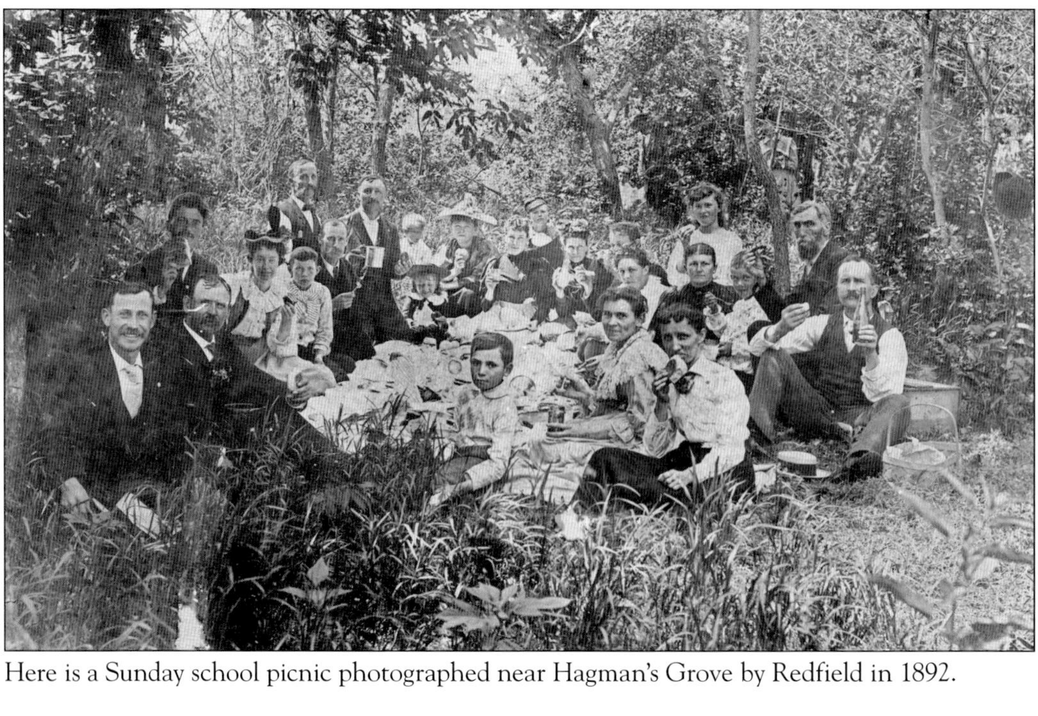

Here is a Sunday school picnic photographed near Hagman's Grove by Redfield in 1892.

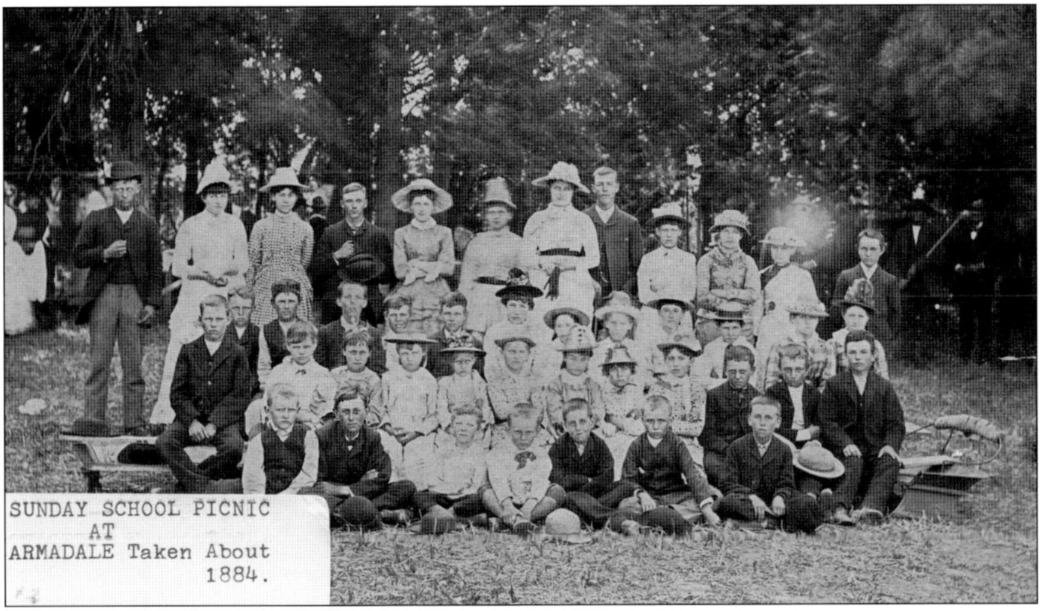

Here is a rare photograph of a church picnic at Armadale Island in 1884. Armadale Island figures in Native American history as well as the history of Spink County. Originally, Armadale Island was farmed by the Mandan people. It was a Sioux campground until it became a stop on the military road from Fort Sisseton to Rosebud Reservation. By the time of this photograph, it was a recreational area with picnic tables, toilet facilities, and a racetrack. Old Settlers' Picnics were held there every Fourth of July for many years. Flooding and tree removal along the James River have obliterated the site.

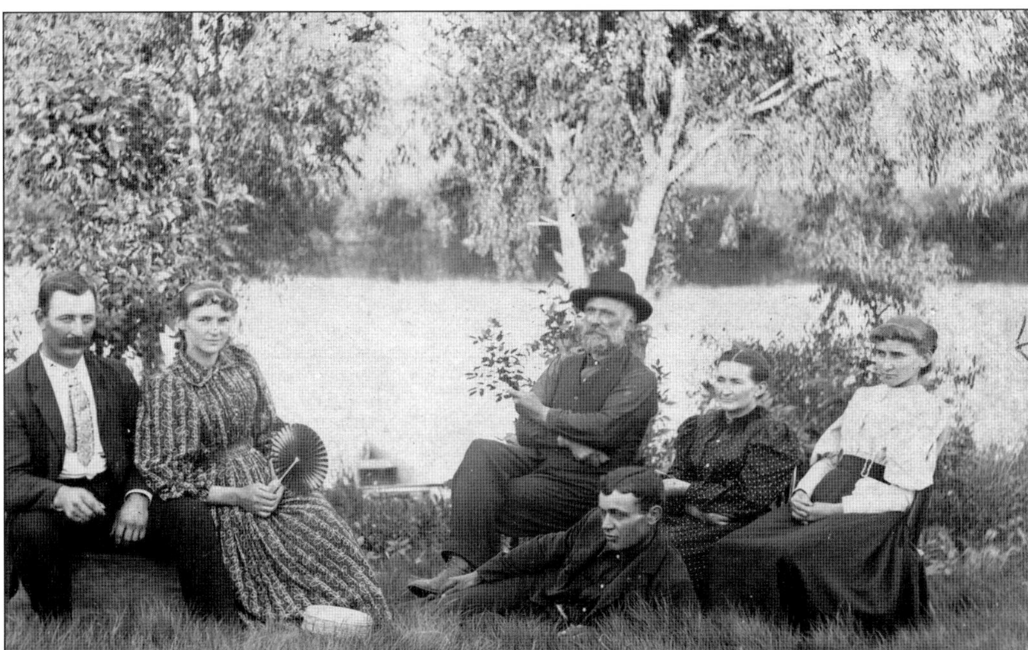

Taken from a family album dated 1918–1920, this photograph shows members of the Schaffer family posing along the bank of Timber Creek.

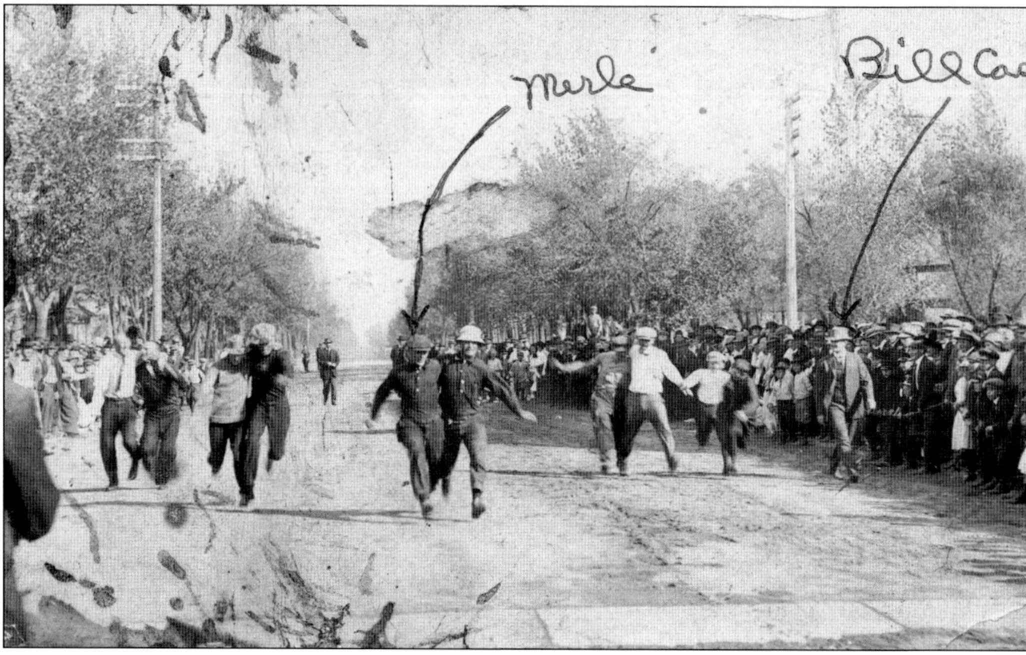

This popular festival competition, a three-legged race, took place in Redfield in 1914. Merle and Freddie Legler appear to have the edge in the race.

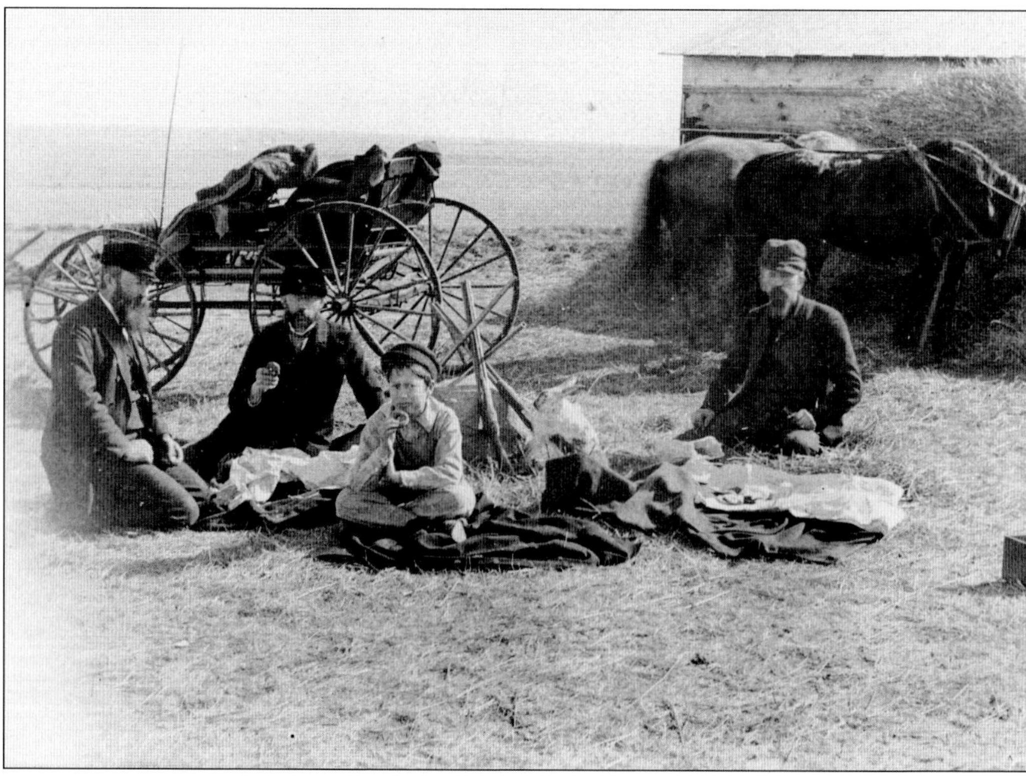

Pictured here is what appears to be a shared, packed lunch by men on a business trip.

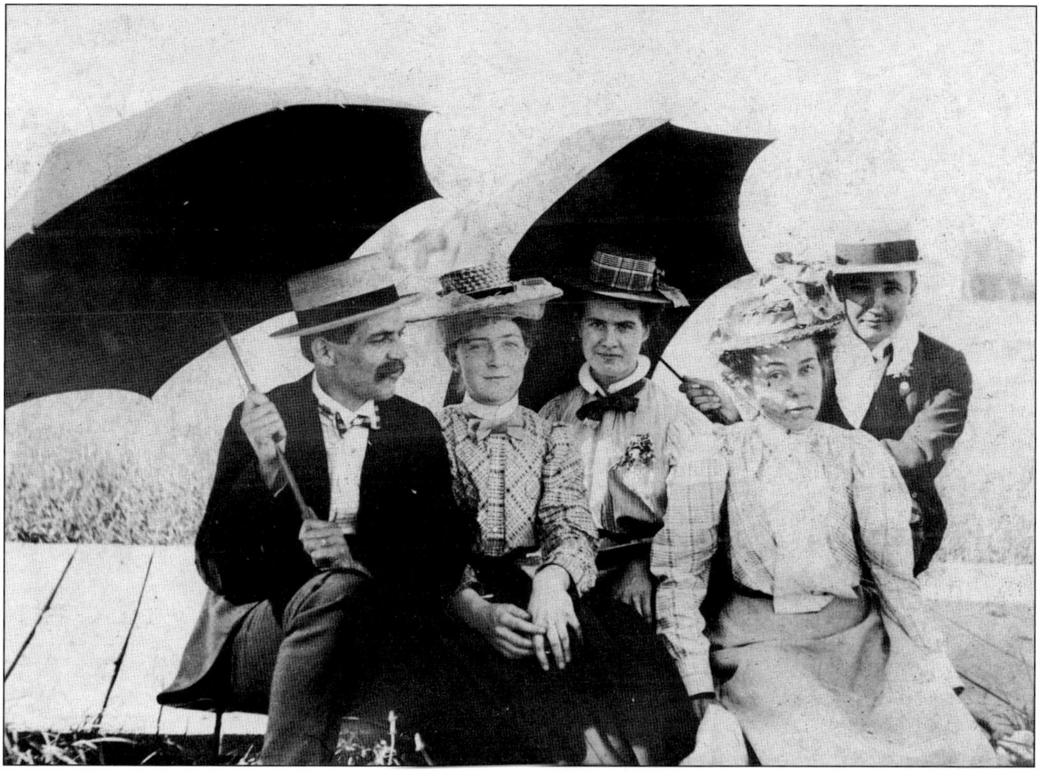

Pictured on this summer outing are Clark Stuttenroth, Bertha Dawson, Lillian Riggs, Ella Blaine, Lillian Bruell, and Will Bruell.

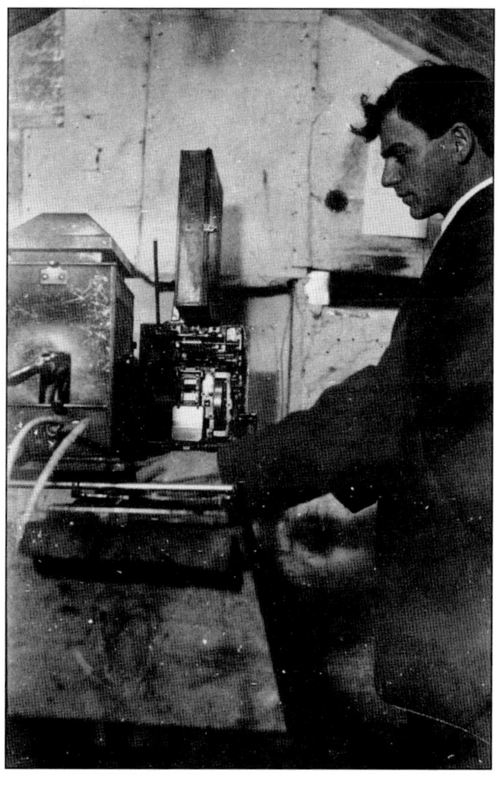

This man is operating a magic lantern. It was an early image projection device, invented in the 17th century, and employed by magicians.

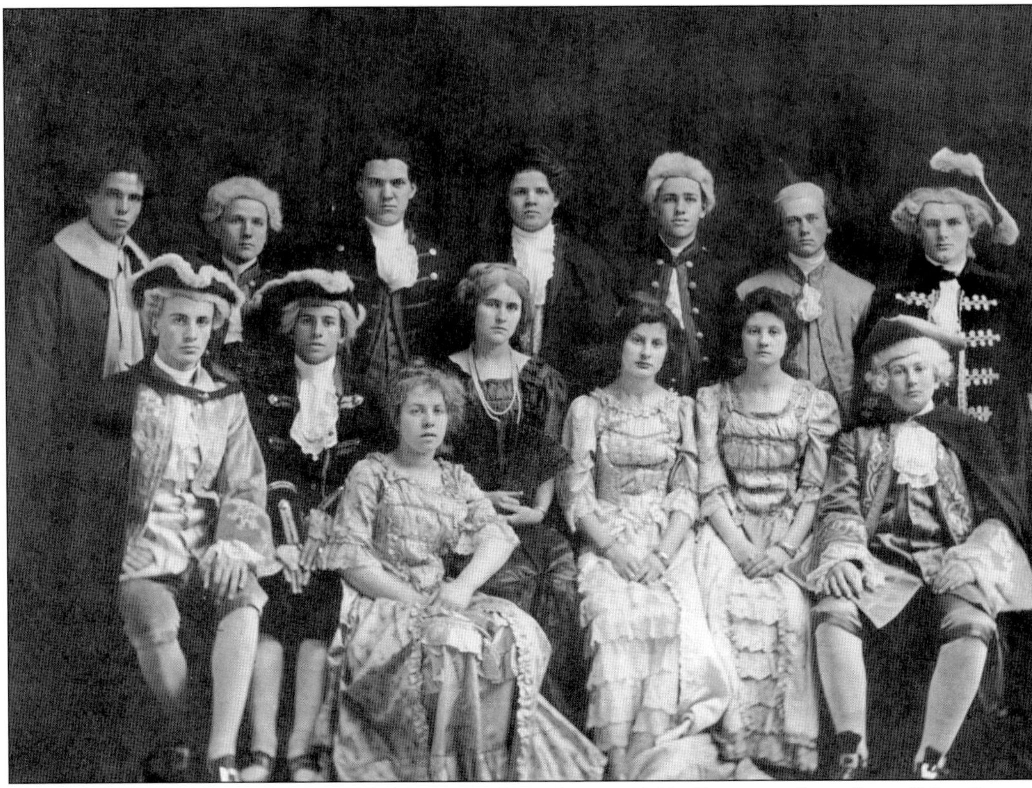

This photograph is from the Redfield senior class play in 1914. Cast members from "She Stoops to Conquer" pose in their costumes.

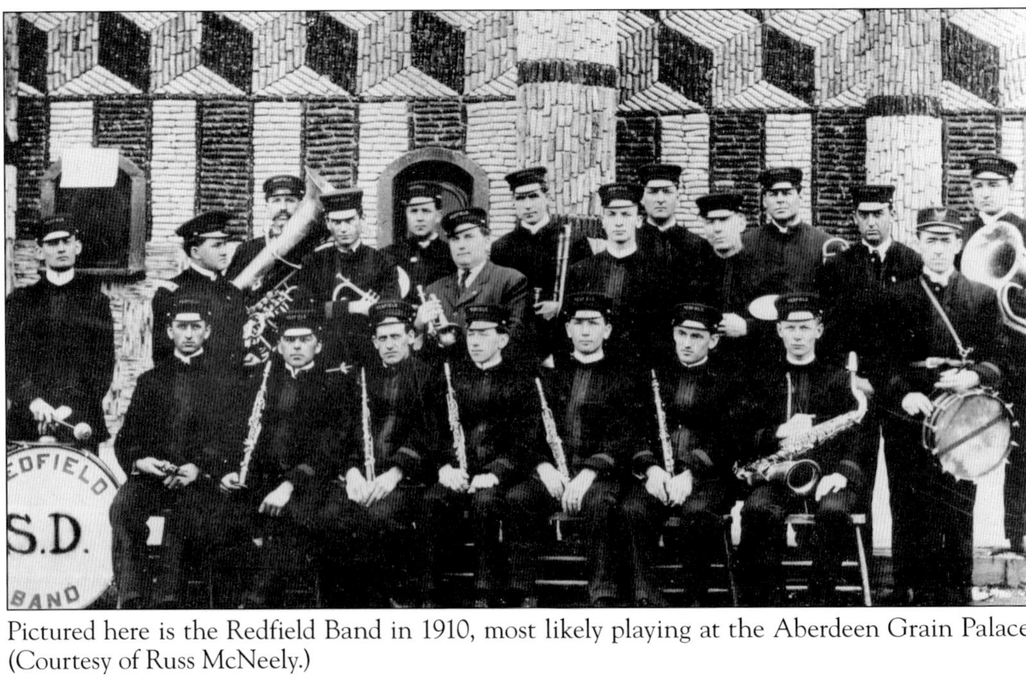

Pictured here is the Redfield Band in 1910, most likely playing at the Aberdeen Grain Palace. (Courtesy of Russ McNeely.)

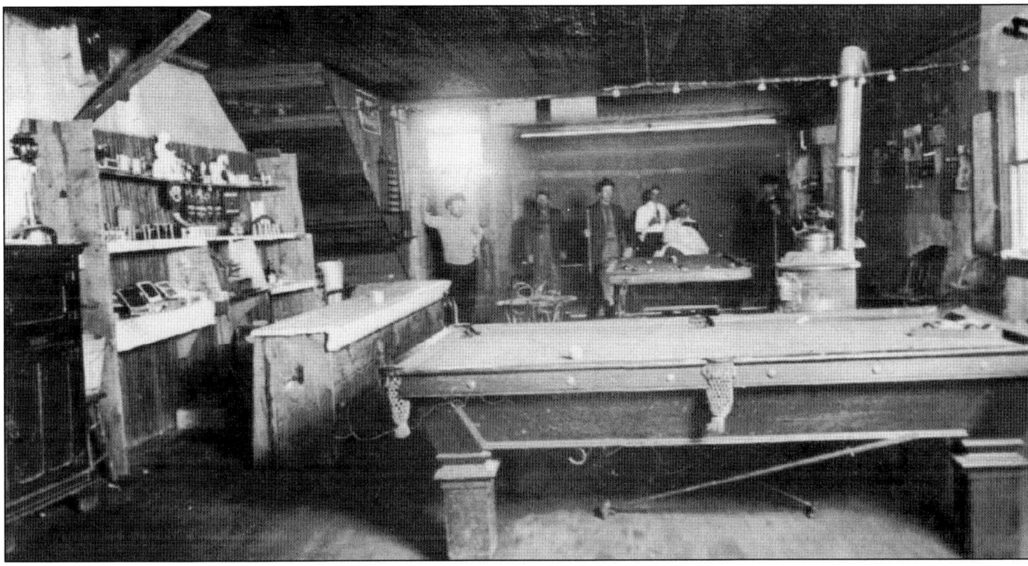

This pool hall combined with a barbershop was a popular hangout for Spink County men. This typical pool hall was probably in Crandall, Day County, just a few miles east of Conde. (Courtesy of Earl Grandpre.)

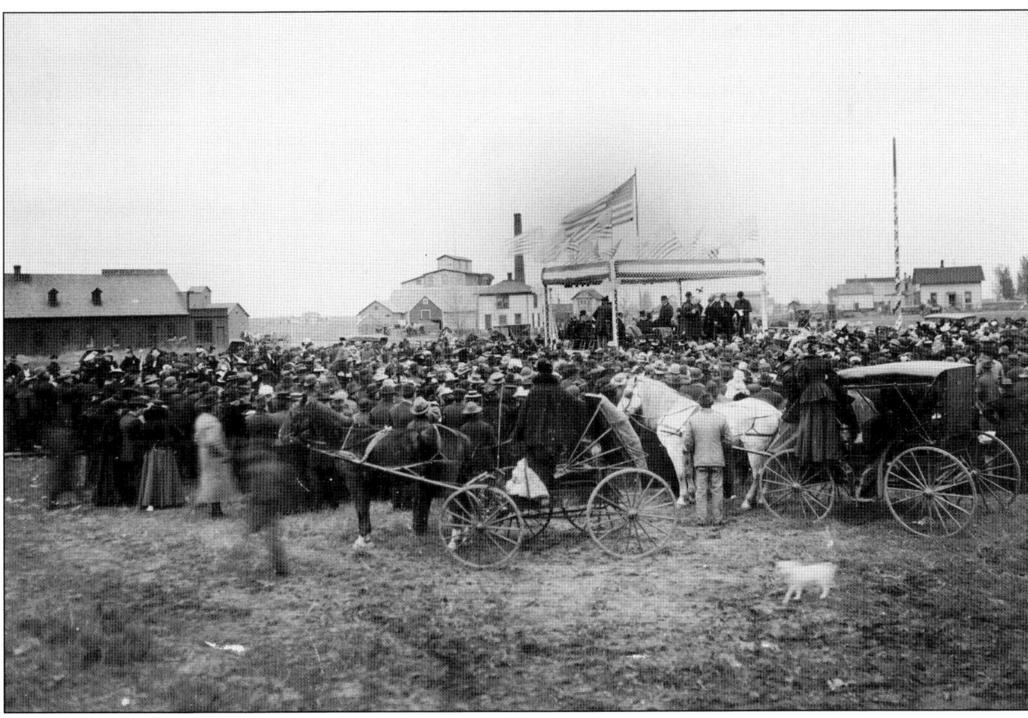

Crowds always gathered for a special occasion. Pictured here, President McKinley delivers a speech in Redfield on October 14, 1899.

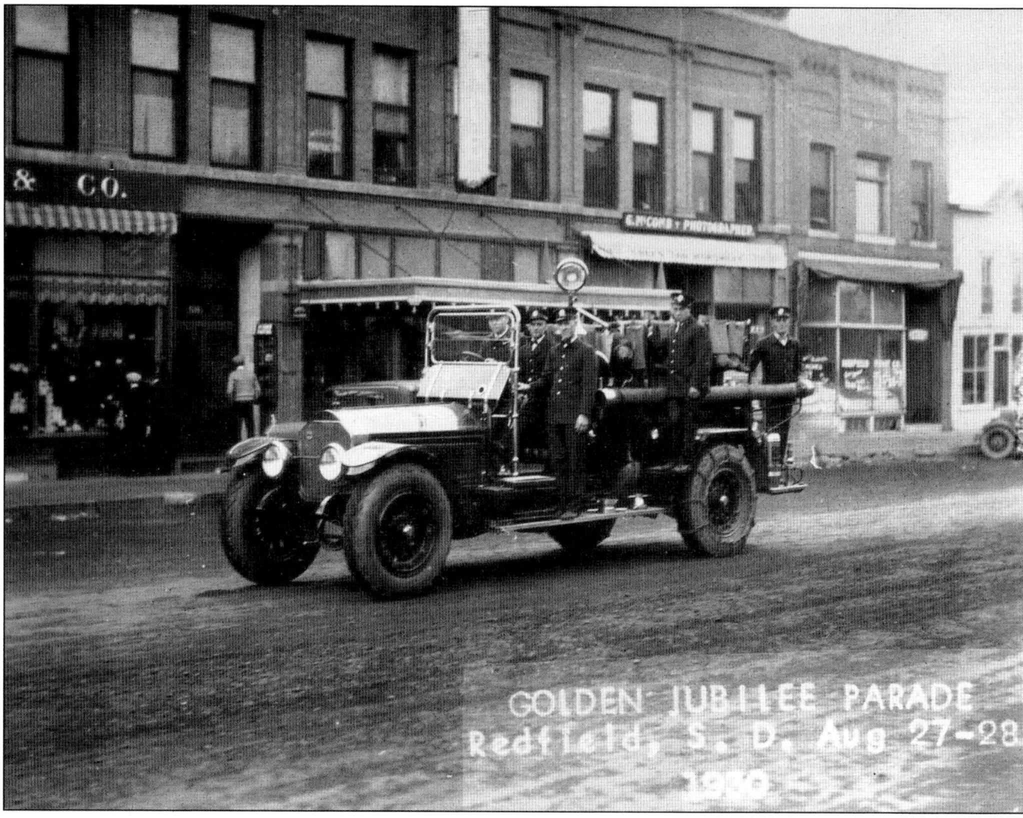

Redfield celebrated its Golden Jubilee August 27–28, 1930, with a parade down Main Street. Among the featured entries was the fire truck that served the community from 1920 until 1970. It continues to make appearances in local parades.

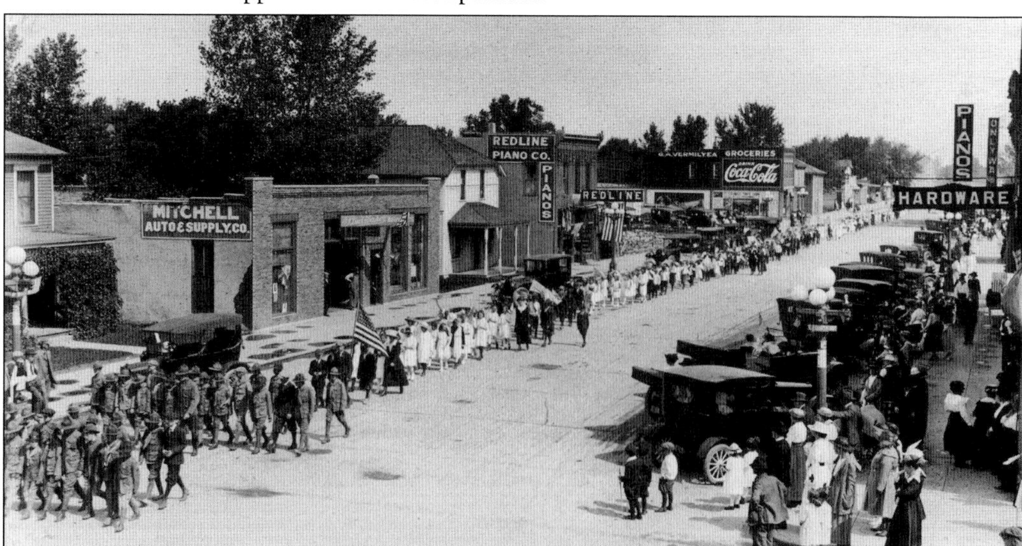

This Redfield parade took place shortly after World War I. A large military contingent leads the parade.

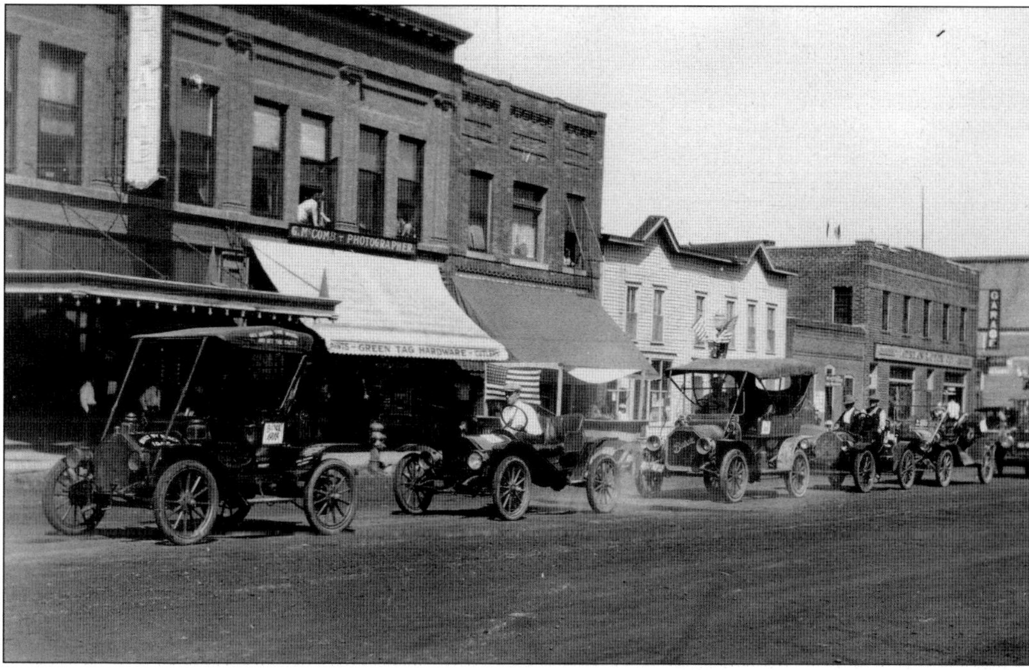

It is hard to imagine that these early autos in the 1930 Golden Jubilee parade in Redfield were already considered "antique" at the time.

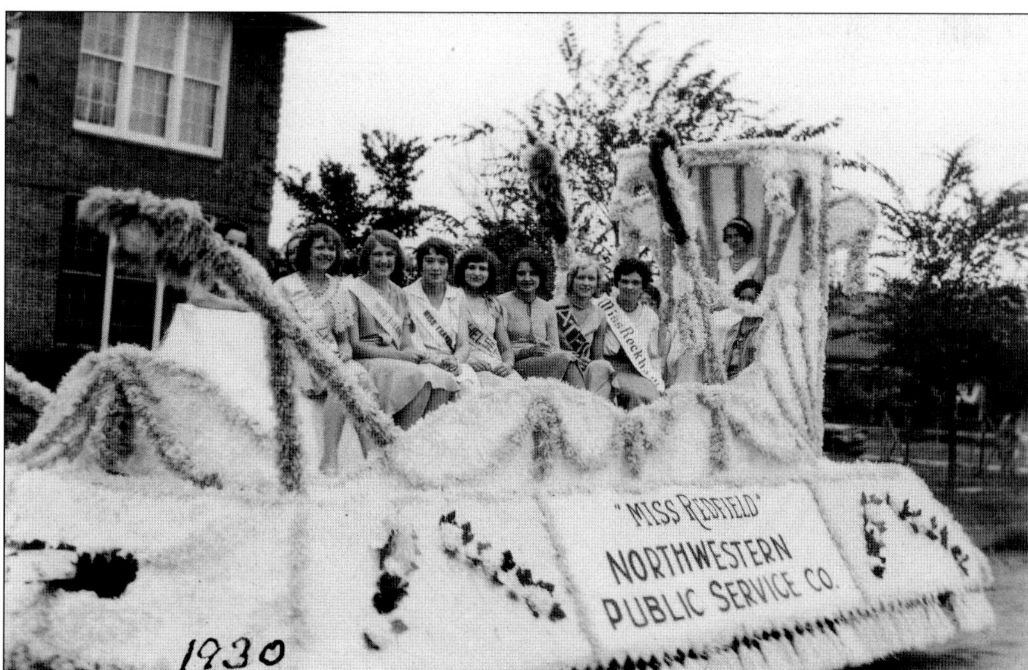

This float featuring Miss Redfield was part of a 1930 parade in Redfield.

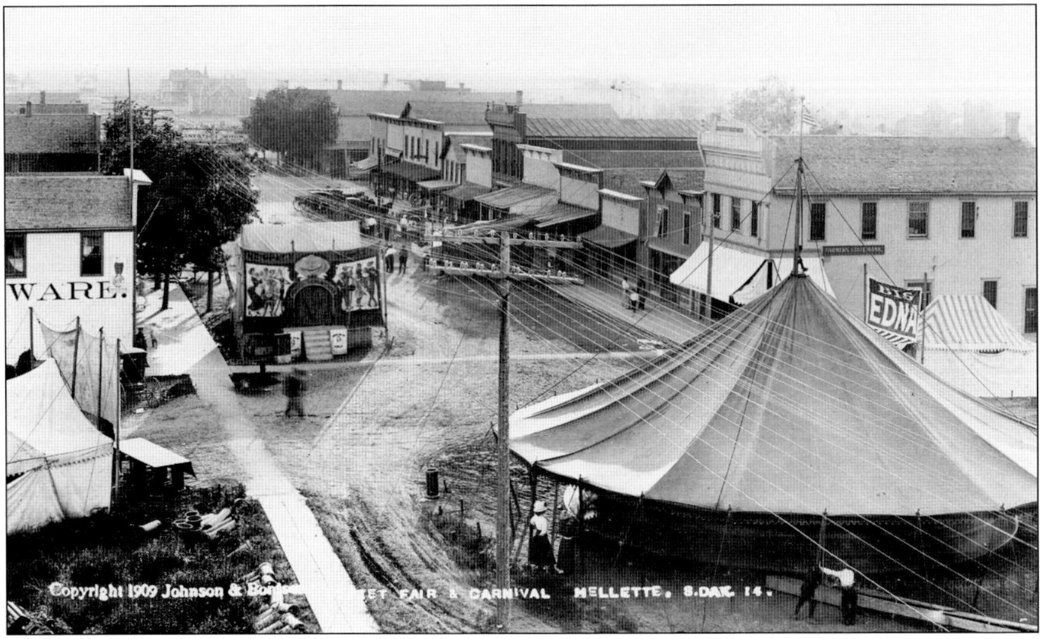

Pictured here is the Johnson and Bordsen Street Fair and Carnival in Mellette in 1909. (Courtesy of Glenn Overby.)

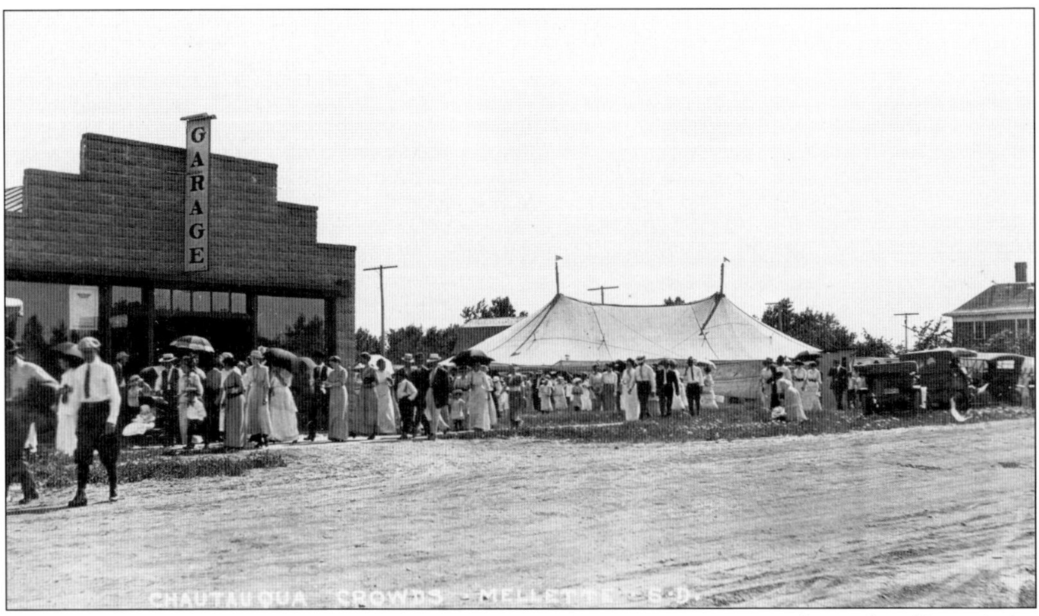

Pictured here is the Chautauqua in Mellette in 1909. Chautauqua was an intellectual and knowledge enrichment phenomenon started in Chautauqua, New York; it developed into traveling shows with orators, dramatic readings, and various presentations considered refined and beneficial to the attendee. (Courtesy of Glenn Overby.)

Eight

Interesting Portraits

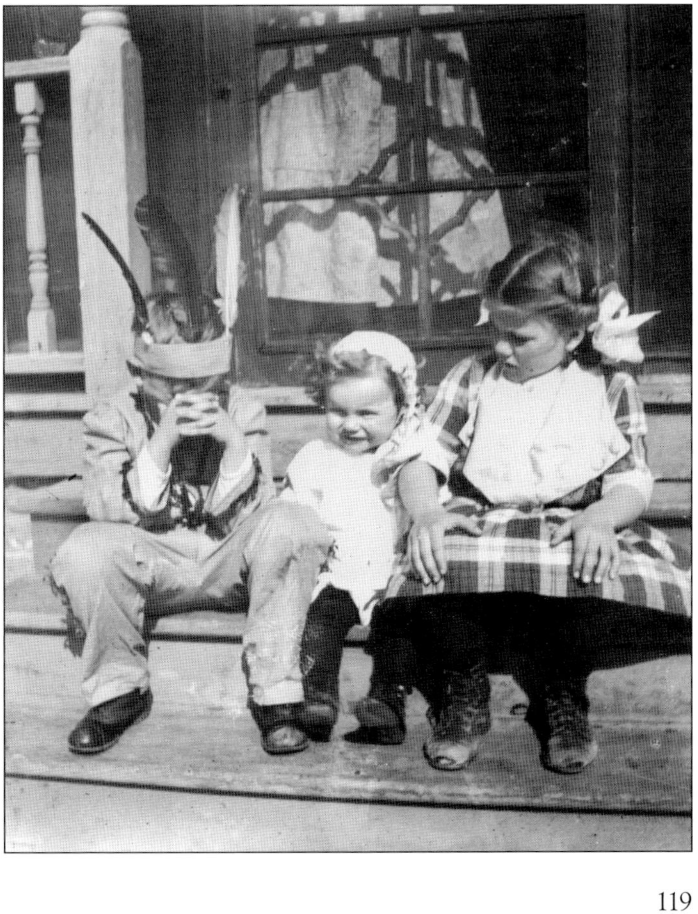

This book opened with a dedication to the early photographers of Spink County. It is, therefore, appropriate to present a sampling of mostly formal portraits taken by those early photographers. Some portraits are of people known and recognized in their time and in their Spink County community. Others are interesting, unique, and perhaps fun. Here is a 1910 photograph of three youngsters by Lenz. (Courtesy of Alan Evans.)

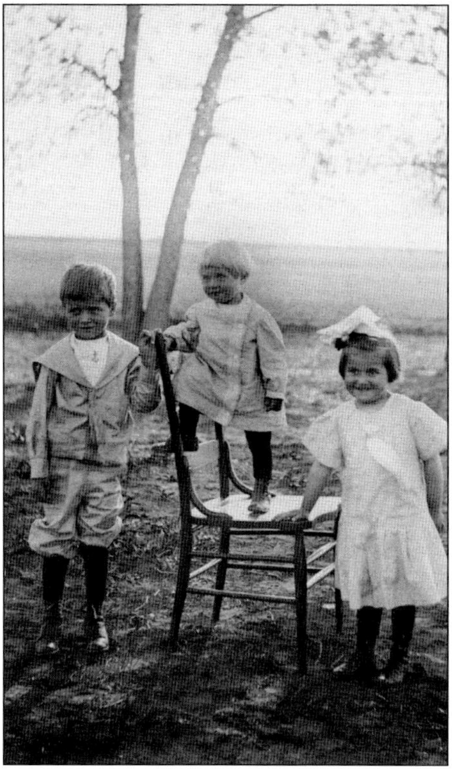

Little Maude Francis poses with her friends, all Ashton residents, by Anderson. (Courtesy of Alan Evans.)

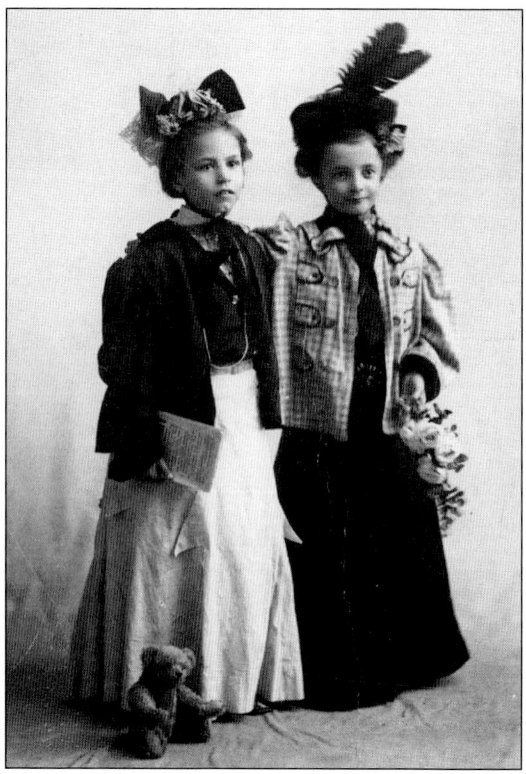

Pictured here are Lucille Issenhuth and Jessamine Coolidge of Redfield, playing dress-up with their teddy bear.

Redfield's first mayor, Daniel Hunt, poses with his wife Addie and their children, Arlington, Georgia, and Ray. Hunt served as mayor from April 1883 to April 1885. In recognition of his service, the city council presented him with an engraved silver dollar, which is now displayed at the Spink County Museum.

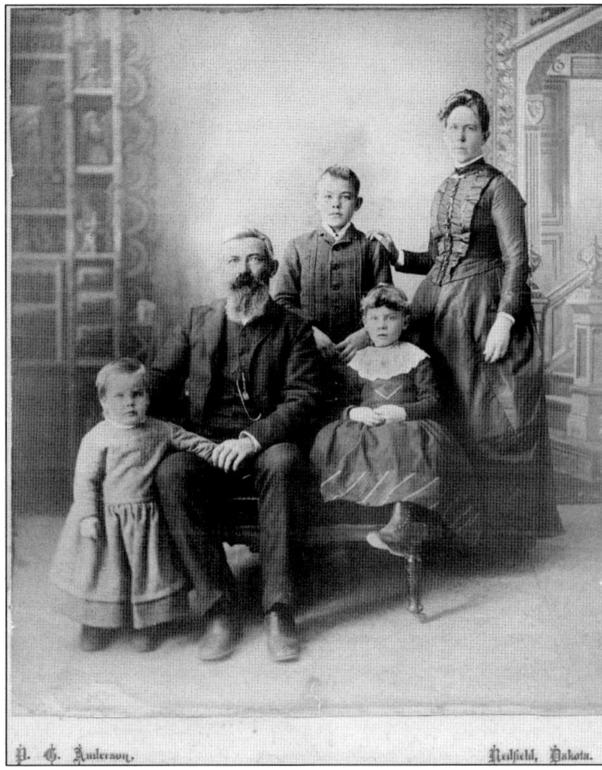

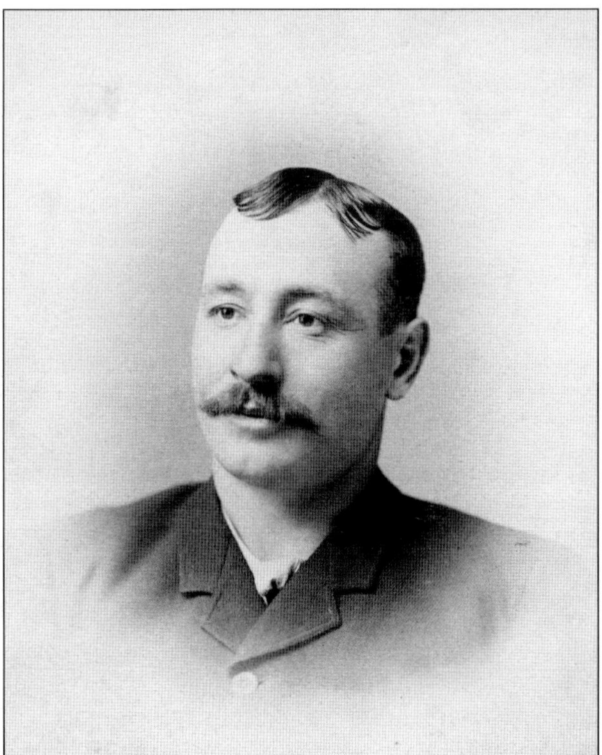

Here is the first sheriff of Spink County, Arthur Lawrence, photographed by H.F. Quiggle in 1881.

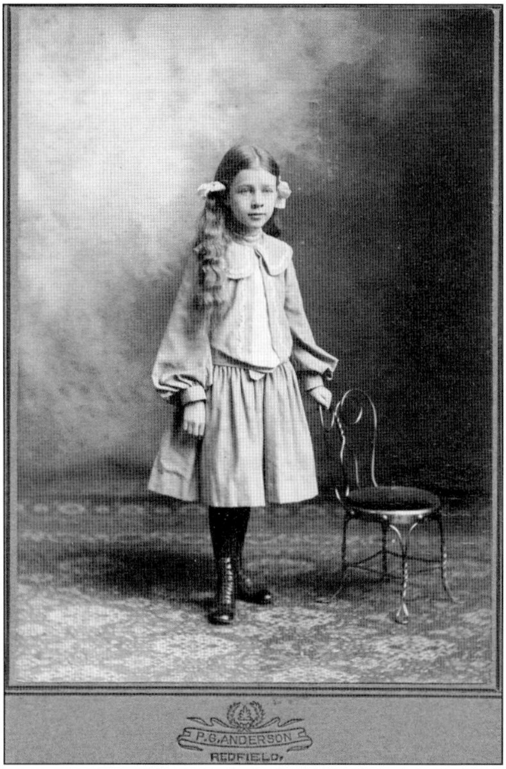

This portrait of Marie Emery was taken by Anderson.

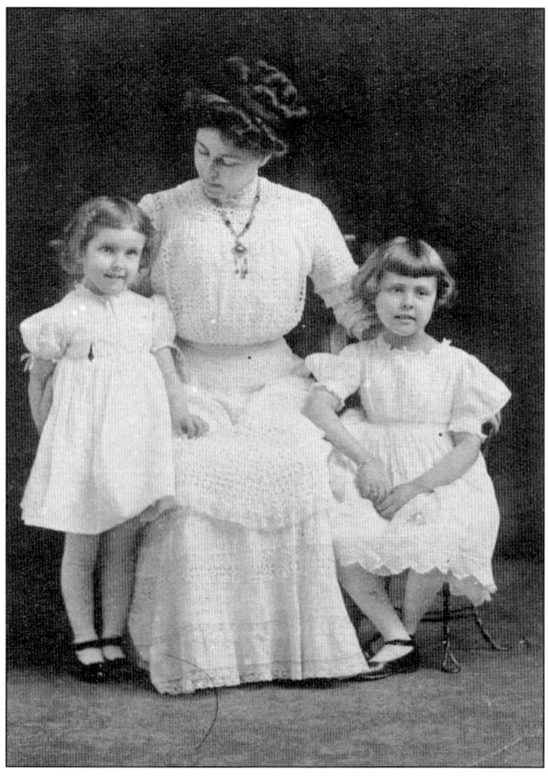

This is believed to be a portrait of Daisy Lindrooth and daughters; the photograph was taken by Lindrooth.

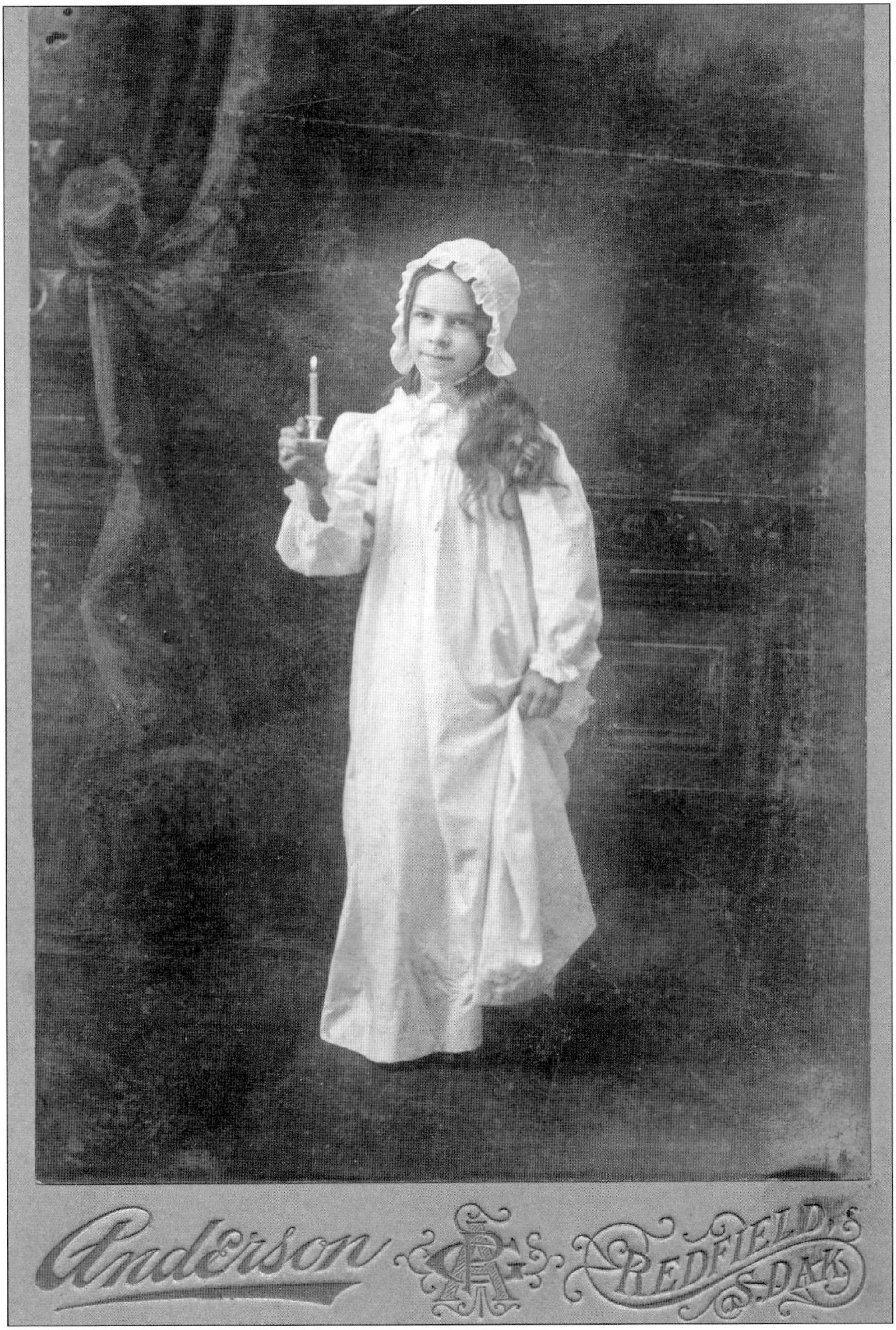

This young girl with a candle is another portrait by Anderson.

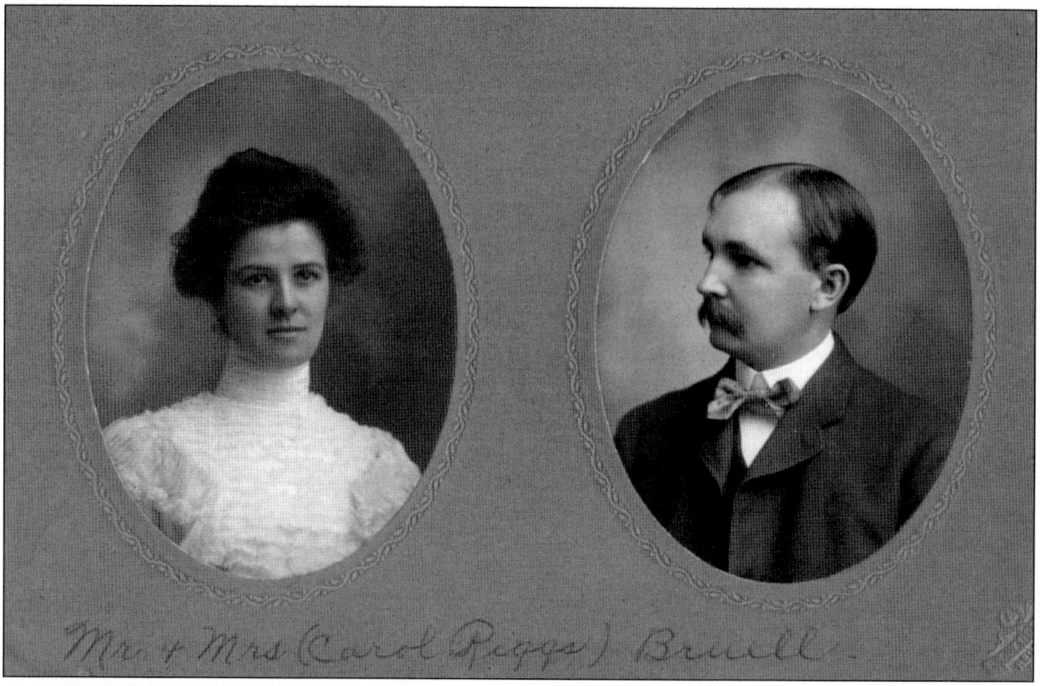

This double portrait shows early residents Carol (Riggs) Bruell and husband William Bruell in 1900. Bruell came to Dakota Territory in 1880 at the age of eight. He graduated from Redfield College, studied law in the office of Howard and Walsh, and was admitted to the bar in 1897. He served in the state House of Representatives in 1923 and in the state Senate in 1925.

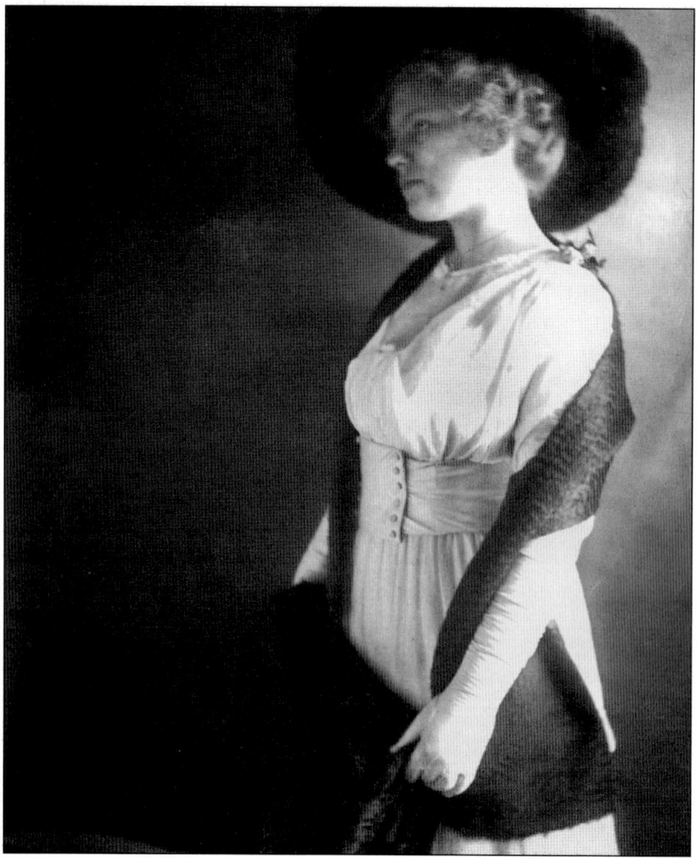

This portrait of a young woman in a fur hat was taken by Lenz. (Courtesy of Alan Evans.)

The Hillard sisters—Daisy Lindrooth, Ella Boub, Bertha Schalkle, and Rose Rowe—posed for photographer Lindrooth.

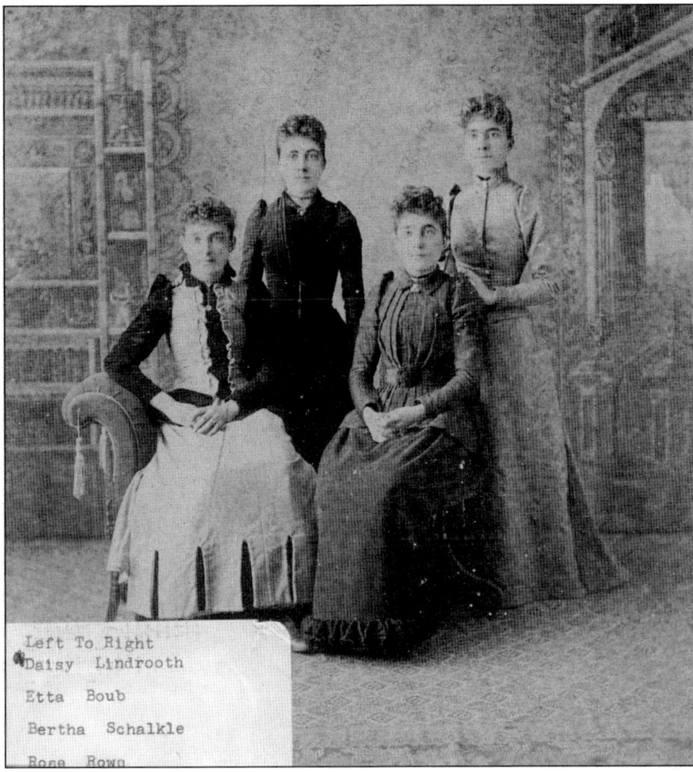

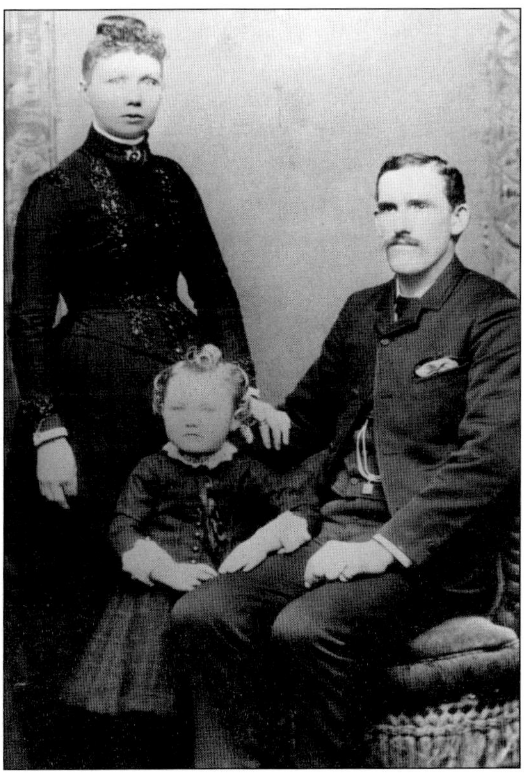

Anna and Shadrach Evans pose with son Ben. Boys wore dresses until they were old enough to wear knickers. Despite the clean and starched appearance, Ben was born in a dugout, and the family likely lived there at the time of the photograph. Shadrach had literally pushed a cart with his belongings from Minnesota to Dakota Territory. To file his claim, he walked from Aberdeen to the land office in Watertown, approximately 100 miles. (Courtesy of Alan Evans.)

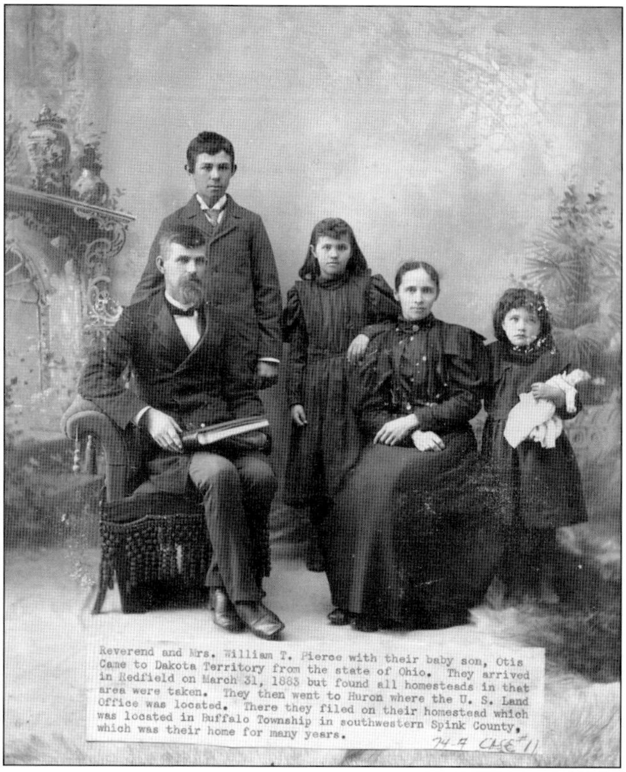

Pictured here are Rev. and Mrs. William T. Pierce and son Otis. They arrived in Redfield in 1883. Reverend Pierce's great-grandson Rev. David Anderson, also a descendant of the Hagman family, was a recent out-of-town visitor to Spink County Museum.

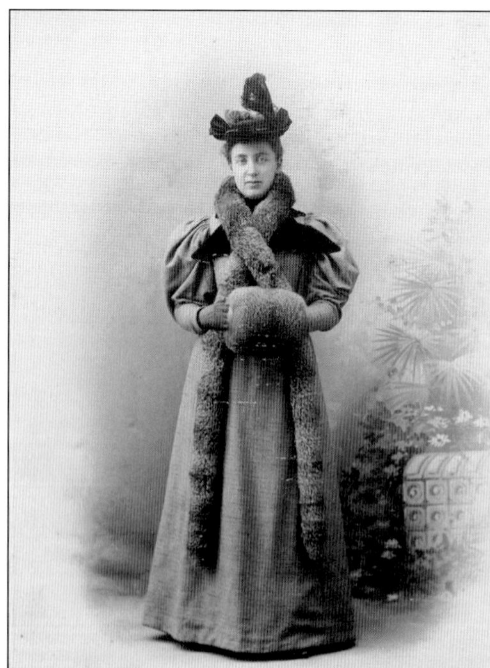

Here is Carolyn Erickson Kutnewsky, presumably the wife of Dr. Kutnewsky (see page 31). This portrait was taken by Anderson.

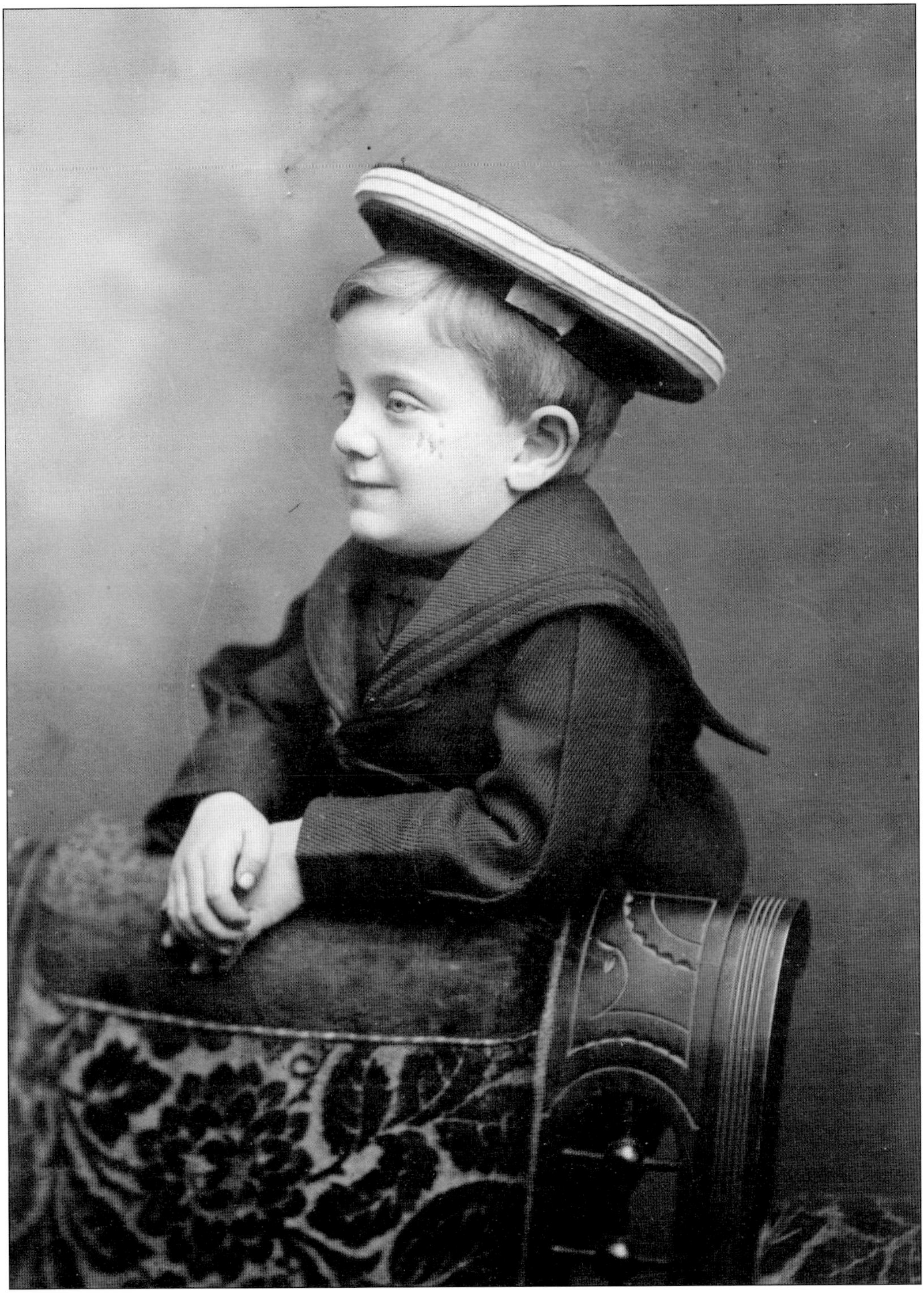

This portrait of a young boy was taken by Anderson.